Walking in the Good Way

Ioterihwakwaríhshion Tsi Íhse

D1257474

Walking in the Good Way
Ioterihwakwaríhshion Tsi Íhse

Aboriginal Social Work Education

Edited by

Ingrid Thompson Cooper and Gail Stacey Moore

Canadian Scholars' Press Inc.
Toronto

Walking in the Good Way / *Ioterihwakwaríhshion Tsi Íhse*: Aboriginal Social Work Education
Edited by Ingrid Thompson Cooper and Gail Stacey Moore

First published in 2009 by
Canadian Scholars' Press Inc.
180 Bloor Street West, Suite 801
Toronto, Ontario
M5S 2V6

www.cspi.org

Photograph on page 132 by J. Nauta, Museum of New Zealand Te Papa Tongarewa, MA_F.001092/01-03, Part 12

Every reasonable effort has been made to identify copyright holders. CSPI would be pleased to have any errors or omissions brought to its attention.

Canadian Scholars' Press Inc. gratefully acknowledges financial support for our publishing activities from the Government of Canada through the Book Publishing Industry Development Program (BPIDP).

Library and Archives Canada Cataloguing in Publication

Walking in the good way = Ioterihwakwaríhshion tsi íhse: aboriginal social work education / edited by Ingrid Thompson Cooper and Gail Stacey Moore.

Includes bibliographical references and index.
ISBN 978-1-55130-351-2

1. Social work education—Canada. 2. Indians of North America—Education (Higher)—Canada. 3. Social work education. I. Thompson-Cooper, Ingrid II. Stacey-Moore, Gail III. Title: Ioterihwakwaríhshion tsi ihse.

HV11.W352 2008   361.3'071171   C2008-904689-7

Cover art: K.C. Adams
Book design: Susan MacGregor / Digital Zone

09 10 11 12 13   5 4 3 2 1

Printed and bound in Canada by Marquis Book Printing Inc.

In memory of Marie Wilkinson, 1952–2003

Dr. Marie Wilkinson was a senior lecturer in the Department of Social Work, Social Policy, and Sociology at the University of Sydney from 1991 to 2002. Prior to this, Marie worked for 16 years as a frontline social work practitioner, educator, and policy maker in child welfare and mental health. In both her academic and practitioner roles, Marie brought a heightened sensitivity to the manifestations of disadvantage and injustice. Marie was passionate about integrating Indigenous issues into the social work curriculum and was working on this until her untimely death.

Ioterihwakwaríhshion Tsi Íhse

Ioterihwakwaríhshion Tsi Íhse—Mohawk meaning "Walking in the good way"
Pimatisiwin—Asinhinabe meaning "Walking in a good way"
Mino-pimatisiwin—Cree meaning "The good life"

Pimatisi is the root Algonquian word for a life. It identifies an approach to life. The key concept is that life is a gift, and therefore has intrinsic value. To develop that life into a good life, a human being approaches or travels on the good road. A human being retains and maintains good relationships with the animate and inanimate beings. This implies a latitude or scope of choices of personal responsibility (Hart, 2001; Young, 2003).

Contents

Untitled painting of a bird, by K.C. Adams

Wa'tkwanonhwerá: ton*

William S. Rowe

Growing up as a non-minority in Canada in the mid-20th century presented few opportunities for the kind of cultural immersion needed to be instinctively culturally competent in the development and provision of human services for Aboriginal Canadians. Depending on one's geographic location—rural, urban, north, south, east, west—one would likely know some Aboriginal Canadians, interact with a few, and establish relationships with very few, if any. Stereotypes were omnipresent and reinforced through the media, school, the workplace, and the marketplace. If one was fortunate enough through a personal friendship to get a glimpse into the world of Aboriginal Canadians, it was unlikely to be a revealing picture of the myriad struggles and challenges facing the majority of them at the time.

A transformative experience in my own life occurred when living in Thunder Bay, Ontario, in the early sixties. My father was a senior administrator at the provincial correctional centre (also known as the "Prison Farm"), and, as a result, we lived on the grounds. The facility was classified as minimum security and, as such, inmates were simply a part of my daily life. I had lived on or close to correctional facilities all of my life and it was obvious that Aboriginal Canadians were greatly overrepresented in the general prison population. At age 16, something moved me to inquire about this, and I discovered that the average Aboriginal-Canadian prison population was between 60 and 80 percent of the entire prison population at any given time in a location where Aboriginal Canadians as a group were less than 5 percent of the population. Intrigued by this situation, I skipped classes over the next two days and sat in on the local provincial court proceedings. I observed Aboriginal Canadians being regularly sentenced to jail terms for equivalent or lesser offences than their non-Aboriginal counterparts, who were given fines, probation, or suspended sentences. Most of the Aboriginal Canadians were first offenders, and most of the others were repeat offenders. It was hardly a scientific survey, but it left a lasting impression of what appeared to be official (systemic) discrimination.

A number of years later, when a relative sent me information on our family tree, I discovered my great-grandfather was married to a Mohawk woman named Bruyere in the Montreal area. Upon further investigation, I discovered that my great-grandfather had passed away in Bordeaux Prison. These discoveries, which had not been

---

* Welcome (Mohawk).

passed on by my grandparents or parents, made me wonder how many other Canadians had similar roots that they did not know about.

Later travels, study, and professional activities would add many layers of knowledge to my early sojourn into social research. Some of those experiences included providing services to children and adults in most provinces in Canada, many US states, the UK, the Middle East, South Asia, and New Zealand. In all cases the range of human services provided to indigenous peoples and distressed minorities by professionals were unlikely to be from those who were either from or who were able to identify with those same groups. The solution has been obvious for some time. Culturally competent human services are best provided by qualified and committed people from the same groups of the people they seek to serve. How to achieve this, on the other hand, remains an elusive goal even to this day.

This book is a significant contribution to that effort. It does not and cannot detail all the actions that have been and are taking place in Canada. In my own experience countless Aboriginal Canadians have patiently tried to raise my level of understanding and educate me as to the means by which I could best use my professional privilege to be helpful. Part of my education came through the happy coincidence that I was the director of the School of Social Work at the Memorial University of Newfoundland when we had an opportunity to start a social work program for Inuit community leaders of Labrador. Summarily I became director of the School of Social Work at McGill University and worked with faculty and Aboriginal community leaders to help establish the Aboriginal Certificate Program and ensure that it would be recognized by the university.

Many efforts are as geographically bound as the very people they are attempting to serve. A large, primarily urban setting like Kanawake bears little resemblance to the environment of the nomadic Innu of Labrador. Northern communities without road access have very different circumstances than some of the well-defined and politically sophisticated First Nations communities in the Prairie provinces and British Columbia's Lower Mainland. Programs at the Saskatchewan Indian Federated College, now known as the First Nations University of Canada, the University of Calgary, the University of Victoria, McGill University, the Nicola Valley Institute of Technology, Thompson Rivers University, the University of Manitoba, and Laurentian University have made major advances and remain committed to capacity building of culturally competent human service professionals. Although this is by no means an exhaustive list, they are rather good examples of significant successes that must be recognized and replicated, where possible.

This work carefully and sensitively describes a number of efforts that have taken place over 25 years during a time of tumultuous change. The contributions provide accurate accounts, keen analyses, and powerful insights, embracing both missteps and challenges, as well as successes. Urtnowski and Zapf's descriptions of program development in Quebec and Alberta demonstrate the unique challenges and lessons learned, particularly that one size does not fit all and that program development is possible only through the establishment of both institutional and individual trust. Mastronardi expertly identifies the culture clash that ensues when a school of social work engages with a northern community to provide a social work program that can only be properly delivered in Inuktitut and requires significant input to the curriculum both in content and method by the individuals and communities it will serve. This whole process is made vivid by Annahatak's reflections on her time as a community worker in Nunavut.

Garwood and Stevenson's discussion of Aboriginal healing practices provides further insight into the deep cultural context that is both unique and fundamental to the development of effective Aboriginal social work. In the chapter, "Walk a Mile in Social Work Shoes ...," Acco and Garwood take this a giant step further in outlining the critical need for Aboriginal experiences to be validated (this is also addressed in Mastronardi's chapter). Given the systemic prejudice that exists, a strong sense of self is necessary to combat the forces of assimilation. They also describe the advantages and disadvantages of the adaptive court system, both in the North and in metropolitan settings. Finally, they give us a list of principles to help reduce the prejudicial barriers that contribute to systemic racism and prejudice. Thompson Cooper, Dobson, and Stacey Moore present a teaching as healing model that draws on the wisdom of both traditional psychology (Rogers, as cited in Wright, 1993), and Feehan and Hannis (1993), to mention only a few. This model recognizes that both the student and the teacher change in the process, which is often hard for traditional educators to accept.

Stacey Moore's chapter gives a first-hand account of the conceptualization, negotiation, initiation, implementation, and, finally, integration of a Certificate Program in Aboriginal social work practice. She describes this as a "think piece," not a "blame piece" and achieves that goal very well. All of this is placed in the context of Aboriginal professional social work and education in general. Grenier's qualitative analysis of focus group testimony from current and former students in an Aboriginal social work education program helps us understand the challenges that students and graduates face as they struggle with perceptions of marginalization and devaluation in the traditional academic institution.

The perspectives from Australia and New Zealand are particularly helpful since these countries face many of the same obstacles as Canada, and have generated some creative mechanisms that are instructive to all. My own experience of learning about the overrepresentation of Aboriginal Canadians in the prison system is validated by Anglem's reporting of a 50 percent prison population of Maori in New Zealand, even though the Treaty of Waitangi (1860) was visionary compared to Canada's Indian Act (1876), which I believe illustrates the complexity of the situation. In addition, the description of the Australian program at Charles Sturt University, and its suspension and relaunching, demonstrates the universality of these challenges.

The honest and uninhibited reflections of the educators, students, and alums in this important work provide an uncommon glimpse into the world of professional education and a profession that is ambivalently struggling with one of its greatest challenges. Clearly this book will provide direction for some and validation for others, but perhaps, most importantly, a stimulus to the much-needed discourse on Aboriginal social work education.

A class in Nunavik in the early 1990s with teacher Annie Alaku. Space permitting, Inuit community worker students always preferred the floor to the formality of desks.

Chapter 1

Walking on Thin Ice:
The Evolution of the McGill Certificate Program in Northern Social Work Practice

Liesel Urtnowski

> Social work started from the White people. Since Inuit cannot fully adapt to the lifestyles of White people and White people cannot fully adapt to the Inuit lifestyle, Inuit, through their knowledge of their fellow human beings, must work on social work. They must adapt White people's ways of doing social work so it can be applied to Inuit.
>
> —Tamusi Novalinga Qumak
> (personal communication, 1984; translated from Inuktitut)

In recent decades a number of Canadian schools of social work have initiated programs to provide culturally sensitive social work education to groups of Aboriginal peoples. In large part these programs resulted from recognition by Aboriginal groups as well as by some schools of social work that the dominant society's models of social work practice cannot be directly transplanted to the Aboriginal context. The programs have evolved to reflect varying degrees of Aboriginal control of curriculum, learning materials, and teaching methods (Castellano, Stalwick & Wein, 1986; Brown, 1992).

As the need for such programs became apparent to some of us, the difficulties in balancing the various claims (e.g., governmental, academic, communal, personal) of the participants also came into focus. Between 1981 and 1999 I was intimately involved in this process as the designer and coordinator of the McGill University Certificate Program in Northern Social Work Practice. The field was new and there were few models for what we were attempting.[1] Ultimately the realization of the project depended on the self-awareness, attentiveness, and co-operation of southern instructors and consultants, some non-Inuit social service agency managers in Nunavik, and Inuit community workers.

The Certificate Program now offers most of its courses on-site in the Inuit communities of Nunavik—Arctic Quebec, the northernmost third of the province—and in Inuktitut, the working language of the community workers. The cost of training in the North is extremely high, and the logistics are complicated by the distances and the capriciousness of the weather. In these conditions, the Twin Otter aircraft bringing workers and instructors to a settlement chosen for a course can be grounded or delayed, causing absences that require subsequent makeup sessions. Despite the challenges presented by distance, lack of educational background, and cost, by June 1999, 17 Inuit community workers had completed the 30-credit program (10 courses) while 32 more were at various stages of completion. With only three course offerings per academic year, interruptions due to weather, illnesses, and family problems, as well as high personnel turnover in the job, it takes longer than three and a half years to complete 30 credits. Nevertheless, one of the certificate graduates was able to continue her studies full-time in Montreal and, after another two and a half years, became the first Inuk BSW in Nunavik. She is now a social work supervisor in Kuujjuaq.

In the following pages I take a retrospective look at how the program came about, what my objectives were, and how I approached the development of curriculum and course content. The academic requirements of the university and the expectations of the two Social Service Centres in Nunavik that employ the workers were important and are discussed. However, what was of paramount importance to me then, and remains so now, was that the program be responsive to the unique context of the North and the specific needs of the community workers, and, further, that the process by which the community workers play a central role in defining their own educational needs be built into the program.

What transpired involved a process of call and response, back and forth, between me and the Inuit community workers, and (through me) between the community workers and the university and social service agencies. Because the program could not have been developed successfully without their input, interspersed among my reflections and observations are the voices of the Inuit workers. (In most cases, out of respect for their privacy, I have not included their names.) Throughout, I attempt to address a central and ongoing contradiction faced by the community workers: their need for acceptance and validation by the social service bureaucracy on the one hand, and for the approval and support of their own communities on the other. In my view, this tension is profound and permeates almost all aspects of our work together.

Nunavik: Physical and Social Context

I remember when men used to go hunting a lot by dog team. The meat would be shared. If a man killed caribou, everybody would gather in one small house. It would be full and we would eat all together. There were no stores, so we lived the hard way. We girls were left with our mother to learn how to sew. Now that is all changed. Men hunt less and go to jobs. Even our mothers are working. My mother says she's tired of working, but food, housing and clothing are so expensive. My younger sisters don't know how to sew because my mother didn't have time to show them. (Community worker, class project, 1983)

The 14 communities of Nunavik are sprinkled along the 1,500-kilometre coastline of eastern Hudson Bay, Hudson Strait, and Ungava Bay, north of the treeline, between the 55th and 62nd parallels. In the 1990s, some 90 percent of the almost 9,000 inhabitants were Inuit. The population is unique among North American Native groups for the extent to which it continues to use its indigenous language: Almost all Inuit continue to speak Inuktitut in their daily interactions within the family and in the villages.

The South is geographically remote. The southernmost Nunavik village, Kuujjuarapik, is more than 1,100 kilometres from Montreal; the northernmost, Ivujivik, almost 1,900 kilometres. Since the region has no roads, all travel is by air and thus costly. In the 1990s, only Kuujjuaq and Kuujjuarapik had airstrips for larger jets; the other communities were served solely by Twin Otters.

Internet connection was gradually set up for medical and government organizations in the very late 1990s. Until then, communication was limited to telephone, fax, or a very slow mail service, making contact laborious and often frustrating.

These isolated villages vary in population from about 160 inhabitants to nearly 2,000. The population is young. In 1987, during the time covered by this memoir, 55 percent of Inuit were under 20 and only 4 percent were over 60. In 1992, 41 percent of the population were under 15 (Santé Québec, 1994). The birth rate was four times the national average.

Until the mid-1900s most Inuit of northern Quebec were still nomadic or semi-nomadic, although they had been trading furs for many decades at Hudson's Bay Company stores in exchange for goods such as guns, pots, tea, sugar, and flour. As people gradually moved into permanent settlements to be near a Hudson's Bay store and perhaps a school, they also began to rely more on imported foods and goods. By the 1970s, almost all Inuit in Nunavik had taken up permanent residence in coastal settlements. Many Inuit families chose to move into the settlements because they were denied the Family Allowance unless their children attended school. Of course, housing and proximity to nursing stations were also valued by Inuit. As they moved into the settlements, an increasing number of Inuit took on regular paid jobs. All these changes encouraged a more sedentary life. Instead of coming into the settlement to trade or join seasonal celebrations, people travelled out of it to hunt and fish.

The traditional economy (hunting, gathering, and trading) now runs parallel to a money economy. A few Inuit are employed by the Northern (formerly Hudson's Bay Company) stores, some local businesses, a nickel mine, and co-operative retail stores,[2] but most jobs are found with governmental or para-governmental organizations. The unemployment rate is high, especially in the smaller communities, and about 20 percent of the population receives welfare. The cost of food and all goods imported from the South is expensive, and while much of the diet consists of traditional foods, younger people often prefer imported foods. The work of hunting has also become more costly. In the words of a male community worker who trained under the Certificate Program:

> We have to have full-time jobs in order to afford hunting gear, gasoline, and a skidoo. Hardly anyone uses dog teams anymore. But when we have to work every weekday, we can only hunt on weekends and that doesn't provide enough game to feed the family for a whole week. So we have to buy food at the store too and hold full-time jobs.

Since the move to settlements and the establishment of more regular contact with the South, the communities have suffered from the encroachment of the dominant political and economic system, whose cumulative effects are evidenced today by increases in family disputes, depression, suicide, generational differences in expectations, violence against women, and drug and alcohol abuse.

If the birth rate is four times the national average, so is the suicide rate. Among men 15–24 years old, it increased three to four times from the late 1980s to 1995 (Régie régionale du Nunavik, 1995) to reach 211 per 100,000, about four times that of the rest of Quebec. In 2000 the overall suicide rate in Nunavik was 82 per 100,000; in the rest of Canada it was 13 per 100,000 (Inuit Tapiriit Kanatami, 2000). This is only one indication of the severe social stress and disorganization brought on by increased contact with the South and its foreign institutions and the concomitant loss of Inuit control over many aspects of daily life.

For instance, Inuit were coerced into regular school attendance (either in their small communities or in residential schools in Churchill, Manitoba, or in Ottawa). A male community worker, born in 1948, wrote in a 1984 class project describing his experience in the community of Salluit:

> In 1957 the government came and started to build a schoolhouse. And at that time the government started to drag me out of my igloo. So just imagine, driven out of your igloo into a house is already too much. The teachers were very strict in school. So I'm trying to be very gentle to my children because of the shock somebody did to me. So I've been working on and off in the white way which is not satisfactory in either of the two ways of life.

Changes in social relationships resulting from the introduction of technology and wage work, a sedentary village life, and the erosion of the Inuit economic base have also weakened traditional helping approaches and mechanisms of social control. A female community worker, who trained in the program, wrote in a 1983 assignment:

> In my community [Kangisualujuaq, on the east shore of Ungava Bay], there were not too many problems until Government came in 1959. Before, we used to share food and there were no drugs and no alcohol problems. Then we started to make money for food and clothing. Before, everybody used to help each other with everything. When Government came to North, then they told us what to do and Inuit followed what they said.

Encroachment by southern interests also had a very physical aspect. In 1985, another worker wrote about her community, Puvirnituq on Hudson Bay:

> In the 1970s government really started coming in like a river. People didn't have time to think or look at what the government was doing to the land, for people were busy doing what the government had brought in, like gambling and drinking. But then we came to our senses and began to try to pull away from the James Bay Agreement [1975]. The government was trying to take the land, which was the resource for me and my people.

Some community workers have said that younger Inuit are more seriously affected by these disruptions than those over 50, as suggested by the high suicide rate among the young. Older people, they say, tend to be more rooted in traditional Inuit culture and therefore seem to suffer somewhat less identity confusion. While older people also have problems with substance abuse, they tend to retain traditional skills (hunting, fishing, and sewing). Many are distressed by the loss of these skills among the youth. In turn, many young people, as a result of the invasion of southern cultural forms, no longer rely on the guidance of elders. As well, many of the young drop out of school and a large number turn to alcohol, drugs, and gasoline sniffing. Their parents and elders are not sure how to approach these new problems, especially since they themselves are too often grappling with problems of depression, alcohol abuse, or family violence. As social problems become more severe, communities rely increasingly on the interventions of the Social Service Centres and their Inuit and non-Inuit workers.[3]

Origin and Development of Social Service Structures: Local Reaction

From World War II until the 1960s, according to one Inuk elder, Inuit contacts with *Qallunaat*[4]—White people—were mostly with federal officials; a few nurses, teachers, and missionaries; and Hudson's Bay Company employees. Most Inuit were then still living on the land, moving from place to place according to the seasons and the migration of animals. In the 1960s, in keeping with its policy of increased sovereignty over the North, the Quebec provincial government began to take a more active interest in the region. At about the same time as families were moving into the first houses being built in the small coastal settlements, provincial schools were established and federal nursing stations were brought under Quebec control. As the role of the state became more pervasive, Inuit became subject to a social service system alien to their cultural practices. Whereas previously elders were asked to mediate disputes or advise on solutions to individual problems, "helping" was now to be organized through the state models of social service delivery.[5]

In 1979, a tiny hospital in Kuujjuaq was incorporated as the Ungava Bay Hospital and Social Service Centre. Meanwhile, the Kativik Regional Council (later Regional Board) of Health and Social Services was created with coordinating and planning functions similar to those of other regional councils throughout the province.[6] In 1983, because of its great expanse, the region was divided and a second Social Service Centre was created in Puvirnituq to serve the seven westernmost communities, along Hudson Bay and Hudson Strait. From then on, the centres in Kuujjuaq and Puvirnituq operated as separate entities with little communication between their community workers; the two groups of workers rarely met except to take courses.

Public housing, nursing stations, and airstrips in each community were generally welcomed by the Inuit, who benefited from some health care and were freed from periods of intense hunger. They valued the medical, social, and economic development impetus from the *Qallunaat*. At the same time, government services, controlled by forces beyond the region, aroused strong feelings of dependency and alienation. In the words of a male worker:

> My father used to trap foxes to trade and buy what we needed and fish with the nets and catch lots of them. When he came back he used to share with all the families in the settlement. All the brave hunters used to do that. Today, in the same settlement, there are a number of men fishing with the nets and catch more than my father and they share as my father did, not because they want to help people as my father did, but they want the money from the [government] Hunters' Support Program [hunters were paid for their catch even before sharing]. Since they can get this money nobody feels to give away their catch.

The ways in which programs operated left control largely in the hands of the *Qallunaat*, thereby perpetuating the historical relationships of colonialism. For instance, when the first few Inuit were hired as community workers in the late 1970s, they were expected to translate for the three non-Inuit professional workers. This was soon recognized as next to useless by Inuit workers and clients. Among other problems, the non-Inuit were perceived as intrusive in their questioning of Inuit clients as they based their assessments and decisions on assumptions of the dominant culture, and put the Inuit community workers in embarrassing positions by asking them to translate inappropriate statements or questions.

Subsequently, during the 1980s, the Inuit workers gradually acquired more responsibility for dealing with problems of individuals and families. Yet Inuit workers continued to be troubled and angered by the non-Inuit workers' control. As Inuk worker Lolly Annahatak wrote in a 1995 essay entitled "Reflections of an Inuk Community Worker" (the complete text of her comments is in the next chapter):

> Often non-Aboriginal workers do not understand or cannot accept that an individual's needs may be perceived as secondary to a family's needs and rights. On the other hand, sometimes family members do not accept that they cannot dictate to an individual as they did in the past. (p. 1)

This worker recognized that Inuit differ from non-Inuit, and even among themselves, in their assessment of whose rights should prevail and in what context, but reject the privileged position of non-Inuit in determining such rights.

Delivering social services to Inuit people through the legal and organizational structures that serve the rest of Quebec poses other problems. Supervisors and administrators are mostly non-Native professionals from social work or related disciplines. Services in each small community are provided by Inuit workers who are geographically far from their supervisors. In the 1980s and 1990s the Inuit community workers had little (if any) formal education—most had not completed high school, and a few in their fifties had very little formal schooling whatever. Yet, because of their knowledge of the culture and language, these workers have been indispensable to the effective delivery of social services in Nunavik. Services offered include those related to the federal Young Offenders Act (replaced in 2002 by the Youth Criminal Justice Act), the provincial Youth Protection Act, foster placement for children with special needs, increasingly frequent crisis intervention (especially for battered women), and home care for the elderly and the disabled. By the early 1990s, each community had at least one part- or full-time worker hired to provide child welfare services under the Youth Protection Act and one worker who focused on adult services under Quebec's CLSC (Centre local de services communautaires) structure.

Genesis of the Certificate Program in Northern Social Work Practice

With the passage of the Youth Protection Act in 1979, no area in Quebec could be exempt from the administrative jurisdiction of a Social Service Centre, a major part of whose mandate was the application of the Act. The expected increase in youth protection referrals—coupled with a general rise in social problems and the remoteness of the communities—made it all but impossible for a Social Service Centre in Nunavik to fulfill its mandate without having Inuit workers stationed in each community. The handful of White workers in the North could not hope to cover all the communities. Further, they could not communicate directly with most of the population, nor could they bridge the gulf between Inuit ways of helping and southern social work practice.

By 1981, the *Qallunaat* director of social services for the entire Nunavik region had hired two university social science graduates (not social workers) to respond to social crises on both the Ungava and Hudson coasts. However, because almost all of the direct work had to be done in Inuktitut and with knowledge of cultural practices, she also began hiring Inuit community workers for some of the settlements to assist the *Qallunaat* workers. This necessary change led to the need for social work education for the newly hired Inuit workers. Eventually the Quebec government agreed to pay training costs under the terms of the James Bay and Northern Quebec Agreement of 1975.

In 1981, two years after the Social Service Centre was established at Kuujjuaq, the director of the centre asked the McGill School of Social Work to collaborate on a training program for the community workers, an initiative for which I accepted major responsibility. In retrospect, I can see that I responded with rather naive enthusiasm to such a challenge. My knowledge of the lifeways of Aboriginal peoples was limited to having taught a few First Nations students in our Bachelor of Social Work program. Although I had cross-cultural experience as a social worker in Latino communities in New York City and in Mexico, my lack of credentials to teach social work to Inuit students far outweighed my qualifications. I needed to educate myself; the director of the Social Service Centre readily agreed that the matter of training needs should be explored with the community workers themselves. I therefore met with them in early 1982 when they were flown into Kuujjuaq to be introduced to the Youth Protection Act and to be offered a program of training in social work.

The concept of social services was almost totally new to the Inuit; the tension in the community workers' position was palpable. During our meeting I became aware of their sense of subordination. Some were passive, while some wondered whether the community would understand and accept the law. One said that Inuit had their own appropriate, though unwritten, family laws; another was unwilling to accept the task of convincing his community of the need for this White man's law—he lamented that he was already being accused of acting like a White man. A third worried that the law would make people feel that they were incapable of caring for their own children.

Yet they clearly hungered for information on what social workers do in the South. They recognized that for them these were new times with new problems, calling for new interventions and new tools. When it came time to discuss a program of study, the community workers, six women and two men, told me a little about their work, which they had been doing for about a year. They explained that the job posed a number of problems for them. They wanted to know how to get people to stop drinking; what to do when men beat their wives or girlfriends; how to deal with people who sniffed gasoline, took dope, or suffered from depression; and how to resolve marital conflict. They asked what happens in psychiatric hospitals, since Inuit had been sent to Montreal for treatment of strange behaviour.

We agreed that if they found southern values and methods to be inappropriate or irrelevant they would tell me, and we would figure it out as we went along. They suggested that if I wanted to become acquainted with their lifeways, I should arrange to live for a while in one of their communities. I was to hear this advice again and again in the years to follow. Observation rather than simply listening to an explanation exemplifies the Inuit way of learning.

On the last day of our meeting in Kuujjuaq, the workers asked that I return as soon as possible to begin teaching. It was my feeling at the time that, compelled to work under a system imposed from the South, they were grasping at any help and support that might be offered them.

At the end of the first course, the workers unanimously proposed that courses be hosted by different Nunavik communities on a basis of rotation. In this way, they felt, they would gain credibility in the communities: Residents would be able to see for themselves that the job required special training and members of the community would become accustomed to social services as an institution, and our students would not be isolated from the social context of their learning. The workers preferred to board with Inuit families and eat traditional food, although a few years later they did ask that one course be given at McGill so they could also feel part of the university. Community locales offered advantages for the instructors, as well: We would have the opportunity to be participant observers, and we would have the benefit of the knowledge and guidance of community elders and leaders.

The teaching took the form of two-week intensive courses on various topics of practical application (decided upon among us) given by southern instructors (at first usually myself and a colleague), and offered about every three months at a gathering of students and instructors at a community in Nunavik. Along with the courses each student underwent a two-week fieldwork practicum under the supervision of a southern instructor (initially, most often myself).

Over time I began to realize that these community workers needed and deserved recognition for the studies they had undertaken and respect for the skills they were acquiring. The idea for a Certificate Program in social work, patterned on the McGill Certificate Program in Northern and Native Education, took hold.

Inception of the Certificate Program

From 1982 through 1999 I was coordinator of what came to be known as the Certificate Program in Northern Social Work Education. It received the McGill Senate's final approval as a Certificate Program in 1987, and community workers were given retroactive credit for courses they had already taken. Originally funded by Manpower Canada and subsequently by the Quebec Ministry of Social Affairs (through the Regional Board of Health and Social Services), it was transferred in 1992 to the Ministry of Education.

The program grew naturally from the courses the community workers had already been attending. The general pattern of intensive courses, fieldwork, etc., was effective and was retained. What became immediately pressing was the question of curriculum.

Preparatory to generating curriculum for the first phase of the program, I attended a conference at the University of Saskatchewan at Regina. Present at that conference were leaders of First Nations and Métis communities and some non-Aboriginal social work professors. From the report of that conference, entitled "Indian and Native Social Work Education Project" (1982), I adapted the following questions as a guide for my own reflections:

1. What are the needs and philosophy of those who will be affected by our educational efforts?
2. What are the social and cultural characteristics of Inuit society that must be incorporated into the teaching?
3. How can social work education in the North contribute to eventual control of social service delivery systems by the Inuit themselves?
4. What knowledge and skills will Inuit social service workers want and require in order to develop social welfare and social service programs to suit the needs of their own communities?
5. What are Inuit presently doing that they consider social welfare activity?
6. What are the traditional ways of learning and of teaching?

Meanwhile, and almost from the first moment, another series of questions and problems arose. To paraphrase the late Jack Cram (1978) of the McGill University Certificate Program in Northern and Native Education: How could English-speaking instructors convey education concepts to students whose first language was Inuktitut, whose English was for the most part very basic, and whose level of formal education was in many cases limited to elementary school?

Since many of the workers had spent the first six to 10 years of their lives in tents and igloos before government services and policies pressed them to move from the camps into settlements, their early formal schooling had been irregular. They could all read and write Inuktitut and some English, but their skills were not equal to the task of reading social work texts or writing essays. Ideally, they would have been offered more basic education in both Inuktitut and English before taking on the social work education program, but the situation was urgent, and they did have experience as workers in their communities and they were willing to risk the experiment.

There was also a corollary to Dr. Cram's question, and it was just as pressing. How could southern non-Inuktitut-speaking instructors who had little or no education in the lifeways, concepts of time, and cultural values of the Inuit hope to understand the needs of their students? How could we even assess the appropriateness of the education we were offering?

Clearly if solutions to any of these questions were to be found, it could only be by recognizing the needs of the partners in the project, through consultation, and by practical experimentation.

Developing Curriculum: Preconditions and Expectations

A number of major considerations shaped the Certificate Program's educational objectives and determined curriculum content. From the outset, a balance had to be found between three sets of needs: (1) McGill University requisites for a Certificate Program; (2) Social Service Centre job requirements; and (3) the educational needs of the Inuit workers.

1. University Requisites for a Certificate Program

The academic and administrative requirements of McGill University School of Social Work regarding admission standards, credits, and student evaluation closely parallel those of other social work schools in Canada. The community workers met few of the entrance requirements, but the McGill Centre for Continuing Education agreed in 1987 to accept as students those workers who were at least 23 years of age, held at least half-time positions as community workers in a Nunavik community, and had been recommended by the administrator of their Social Service Centre. Appraisal of high-school records was waived since most students had not finished high school. It was also agreed that after completing 10 courses the student would be eligible to apply for advanced standing in the Bachelor of Social Work program.

I had to retain the course titles and numbers of social work courses, but fortunately was not pushed to reveal how I would proceed to formulate and create course content. So, for instance, while a course offered at the university might have a theoretical slant, a course of the same title offered in Nunavik could be designed with more practical content.

Student evaluation was another area that demanded elasticity. The university system requires that marks be given for each course, but there is no requirement that students produce university-length papers as course assignments. For these we could substitute more appropriate methods for assessing student progress (e.g., end-of-course exams; short written pieces based on experiential assignments; community research projects). It is noteworthy that the Inuit students in the early period did not care about marks. There was evidence neither of competitiveness among them nor of interest in their teachers' formal evaluation of their work.

I had to negotiate all the above administrative requirements without the direct input of Inuit. Distance, culture, and language precluded their participation at that point. I could only make every effort to bring about the most flexible arrangement possible and then inform the workers. I was fortunate in that my strategy of maintaining sufficient vagueness was accepted by the university; explicitness was not demanded of me.

It took some years to develop and receive approval for the final curriculum plan, course list, and outlines, since these were negotiated with the first small cohort of students and discussed with social work professors who taught those courses at McGill but were not inclined to travel to the Arctic.

2. Social Service Centre Job Requirements

The two Social Service Centres, which employ the workers and expect them to function with relative autonomy in their home communities, are heavily concerned with legal mandates with regard to youth protection, young offenders, foster care, mental health, violence against women, and services to the elderly and disabled. Technical aspects of social service delivery are paramount in their model. Presiding over the Social Service Centres is the Regional Board of Health and Social Services. The board, whose director for most of the duration of the Certificate Program was an Inuk woman, actively supported the program, although it was not involved in planning curriculum.

The Social Service Centres co-operated with efforts to plan courses and agreed to the paid release of workers to attend the courses. However, the expectation that the courses could prepare the Inuit workers to function according to the models and standards of mainstream social work and to adhere to technical agency requirements—almost instantly—was problematic. We could only meet them in part, and only slowly.

For example, thorough recording is especially necessary in cases of youth protection and young offenders, in which evaluations are central to decision making by the agency and court. So, while administrators and supervisors were aware that Inuit were working in a system that is strange to them and that Inuit culture does not have a written tradition, they expressed frustration with the lack of verbal or written information from Inuit workers about their clients.

Consequently, they expected more teaching of the writing of detailed psychosocial assessments (Dulac, 1996). One administrator commented: "It takes them hours to collect their thoughts and write one page. Clearly it is a matter of schooling; not many had the opportunity to attend secondary school." Perhaps so, but this might also be an example of differing social perspectives. An alternative explanation could be that Inuit workers resisted offering extensive information to non-Inuit employers about members of their communities who might also have been relatives. In the context of legal and policy frameworks, workers may feel more allied with their clients than with non-Inuit supervisors and managers. The context in which they are required to offer information is one of unequal power, in which Inuit cultural values and practices are vulnerable to negative judgment by non-Inuit social workers and managers.

Another concern of non-Inuit managers was that the Inuit workers hesitated to confront their clients, to question them more closely, and to follow up on difficult cases. The Certificate Program, they said, should focus more heavily on teaching the techniques traditionally used to deliver a product consistent with law and professional practice. The non-Inuit administrators did not ask that we facilitate an interrogation of mainstream practices where they collide with Inuit values and practices.

We had to find a way to extract and teach what was of value in professional techniques such as good reporting, active intervention, and follow-up without losing sight of valid Inuit concerns.

3. Educational Needs of Inuit Community Workers

To do their jobs the Inuit community workers needed both a broad education in traditional areas of social work—direct intervention, social welfare, and community development—and a critical understanding of legally mandated social services, most of which were quite new to them in the early 1980s, and which continue to pose special problems in their practice. They expressed the need for better understanding of the Youth Protection Act, the Young Offenders Act, and laws pertaining to physical abuse of women, as well as for information about suicide and alcohol and drug abuse. They wanted to know what concrete actions could and should be taken about these problems. At the same time, they wanted to express their resistance to these "White man's laws" and to discuss the "Inuit way" of resolving social problems.

Traditional Inuit helping practices respond satisfactorily to the needs of many members of the Inuit community. At the same time, the increased incidence of serious social problems resulting from powerful influences from the South, coupled with legal requirements imposed by the newly instituted social welfare structures, led the workers to call for training that addressed both the needs expressed by members of their communities and the demands of their job description. In this program, consequently, assignments were, and remain, practice-based, with follow-up in the form of a credited two-week intensive practicum in Inuit communities (or in Montreal, if the worker prefers and is sufficiently fluent in English).

The training needs of these workers are special. Inuit have to learn the White system and at the same time find their own place as trusted community members and even leaders. They are constantly in the process of blending Inuit and non-Inuit ways of working, with the ultimate goal of control over their own social services. Any teaching program would have, therefore, to attempt not only to communicate southern models of social work practice but also to encourage workers to articulate Inuit ways of helping and solving problems. Course material and information had to come from the communities as well as the university and the social services.

Developing Curriculum with Inuit Workers: Preliminary Observations

What and how to teach were questions that crystallized the divergent expectations of the three major players—Inuit, the university, and the Social Service Centre. Fortunately, I had considerable freedom at the outset to balance the three sets, but it was impossible for a non-Inuk to completely determine Inuit training needs. Ideally, I would have had the opportunity to consult with elders and community leaders, in addition to my consultation with the community workers and the director of social services, but time, distance, and cost precluded such a wide-ranging approach.

With consultation, I decided that the aim would be to help community workers develop whatever knowledge and skills they might require in order to contribute to the betterment of their communities, to deal more confidently and effectively with non-Inuit organizations, and to begin thinking about what kinds of social welfare procedures and social service programs would respond to the needs and values of their own communities.

To that end, Paulo Freire's popular education model seemed appropriate as a tool for developing course content and as an approach to the teaching process itself (Freire, 1970, 1985; McLaren & Leonard, 1993). His model starts with people's everyday experiences, problems, and hopes, and then helps them to examine and understand the conditions of their lives. It encourages a participatory process, developing critical thought and creative expression, and linking analysis to action. In relation to social work, it helps to break down the separation between practice and theory and between direct practice and social policy. It also advocates less dependence on experts and more trust in people's own descriptive, analytical, and action skills. The model builds on the experience and knowledge that members bring to the group. I decided to begin with the workers' daily experiences, to explore some southern content, and to revise as we went along.

My limitations were immense. To prepare myself as best as possible, I extensively researched (and continued to do so) the history, cultural practices, and social conditions of the Inuit. In 1982 and 1983, I co-taught a few courses in Nunavik, one with a social work practitioner who had lived among Inuit on Baffin Island. During that time I also spent a total of about four months divided among a few communities, working alongside the Inuit workers. While focusing on the immediate concerns of the workers, I was able to draw out the culturally based practices upon which they already relied and to test some mainstream social work principles and methods, which most of them were eager to examine and to try to apply. During the 1980s I also spent some weeks in additional communities with workers ready to do the practicum. This credited course allowed me to test the usefulness of course content and reflect further on curriculum. The entire process of developing the Certificate Program was one of action and reflection, always a layering, always a revision as a result of new learning on everyone's part.

Developing Curriculum, 1982–1989:
Interaction, Observation, Reflection

Although only a sojourner in the North, I was able to learn about the complex nature of community work. I learned that in these small communities where everyone is known to everyone else, the pressures inherent in responding to problems are immense. The expectation of the Social Service Centre that workers intervene in any situation of abuse, including one instigated by a relative, was particularly distressing. Such an encounter was to be avoided if at all possible. The work was especially painful in the smaller communities where, at the time, there was only one community worker. In communities with two part-time workers, cases could be shared and the pressure somewhat relieved.

A further stress was the tendency for community members to expect service at any hour of day or night. Almost all the workers were women who meanwhile had families of their own to care for. They would be called out to do anything from ordering children home late at night to dealing with aggressive or mentally ill people. In communities that had no police constable, or where the constable was temporarily absent, community workers were particularly likely to be called upon for policing interventions.

Workers complained that community members did not understand their role and that they had insufficient support and guidance from supervisors about expectations and difficulties. These distant supervisors and managers were rarely available outside office hours. In some communities, the community council would aid the worker in difficult situations. In many communities, the council was of little help to the workers, preferring instead to refer problems to them.

The equivocal position of the workers was also a source of tension. Community workers frequently found themselves having to defend laws, policies, and forms of intervention that were neither accepted nor understood by members of their communities. One Inuk worker said: "We have always handled problems within the family and a social service worker meddling in family affairs is difficult to accept. There are times when we do not feel comfortable discussing a problem with clients older than ourselves, especially with men." Another worker reported that a father of a seriously misbehaving boy told her that, since he would never go to her house to discuss her children's problems with her, she should not meddle in his family affairs. Despite explanations, this father could not see the worker as other than an Inuk community member; the role of "government worker" was abhorrent and foreign to him.[7]

A worker in a small community expressed his dilemma in the 1980s by drawing a picture of his head divided into quadrants. He explained that in the worker-client relationship he had four identities simultaneously: (1) to the people in his settlement of about 600 he was either a relative or a friend; (2) as an Inuk he was loyal to his people and their traditions; (3) as a helper he did his best for the community; and (4) as an employee of the government he had to work in its interests, although it had been acting against the best interests of the Inuit. How could he be an Inuk, he asked, a member of the community, while in the control of the Social Service Centre?

All these factors led to a continuing high rate of burnout and staff turnover. Yet, while most workers viewed the "White man's laws" as inappropriate and badly administered, they simultaneously sought in *Qallunaat* forms of intervention that might control some very destructive behaviours in their communities. A number of workers told me that legislation "is all we have right now to separate aggressive people from their victims. When we lived in the camps, we had ways to deal with such behaviour; since moving into the communities these ways don't always work anymore." As a last resort, then, the Inuit workers see some value in appealing to legislation. In the classroom, meanwhile, there is the opportunity to discuss useful traditional ways as well as those *Qallunaat* methods of intervention, which many see as having helpful elements.

In my early visits to the communities, workers often wanted to watch me work and arranged joint meetings with a few English-speaking clients. Some workers also had me meet with unilingual Inuktitut-speaking people while they translated, thereby helping me to become more acquainted with their culture. Others used some of our time together to speak about their personal situations.

Of particular interest to me were the workers' reactions to my efforts to elicit expressions of feeling from some of the clients. Several workers felt this was "not the Inuit way," but a few workers speculated that community living, as well as contact with *Qallunaat*, had brought a new view that lent some legitimacy to the expression of feeling about subjects that had been kept hidden previously. In 1984 two workers, who had watched me with the same family, differed in their assessment. The first said: "I want to learn more about how to go into a person's feelings. Inuit are all words and no feelings." Her colleague said: "No, it would be better if we did not learn *Qallunaat* ways of interviewing. You should learn to speak Inuktitut." In another community a worker commented: "There is a way that you can talk with clients that brings out emotions that I didn't think existed in Inuit, especially in older Inuit. There are some Inuit who never talk to each other about what they feel or what they think."

The question of who would speak of emotions, and when and where and with whom, turned out to be much more subtle than these comments imply as I was later to discover from these same students, in the classroom, speaking in their mother tongue.

Between English and Inuktitut

In my use of Freire's communication-intensive model, the question of language became more and more critical. I had quickly learned that Inuit ways of teaching and learning differ from our system of formal education, which focuses on developing skills in abstract and linear reasoning leading to conclusions often removed from the context of daily life. Inuit knowledge, on the other hand, comes from daily observation, from practising whatever skills are necessary to group life. "[Inuit pass] along knowledge through observation and imitation embedded in daily family and community activities, with integration into the immediate shared social structures as the principal goal" (Stairs, 1993, p. 86). Stories and experiences are used to illustrate principles, but it is up to the listener to draw conclusions. The daily life, traditions, customs, and stories—the knowledge of the Inuit—are embedded in their language, Inuktitut, and Inuit survival is intimately linked to the knowledge contained in that language.

While educational institutions have shown renewed interest in the retention of Aboriginal languages, the degree to which knowledge and language are interwoven has been less often understood or acted upon. Although I had become somewhat aware of this issue as a child of immigrant parents, I became more sharply cognizant of the fact that language is not simply a matter of words and phrases and that Inuit need to use their own language to grapple with the difficult issues inherent in the practice of social work.

The limitations that the English language imposed on our communication were obvious. What also became clear was that many of the everyday values and concepts of Western professionals are as foreign to Inuit culture as the words of our languages. Even when words were understood, meanings were often unclear. And because we were operating from within different cultural-linguistic contexts, often Inuit workers could not convey their meanings in a way that made it easy for me to apply social work principles and concepts to their work in any straightforward fashion. For instance, Inuit express the high value their culture places on individual autonomy by not asking intrusive questions about a person's inner world, family relations, or personal motivations; they do not inquire about or discuss someone's personal problems until that person requests assistance. On the other hand, the needs of the family and the immediate community often supersede those of the individual to a much greater degree than in the South. And when interventions for unacceptable behaviours are necessary for the Inuit, they are almost never openly confrontational. Traditional social work practice often relies on direct questioning in sensitive areas; is often in the position of intervening against the wishes of some of the parties in difficult situations; and, in its legal aspects, can be quite confrontational. So, while we all agreed that, for example, caring for children, the elderly, and other vulnerable people was fundamental, we had to work hard to find adaptations of the varying ways of intervening. As Tamusi Novalinga Qumak, a highly respected elder, expressed it in the quote at the beginning of this article, "They [the community workers] must adapt White people's way of doing social work so it can be applied to the Inuit."

Our two cultures may agree that the object is to help troubled individuals, but several factors affect the delivery of social services—among others, the conditions under which help is offered, the manner and timing of the approach, and the identity of the helper vis-à-vis the client. The same is true in the classroom. During the early stages of the program, a *Qallunaat* co-teacher and I taught the first few courses in English. At the time, the six to 12 Inuit workers all spoke English well enough to follow the courses in English. However, as the social service organization expanded to cover all 14 communities, some of the Inuit workers hired spoke little or no English. Furthermore, it had become increasingly clear to me that classes should be taught in the students' own language to maintain and promote their identity as Inuit.[8]

It was time to deliver the courses in Inuktitut.

Teaching in Inuktitut: From 1989 Onwards

And so it was that in 1989 I began to prepare all courses at McGill with pairs of experienced Inuit community workers, who would begin to teach the two-week intensive courses in Inuktitut in one of the communities a few weeks later. As consultant on the specific subject matter of a course, I often chose a non-Inuit practitioner who, preferably, had worked with Aboriginal peoples or, for one course, was Aboriginal herself. During the course preparation (10 days of intense and concentrated work for each course, each time it was offered) we shared information and ideas. The Inuit instructors brought examples of practice situations that challenged some general social work principles. These might take the form of how questions are posed to clients, or of how one might follow up an initial contact with a troubled client or family, or of confidentiality in a small community. From our side, we tried to teach the Inuit instructors social work skills in a manner respectful of their concerns and the constraints under which the community workers worked.

The issue of adapting *Qallunaat* interviewing styles to the Inuit context is a complex one. Inuit teachers often told us "you can't say it that way in Inuktitut," which undoubtedly referred as much to the cultural appropriateness of an intervention as it did to the translation of words. As a form of resistance, this frequent comment also challenged Inuit teachers to articulate and develop "the Inuit way" toward a model of social services for Nunavik.

For example, while preparing a course on mental health, we had to be aware of different conceptions and understandings of mental health and illness. The teachers recognized that interpretations of behaviour and notions of causation and treatment differed considerably between the two cultures as well as among the Inuit themselves. There is space in courses for the expression of all views and some students have presented situations in which devils were exorcised, as well as examples of interventions involving a change of environment to another community, or referral to a southern psychiatric consultant or facility. It is left to the bicultural teachers and the workers themselves to sort out which interpretations and interventions are most appropriate for their communities at the time.

The Classroom from the Back

While the first two-week intensive course was being delivered in Nunavik, in Inuktitut, by the Inuit community workers, the consultant and I were available at all times for clarification, support, or administrative assistance. Sitting behind the students as the two Inuit teachers taught and responded to the students, I literally took a back seat. I had to relinquish control of the teaching process, something a university teacher rarely does. I saw that students participated more actively than before, but could not know what was being said. Barred from the thoughts and exchanges they expressed in their own language, I felt both a sense of profound loss and a deep appreciation of the appropriateness of the change.

I also learned a great deal. One of the first revelations had to do with the question of emotional expression. Many non-Inuit students in my McGill classes have experienced abuse and painful family relationships. Some have talked to me privately about such troubles, but rarely in the classroom. They have respected the established boundaries of the academic context. Not so the Inuit. I was astonished to see, as soon as courses were delivered in Inuktitut, an outpouring of emotion—crying, even wailing—followed by quiet expressions of comfort from classmates. Sometimes, especially when the subject was sexual abuse or suicide, one person's pain would spark expressions of anguish in a second, third, and fourth member of the class. Once, I saw tears flowing down the cheeks of 16 faces—the entire class—as the students responded to each speaker. At the suggestion of the Inuit teachers we instituted Healing Circles on two or three evenings during the two-week session as a way for some of the more troubled workers to benefit from the support and caring so freely offered by their Inuit teachers and classmates from other communities.

Our notion of proper student behaviours in an academic setting is challenged by these Inuit students, who disclosed their personal histories and their inner worlds in the social work classroom. They reported to me that they were learning a great deal from one another through the telling of experiences in their own language, although, from my side, I could not be sure which, if any, basic concepts or social work principles were illustrated and implicitly coming through in their exchanges.

The next revelation was how the spirit of unity and support I observed during personal disclosure of painful experiences was extended to the classroom process in all areas of the courses. In my university classes, students debate and argue as they wrestle with theory and course material. Usually differences of opinion among the Inuit students were not apparent to the *Qallunaat* observer. Speakers, whose stories were sometimes rather lengthy, were respectfully listened to and never interrupted. Social cohesion was evident. Furthermore the collective interest in bettering their communities was always at the forefront as they shared their experiences and struggled to develop new tools.

The role of the two bicultural, bilingual Inuit teachers was central to the preparation, teaching, and development of the curriculum. Because they lived and worked in their culture, they brought not only their knowledge of Inuit lifeways and world view, but their understanding of the social effects of neo-colonialism in its various forms such as written laws, technological change, and bureaucratization. In the classroom they behaved according to Inuit norms, teaching and responding to students in a manner congruent with cultural precepts. More importantly, they clearly brought their identity as Inuit, which served to reinforce pride and solidarity among the students. As Louisa May (1996), the bilingual, bicultural Inuk director of Youth Protection for the Ungava coastal communities, stated it:

At times it becomes difficult for us to find a way to adapt the *Qallunaat* ways to our own way of dealing with social problems.... [I]t was clear that courses had more impact on [students'] understanding of the subject matter when it was given by an Inuk teacher in Inuktitut than by an English-speaking *Qallunaat*.... Students could more readily discuss and share how social problems were viewed, experienced, and felt in their own language and from the perspective of their own culture. They were then able to develop tools and learn more about how they might deal with social problems in their communities. (oral presentation)

In their evaluations at the end of each course offering, the students expressed a high degree of satisfaction while commenting on teaching methods. They particularly appreciated role plays of real situations—sharing and learning from each other's experiences—and joint sessions with non-Inuit Aboriginal social workers during a course in Montreal. Most said they learned from victims and survivors speaking about their ordeals, the help they received, and how they found the strength to carry on. The Inuit teachers would assist students in drawing useful concepts from the presentations.

Students consistently showed a strong interest in hearing from respected local elders on the general topic of a particular course. The elders represent an invaluable source of knowledge in traditional methods of helping, rules of communication, acceptable processes of decision making, and the characteristics of a good helper. At least one elder was invited to present in each of the courses. They told stories of how particular problems, such as depression, sexual abuse, or child neglect, were dealt with in the near past and offered principles for such dealings. Although there are now new and more severe social problems, traditional helping processes survive and are, as much as possible, being incorporated into the new system by the workers. They form the basis of the worker's identity as an Inuk helper and contribute to a sense of continuity between the old ways and the new, largely imposed, ways. The students also noted that views, definitions of problems, and suggested solutions sometimes differed among elders, especially according to gender.

Community workers, while articulating their struggles during classroom time, were only too aware that the social service structure is laid down by Quebec law and that there was little hope of changing this structure. The neo-colonialist process was clear to them, although not named as such. Resistance to their subjugation at work was expressed in various ways, for example, by not reporting methods of intervention in every case; by solving problems with help from other community members such as the mayor, an elder, or a council member; or by explicitly expressing their disagreement to supervisors and managers.

In 1996 I asked a researcher at the McGill School of Social Work Family Centre to design and carry out an evaluation of the Certificate Program. He interviewed students and Nunavik *Qallunaat* social service managers. His findings confirmed my own impressions and are still relevant. Regarding the students, he (Dulac, 1996) reported that they continued to seek information about the laws and procedures related to the Youth Protection and Young Offenders Acts, including court appearances, knowledge about descriptions and treatments of major mental illnesses, and factual information about methods of birth control and about structures of government. They wanted to learn about and practise *Qallunaat* intervention methods and techniques. For some, this included an emphasis on psychological concepts related to human development. Their overriding aim, they said, was to help community members and themselves deal with severe personal pain and problems in family relationships. They expressed continued insecurity about intervening in crises such as attempted suicide, sexual abuse and assault, and wife abuse and increasingly saw these as requiring community initiatives, as opposed to their own individual intervention. Agency managers, for their part, spoke about the difficulty Inuit workers had in confronting clients, in writing reports, and in following up on cases.

Dulac noted that, although the students did focus on the development of knowledge and skills directly related to their job descriptions, they also articulated their experience of subordination within the social service bureaucracy. They actively sought to talk about renegotiating their position, rather than merely devising strategies to adapt to imposed programs and policies. They expressed a greater awareness of their potential role in community development and social action, leading them to want information and skills in these areas as well.

Some Concluding Remarks

Clearly, developing and planning courses is beset by many complex needs, desires, and requirements. Aside from the pressures already mentioned, there are those that arise from the obvious fact that the Inuit are not a homogeneous group. Their diversity includes differences in extent of schooling, in income, in travel, and in degree of expertise in a given area; there are differences of opinion by (among other things) age and gender, about numerous values and practices, and there are differences of experience within Inuit culture.

The importance of these differences is best understood by illustration. Throughout this chapter I have only superficially commented on gender relations among Inuit in Nunavik, but they figure prominently in the daily operation of social services. First, although the overall turnover rate in personnel is high, there are few male workers who remain in their positions for more than a brief period. This might reflect the nature of agency social work, since legally mandated services focus mainly on work with individuals and families: the domestic sphere. This division of labour closely resembles that of the South where the majority of social workers providing direct services are women, while the leaders in administrative and in community development positions are most often men. Second, during my tenure, 100 percent of graduates of the Certificate Program were women. Their interest in this type of work, along with their wish for legitimacy, led them to pursue this educational opportunity. Nevertheless, I noticed that their roles as wives and mothers came first. For example, on more than one occasion a student left a course having been called home by a jealous husband; once a teacher could not come in because her husband needed her to make bannock. Generally, these students were more hesitant to intervene with older men than with women. In the cases of battered women and child sexual abuse, the victims were usually female. Nearly all of the workers had experienced such abuse, or knew of someone in their extended family who had. Yet, after one class, the two male workers came to tell me that they had not realized that the abuse affected the women *so* deeply. This indicated to me how difficult it is for workers to confront abusers and how profound the denial is on the part of men. No social work training has a hope of being effective if the difference in the daily life experience of Inuit women and men is ignored.

The interplay of gender relations, traditional values, southern values, neo-colonialism, and the like precludes simplistic approaches to the severe social disruptions Inuit are experiencing, and there are no easy answers as to what tools community workers need in trying to deal with the effects of these disruptions. In the words of anthropologist Jean Briggs (2000), "such an intermingling of traditions and lifestyles, both individually and socially in the community, creates a troublesome tangle of wishes and needs. People disagree about the legitimacy of any given expectation, and, thus, about whether it should be accommodated" (p. 115). The students in the Certificate Program do not stand outside these tensions, they live them every day. As they live them, they try to negotiate them in order to ease the pain of their neighbours while acting as both buffer and conduit between their communities and the social service institutions. Since they find that neither mainstream southern models nor their own traditions provide ready or clear answers to new social problems, the program courses must always include discussion of both non-Inuit and Inuit beliefs and practices.

The educational needs of the Inuit, despite certain constants over the years, are always evolving in response to overall changes in Nunavik, Quebec, and Canada. Furthermore, the Inuit workers continue to move from primarily wanting to acquire the skills and knowledge demanded by their jobs to exploring and strategizing ways of taking charge of interactions and social service policies affecting their communities. As planning for self-government proceeds, there must be room for discussion and debate among the students about the kind of social services they envisage. Inuit continually need to make decisions about what they find useful in southern laws and social welfare policies and structures, and what they will select and integrate from their own traditions. There is some concern that if they lose their familiar world and at the same time accept part of the new without engaging in critical reflection and without being able to control the pace at which changes are brought in, they will feel overwhelmed. There are signs that, while our students individually resist those *Qallunaat* bureaucratic structures and practices that emphasize top-down imposition and intrusion into people's lives, the communities and the whole region will need to join a public endeavour and debate to create a vision of a flexible, dynamic Inuit social service and social work practice.

From the moment of my first contact with the Inuit workers I have been forced to reflect on the values of my own culture and its relationship of dominance vis-à-vis Aboriginal peoples. For example, during the first course the students assumed that since I was a trained social worker and a university professor, and since I was one of the powerful *Qallunaat* from the South, I would also have the power to produce immediate solutions to any social problems they presented me. As they tested me in those early years, there was a noticeable increase in their sense of identity as Inuit with many beliefs and values different from non-Inuit social workers. Pride in their identity and empowerment grew as the group took an increasingly active role in the development of course content. This was especially evident after we hired experienced Inuit community workers as teachers. The frustrations and hopes of many are expressed in the words of Dorothy Mesher (Mesher & Woolam, 1995), an Inuk graduate of the program:

> [You] could say that the *Qallunaat* are just using their Inuit employees to bring the South up North. They want to run everything, and do everything, their own way. I suppose it seems that we're going along with all that.
>
> However, I continue to be an optimist. In the future I still like to dream that these organizations will be completely run by Inuit. Every year we're getting more and more graduates and there's always a few serious ones. Young Inuit will be qualified in the future. So it's my hope that some day it will be different! (p. 105)

The process of developing the McGill Certificate Program and teaching under it drew me into an ongoing exchange across a cultural frontier. The choice to leave this interchange relatively open-ended, to attempt to broaden the spheres of consultation within Nunavik, and to treat Inuit lifeways with respect does not imply that I see the cultural world views that intersect as equivalent in social power. On the contrary, to see myself or the Inuit teachers and workers outside relations of domination and subordination would constitute a serious evasion. The reflections on our own practice as McGill social work educators also need to include our own implication in the process and structures of oppression.

FIGURE 1.1: NUNAVIK

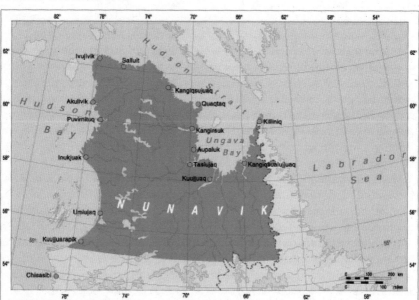

Source: Gouvernement du Québec, Secrétariat aux affaires autochtones

Despite differences, we did communicate, reflect together, and engage. We made progress in connecting and transmitting meanings. I found that sharing elements of our personal lives enhanced our connectedness as people and built bridges in the understanding of each other's cultures and values. This gentle process of working toward common goals greatly enriched my personal development.

I thank the Inuit community workers of Nunavik for their support, patience, and faith in my ability to share with them my experiences, culture, and world view. I also thank them for the many ways in which they have taught me about their lives and their understandings.

Notes

1. In Canada, the McGill Faculty of Education was the only post-secondary professional education program offering on-site courses in Inuktitut. Over the years, the Faculty of Education model (with adjustments and modifications appropriate for social work education) continued to offer practical suggestions.
2. The co-operative movement began in the late 1960s in order to sell the carvings of Inuit sculptors. Later it expanded into general retail stores in each community. It had an ideological bent promoting Inuit self-government and development.
3. The names used here for Quebec government bodies are the English equivalents by which they are known in Nunavik. The official name for a Social Service Centre is "Centre de services sociaux."
4. The origin of *Qallunaat* as a term for White non-Inuit "seems to be from the Inuktitut phrase meaning 'people who pamper their eyebrows,' and it can imply a people who pamper or fuss with nature, or are of a materialistic nature; greedy" (Pauktuutit Inuit Women of Canada, 1989, p. 5).
5. The term "helping" is infinitely complex and can carry varied and even contradictory meanings within Inuit culture. Until recently it did not encompass a great deal of what stands behind the concept of the "social services." For example, it does not include a sense of the power/requirement to enforce solutions mandated by laws and regulations originating in distant government bodies, nor of abstract "professional practice," nor of bureaucratic pressures. For a description of traditional Inuit methods for maintaining social order, see *The Inuit Way* (Pauktuutit Inuit Women of Canada, 1989, pp. 6–9).
6. Conseil régional [later Régie régionale] de la santé et des services sociaux.
7. There may be several factors at play in these examples. In the first place, "the strong communal nature of Inuit culture exists beside an equally held belief in individual autonomy: Inuit place a high regard on the right of individuals to lead their lives free from interference of others. This strongly affects the way people interact. Basically this belief causes Inuit to often feel a certain degree of discomfort when exercising authority over other Inuit even if the position they hold warrants sufficient authority. Conversely, Inuit are unlikely to welcome someone trying to dictate their actions or speak for them without their consent" (Pauktuutit Inuit Women of Canada, 1989, p. 17). Furthermore, as women, particularly young women, the customary rules of conduct related to gender and age may have prevented these workers from feeling confident in a role that granted them the power to act as a representative of the state in dealing with parents and grandparents.
8. Most of the non-Inuit government workers and merchants in Nunavik are now francophone. Since only a handful of *Qallunaat* speak Inuktitut and few Inuit speak French, communication takes place in English, a second language for both groups.

Lolly Annahatak, recipient of an Aboriginal Achievement Award in 2005, with her daughter, Phoebe, and Pita Atami, Makivik president

CHAPTER 2

Intervention Difficulties between Inuit Clients and Non-Inuit Workers

Lolly Annahatak

During my years as a community worker in the North and in serving at Le Module du Nord,[1] situations have arisen where I felt clients were turned off by non-Inuit interviewers who were not sensitive to the cultural background of the Inuk person they were interviewing. I can recall situations where I have felt uncomfortable and stuck when I had to translate questions that were not helpful to the client. I often wondered why the worker for whom I was translating could not understand that the techniques of questioning he or she was using were not appropriate. Often they were too direct or challenging and failed to take into account our perspective of thinking. At other times they were too evasive in responding to questions from the Inuk client.

I now realize that many of the difficulties arise because of our cultural differences and that there is a need to closely examine our relationships as workers (both Inuit and non-Inuit) with Inuit clients. We all come to situations with different perspectives and we need to acknowledge these when working.

Whenever an Aboriginal person is translating for a non-Aboriginal worker who represents a non-Aboriginal agency, the situation is strained at best. If the situation is sensitive, the client can feel "ganged up on" to some extent. Even though the translator is Inuk, she or he is representing a White social service institution and, in the moment, is translating and working for a non-Aboriginal who is questioning the client.

It is fair to say that the culture of Inuit of northern Quebec (Nunavik) is still extremely important to us and defines many of our lifelong rights and obligations. In contrast, most non-Aboriginal workers come from societies where the individual is expected to develop his or her own place and not derive much from, or depend on, the family for support and assistance. In addition, the service they represent is much more oriented toward individual rights than most Inuit have experienced. This can lead to many difficulties in terms of expectations. Often non-Aboriginal workers do not understand or cannot accept that an individual's needs may be perceived as secondary to a family's needs and rights. On the other hand, sometimes family members do not accept that they cannot dictate to an individual as they did in the past.

Inuit culture was very structured. Elders played an important role in decision making and in dealing with problems. This can raise difficulties in social work practice, especially when we focus our problem-solving efforts on the individual (deal individually with problems). Often only a few family members are involved in our interventions and this works against the client, his or her family, and our own objectives by undermining what we are trying to do.

These situations also bring into play many of our beliefs and values. The family was and is, to a great extent, still the most important unit in our culture. Traditionally, family problems were handled within the family and in some instances the presence of a social service worker meddling in family affairs is still difficult for many Inuit to accept. Very sensitive cases, such as dealing with the Youth Protection Act, arise and are difficult to handle.

Another difficulty is that Inuit have a different outlook on time. Inuit have some difficulty accepting schedules as, for instance, at a hospital or Social Service Centre. This makes it difficult for workers to interview people at set appointment times. Inuit usually do not come to their appointments and often show up when they don't have one. This is frustrating for non-Natives.

Another aspect of the Inuit approach to life is that often Inuit people want to talk about many things at once, instead of the one issue on which the non-Native social worker may want to focus. Often the situation that is being discussed may have a very simple solution in the mind of the non-Native worker, but the person being interviewed wants to raise other aspects that the worker is not interested in hearing about.

Another important area in which there can be some problems in communication concerns the Inuit's strong attachment to the community in which he or she lives, while non-Native workers do not usually feel this strong attachment. This can lead to problems when clients are encouraged to press charges against someone. The non-Native worker does not always take into account the effects on an Inuk who presses charges against someone in his or her village. I think this is because most think that you can move away, when in reality most of us have not accepted this option.

The last difficulty I would like to discuss is how social service bureaucracies rely heavily on written documentation. Inuit culture does not have a written tradition. Many workers still have difficulty dealing with clients because written documentation is still foreign to them, and they don't understand the finality of agreeing to something in writing.

Until recently we were isolated from mainstream culture. However, the North is changing rapidly. Younger adults are more aware of both cultures. Television and schooling have played a major role in changing perspectives. Many people are more aware of social problems and of their individual rights. We are beginning to see conflicts between the outlooks of the younger and older generations in our communities. This is causing a great deal of conflict and frustration. Many of our youth are caught between the two outlooks and feel that they do not fit in either culture anymore. There is a need to support them and bring the generations together.

Note

1. This is the organization that deals with medical needs of Inuit in Nunavik.

NICKI GARWOOD

After the hunt, along Payne River, Nunavik

CHAPTER 3

From Igloo to Internet:
Shifting Terrains of Power and Knowledge in Inuit Social Work Education

Laura Mastronardi

As Canadian indigenous peoples endeavour to secure jurisdiction over their own social services, social work education programs offered by mainstream post-secondary institutions take on increasing importance. To respond effectively to indigenous student and community objectives, mainstream initiatives must provide culturally appropriate social work education that addresses "their communal need for capacity-building to advance themselves as a distinct and self-determining society, not just as individuals" (Kirkness & Barnhardt, 1991, p. 5). The challenge for universities in meeting these objectives is considerable, particularly given the historical role of education and social work in the colonization of indigenous peoples. In light of this history, social work education programs designed specifically for indigenous communities provide a unique opportunity to investigate the shifting relations of power between indigenous peoples and state institutions.

If we are committed to walking the path of social justice in the profession and practice of social work, as mainstream educators we need to question whether our knowledge base, curriculum, and the practices of the institutions in which we work actually reflect this commitment. This requires an examination of broader pedagogical and curricular issues that takes us beyond questions of course design and the quality of interactions in the classroom to consideration of the ideological and political dimensions of our pedagogic practice. A commitment to walking on the side of the oppressed compels us to engage critically with the tensions and contradictions involved in the attempt to develop a transformative educational praxis in settings centred in domination.

With the foregoing objective in mind, this chapter provides a critical reflection on the Certificate Program in Northern Social Work Practice, a program of social work education offered by the McGill University School of Social Work for Inuit students in Nunavik, which is the vast Arctic region of the province of Quebec.[1] In this essay, I contend that if our intention is to deepen prospects for Inuit self-determination, we must confront the problems embedded within current practice that reproduce historical relations of domination and oppression between Inuit and Whites. The discussion in this chapter unfolds in the following manner. I begin by locating myself as the author of this text to enable readers to decide for themselves the relative strengths or limitations of my practice critique. I then describe the social and historical context of Inuit social work practice to demonstrate its relevance to educational program design and implementation. In the following section, I describe and analyze how the ideological and structural constraints arising from the program's institutional location reproduce knowledge and social relations of domination. In the next section, I provide a brief narrative of practice and identify specific mechanisms that resist and challenge the reproduction of Eurocentric hegemony to create a space for an Inuit approach to social work to emerge. In the final section of the chapter, I draw upon lessons from my analysis of current practice to suggest pathways toward a decolonized social work pedagogy.

Choosing Marginality

In essence, this chapter offers a critical reading of my own practice experience, which has taken place on the border between mainstream and Inuit cultures. By turning a critical gaze on the Nunavik program, I am implicating my own practice as a former instructor and program coordinator. I believe this is an essential starting point for my exploratory and analytic activities if my theoretical and experiential knowledge is to have any relevance to my ongoing efforts to develop a critical teaching practice "since political agency, experience, and knowledge are transformatively connected" (Bannerji, 1991, p. 91).

At the heart of this endeavour lies the personal contradiction I experience as a White female from a middle-class background, and as an academic and university lecturer attempting to advocate for Inuit self-determination. The history of racist schooling in Canada renders my pedagogic practice, as well as my efforts toward advocacy, problematic. I know that as a White person, I am in a position of relative privilege to the Inuit people with whom I have worked in the northern program and that I need to be constantly vigilant about the danger of appropriating their discourses and voices. At the same time, I believe I have a moral and ethical responsibility to use my position to speak about issues of oppression in social work practice and education.

I am aware that giving voice to my concerns about the current operation of the Nunavik program entails certain risks, not the least of which is the possibility of being perceived by my mainstream colleagues as "selling out." Given the privileges of being in the academy, choosing marginality as one's identification is a political act. Ex-centricity, Mohanty (2003) observes, is about being disloyal to the reconstitution and reproduction of hegemonic processes and dominant ideology. According to Anzaldua (2002), who describes the borderland as a space where one finds comfort in ambiguity and contradiction, the dislodging of hegemonic comfort zones provides a different lens and enables a process of revisioning, an opportunity to explore the possibilities of solidarity and collectivity in the fissures between privileged and marginalized communities.

Working on the margin, hooks tells us, enables the subject to "cross the border" and "to see reality from the outside in and the inside out"; it provides the subject with a "mode of seeing and a way of understanding unknown to those at the centres of power" (1990, p. 149). "Since the border crosser is both self and Other on both sides of the border, working on the margin and acquiring the consciousness of borderlands means possessing contradictory knowledge that cuts across dualistic thinking" (Tastsoglou, 2000, p. 102). Reflecting on my attempts to develop a teaching practice congruent with social justice principles—that is, to learn how to walk my talk—what stands out for me are the tensions and contradictions I experienced between my espoused values and the actual practices in which I engaged as an instructor and program coordinator. This experience serves as a touchstone and point of entry for my analysis of the problems embedded within the Nunavik program.

The Context of Inuit Social Work Practice and Education

To appreciate the complex issues and challenges involved in the attempt to develop culturally appropriate social work education for Inuit students and their communities, we must situate our analysis of the existing program within its social and historical context. Marker (2002) observes a tendency in much of the literature about Aboriginal education "to describe settings and programs in a way that isolates their discussion from larger economic, cultural, and political concerns," and "an exclusionary focus on 'Indians' without looking at non-Native bureaucrats, administrators, teachers, and community members" (p. 30). These tendencies in program description and analysis disguise the fact that Aboriginal education is "about cross-cultural negotiation and power differentials." As a discursive site of Indian-White relations, education remains "a central arena for negotiating identities and for translating the goals and purposes of the cultural Other."

Various depictions of the contemporary Canadian North in the social work literature draw attention to the unequal relations of power between North and South. Zapf (1999b) describes northern Canada as a "product of exploitation, underdevelopment, and colonialism by federal and provincial centres in the south" (p. 44), while Challen and McPherson (1994) note that, in effect, "northern communities have lived in the shadow of overriding concern for the prosperity, development, and needs of larger centres" (p. 196). "Northern life also means a lack of autonomy, the absence of freedom, and the subjugation to external control—that control may be professional, bureaucratic, or economic but it engenders a stultifying relationship of economic and social dependency" (Tobin & Walmsley, 1992, p. 1).

Economic exploitation, cultural domination, and the political control of Inuit by external forces have been the subject of much of the historical, critical scholarship about the nature of internal colonialism in the Canadian Arctic region. Summarizing the central claims of this body of scholarly work, McLean (1997) notes:

> Inuit economic self-sufficiency has been destroyed through a downward spiral that began in the era of whaling and fur trading, and continues in the current era of wage labour and welfare assistance; since the 1950s, Inuit cultural integrity has been undermined through explicitly assimilationist state programs and the integration of large numbers of Euro-Canadian managers, trades people, and professionals; and Inuit political autonomy has been compromised through the constitutional and legal structures imposed by Euro-Canadian governments. (p. 22)

The legacy of dependency and divisiveness brought about by several decades of rapid change under White tutelage continues to cast a pall over contemporary Nunavik. Failed attempts to absorb Inuit into the mainstream of Canadian society are evidenced today in kinship and family breakdown, and high rates of violent death, substance abuse, and suicide, particularly among Inuit youth. The effects of Western domination also include "a profound diffusion of identity, and self-hate or fear of one's own culture," which manifests in "unconsciously vacillating between western and [Native] behaviours, and the loss of cultural vision, which is critical in the formation of one's life" (Colorado, 1995, p. 71).

Although the negative consequences of White colonialism are painfully familiar to Inuit, and we cannot ignore the ongoing systemic oppression that continues to place severe constraints on their lives, we would be remiss in focusing only on their subordination and thereby undervalue their resilience and collective strength as agents of change in their own world. Indeed, perhaps the most definitive feature of life in today's Arctic is the shifting relations of power between Inuit and Whites, which McLean (1997) describes in the following way:

> While economic dependency remains acute, neither unequal exchange nor the extraction of surplus value characterizes many Inuit communities; while a cultural division of labour still pervades wage employment, explicit assimilation is no longer official policy and Inuit are assuming many supervisory and managerial roles; and while sovereignty remains with the federal state, Inuit have attained some degree of self-government through provincial policies and [modern land claims settlements]. (p. 23)

As McLean's analysis implies, in order to maintain a critical analysis of Inuit-White relations in the present-day context, we need to recognize that overt colonial processes have given way to more subtle forms of governance within contemporary arrangements between Inuit and dominant society institutions, including education and social services. As Paine (1977) correctly identifies, the form that the current relationship takes obscures the reality that Inuit continue to be devalued. On close inspection, we can see, for example, that the paternalism characteristic of historical relations between Inuit and Whites has not been diminished by the increased presence of Inuit in the social service sector.

The extension of state-organized social services into Nunavik might best be described as a process of opening the branch plant (De Montigny, 1995). Pursuant to ratification of the James Bay Northern Quebec Agreement in 1975, and implementation of the Youth Protection Act in 1979, the provincial government was compelled to establish a decentralized system to provide social services in the 14 coastal settlements of the Nunavik region, a development that could only be accomplished by hiring Inuit as service providers. Previously they had been employed primarily as language and cultural interpreters for White professionals from the South. The service delivery system that evolved replicates the bureaucratic structure and divisions of labour that typify southern, mainstream practice.

The northern practice context is one in which Inuit practitioners struggle to define their role as helpers at the juncture between Inuit traditions of social welfare and those of the dominant society in an environment controlled largely outside of Inuit influence. Customary Inuit approaches to helping have been displaced by the centring of Euro-Western theories and practices as the dominant social work paradigm. The case management model in current use—including social work processes of intake, case recording, clinical assessment, clinical intervention in the form of individual and family counselling, referrals, and the termination of files—has become a taken for granted way of providing service (Waterfall, 2003). Yet this model of practice is highly problematic for Inuit workers, who find themselves compelled to speak and act in uncharacteristic ways that frequently violate cultural norms. Additionally, this model of social work practice has failed to bring about any significant change in individual and community well-being.

Accountable to both agency and community for their interventions, Inuit workers find themselves in a subordinate and oppositional stance vis-à-vis the service bureaucracy. Their need for validation from both their employers and community members constitutes an intractable practice dilemma—the more they succeed in meeting agency expectations of their work, the more likely they are to be judged unfavourably by community members, many of whom are justifiably suspicious of the "White man's law" (Mastronardi, 1990). Moreover, community members often question the value of social programs and do not have a clear understanding of their purpose. Consequently, there is a lack of recognition, respect, and validation for the profession of social work and the role of social workers. Adding to these stressful conditions in their environment, Inuit workers are also vulnerable to negative valuations of their practice by their professional White colleagues and supervisors. The cultural knowledge that Inuit workers bring to their jobs is not highly valued while their lack of formal academic preparation makes them easy targets for accusations of incompetence.

Despite its obvious lack of fit, agency administrators uphold the need for a conventional service delivery model as a means to ensure practice standards; at the same time, the communities and Inuit workers themselves press for innovation and local control (Mastronardi, 1990). The contrast between agency and community priorities gives rise to competing expectations of workers' practice and thus of their academic preparation as well. Administrators emphasize the need to ensure workers' technical competencies (i.e., to meet bureaucratic requirements of the job), while workers themselves acknowledge the necessity of technical proficiency, but stress their need to develop knowledge and skills as healers and agents of social change.

The foregoing discussion of the Inuit workers' practice context reveals that the design and implementation of culturally appropriate social work education is a daunting challenge. My experience of the Nunavik program is that it functions as a contradictory site that both enables and limits possibilities for an Inuit approach to social work, including the construction of new forms of worker identity, to emerge. Although the program mediates dominant society conceptions of social work practice, it does not fully challenge the prevailing Eurocentric paradigm; the program has both oppressive and liberating tendencies. I now turn to an examination of this inherent tension in the operation of the Nunavik program.

Cultural Reproduction: Ideological and Structural Constraints on the Nunavik Program

The challenge of providing culturally appropriate social work education becomes evident at the practice level where conventional programs designed for mainstream practice settings fail to prepare students for professional responsibilities in indigenous communities. To prepare students adequately for practice in these settings, programs must be designed in close collaboration with indigenous peoples and be grounded in the social, cultural, legal, and political contexts that students will eventually encounter (Canada, 1996c). The history of university-based program development elsewhere in Canada reveals that the active participation of indigenous peoples in the design and implementation of educational initiatives intended to meet their needs is essential to program success.

> [Educational] initiatives may have the term Aboriginal in their titles, but without animating consultation and the plenary participation of Indigenous peoples—indeed without honest acknowledgement of the history of colonial education's privileges and benefits—university programming will continue to be paternalistic, promoting a gendered, classed, and racialized politics of knowledge production and dissemination. This production of knowledge amounts to cognitive imperialism, a form of mind control, manipulation, and propaganda that serves elites in the nation. (Battiste, Bell & Findlay, 2002, p. 83)

How does the social work education program offered by McGill for Inuit students fare in this regard? What opportunities exist for Inuit to represent their interests and priorities in the curriculum?

At the time of its inception, the Nunavik program was loosely structured as a partnership between the university and Arctic communities to afford some measure of Inuit control. In pursuit of this objective, the program has attempted to develop strong ties with the communities through its field-based delivery format, use of local resources, and links with the social service agencies where the students are employed. Although this model has offered some opportunities for Inuit participation, the program's embedded location within the university seriously constrains the extent of their influence. The connection between the program and university is hierarchical, not lateral. Conventional administrative structures and practices within the university, which consolidate decision making in the highest echelons, effectively pre-empt Inuit participation in curriculum policy development and marginalize accountability to their communities.

The claims to autonomy of powerful interest groups within the academy further reduce Inuit capacity to exert any direct influence on the university. Moreover, as Barnhardt (1991) suggests, programs intended to respond to uniquely indigenous concerns are typically treated as "anomalous and considered outside the purview of the university's customary mission," thereby contributing to a stance of scholarly detachment and aloofness from the community they are meant to serve (p. 222). At present, the allocation of power is inversely proportional to the amount of program activity in which participants engage; the power of those who are most active in the program is restricted to a narrow range of operations, while policy decisions become increasingly distant from the classroom and the communities.

Having to implement policy formulated without Inuit participation was a particularly difficult aspect of my work as program coordinator. In effect, my complicity with administrative structures and processes that excluded Inuit as full partners cast me in the role of the colonial White tutor deciding the best interests of my Inuit protégés. The fact that the program's administrative practices are those of a state-dependent educational institution also means that the formation of Inuit students' social work ideologies is determined to some extent by the program's location within the university (Hesch, 1996, p. 285). The relative powerlessness of Inuit to influence curriculum policy ultimately has a detrimental effect on students' learning experience.

The social work curriculum can only be understood in relation to the social, historical, and political contexts in which it is embedded. From a social constructivist perspective, Apple (1989) notes, the curriculum takes meaning from the complicated and complex configurations of dominance and subordination that are external to it. As described elsewhere in this volume by Urtnowski, the social work curriculum for the Nunavik program is based on McGill's Bachelor of Social Work degree program. Attempts to adapt the mainstream curriculum to create a more culturally appropriate learning experience for Inuit students raise the question of what counts as valid knowledge for social work practice and who decides.

In order to access resources and to retain accredited program status, the School of Social Work must emphasize disciplinary knowledge in the Nunavik curriculum. As Leonard (1994) notes:

> Professional socialization into the dominant paradigm of objective, specialized, technical knowledge is the primary task of schools of social work. It is a system of knowledge production and professional advancement based upon methods of accreditation and the establishment of standards of practice. (p. 22)

To appreciate the implications of professional socialization for Inuit students, we need to be conscious of the fact that because "disciplines provide the conceptual resources which 'in-form' thought and action" (Usher & Edwards, 1994, p. 47), they also serve a normalizing and regulating function. "In the process of acquiring the ways of talking that are normally associated with a particular subject position, one necessarily acquires also its ways of seeing or ideological norms" (Fairclough, 1995, p. 39). In order to obtain the knowledge required for certification and job success, Inuit students are thus compelled to acquire and accept a new form of consciousness, an orientation that not only displaces but also devalues their world view. Moreover, professional socialization marginalizes Inuit students' cultural and experiential knowledge.

A professional discourse such as that of social work is based upon expert knowledge as an increasingly close approximation to the truth about what exists in the objective world—our diagnosis, assessment, and interpretation—and because of this, it excludes, with differing degrees of rigidity, outside knowledge … rules of exclusion that have operated so powerfully in social work to privilege forms and sources of knowledge that are Eurocentric, patriarchal, and bourgeois are an essential means of ideological domination. (Leonard, 1994, p. 22)

A persistent challenge in curriculum adaptation has been the requirement to balance the cultural appropriateness of mainstream theory for practice in Inuit settings with the need to avoid creating a seemingly inferior program by straying too far from acceptable standards as articulated in the code of ethics of the Canadian Association of Schools of Social Work (Brown, 1992). However, as Delaney and Brownlee (1996) observe, these standards do not, in fact, take into account the realities of northern practice and the dilemmas faced by Inuit workers. Thus, although "certification and educational training are strongly supported by indigenous communities to improve the quality and standards of service, the means by which certification is currently granted, and the criteria for certification, are sometimes perceived as an assimilationist tool to determine recognition of social workers based solely on mainstream educational standards" (Fiddler, 2001, p. 182). From the university's perspective, "rigorous standards derive from principles of efficiency, cost effectiveness, behavioural objectives, standardized testing, and the rhetoric of meritocracy and individualism" (Apple, 1989, p. 189). As an expression of the ideologies and educational values of the dominant, Euro-Canadian society, these standards are not appropriate for evaluating the success of programs designed for indigenous communities. Their continued application impedes "the reform required to achieve respectful and productive liberation for Aboriginal peoples from the educational apparatuses of colonialism" (Battiste, Bell & Findlay, 2002, p. 83), a point to which I will return in the concluding section of this essay.

Despite the ideological and structural constraints on the Nunavik social work education program that function to protect the hegemony of Eurocentric thought and knowledge, the program's location on the margin of mainstream post-secondary education affords some autonomous space to resist and challenge knowledge and social relations structured in domination. hooks speaks of the margin as "a site of resistance and radical openness … a central location for the production of a counter-hegemonic discourse" (1990, p. 145). In the following section of this essay, I provide a brief narrative and reflection on actual processes of course preparation and delivery that illustrate some of the efforts that have been made to create a space for an Inuit approach to social work practice to begin to emerge.

The Nunavik Program as a Site of Resistance and Cultural Production

The preparation of courses in the Northern Social Work Program is a fully collaborative process involving the program coordinator, a subject specialist (i.e., course consultant), and two Inuit instructors. Preparation entails decision making about teaching and learning objectives, course content, resources for teaching and learning, and methods for course and student evaluation. A concerted effort is made to highlight Inuit content knowledge in each course, to integrate Inuit and mainstream knowledge and perspectives, and to ground the teaching in students' daily practice realities. Pedagogical materials and related activities are obtained from Inuit or other indigenous organizations or are created as required. At the course-planning stage, consideration is also given to maximizing the use of local community resources for course delivery, including the participation of elders, community leaders, formal and informal helpers, and youth. Emphasis in course planning is placed on experiential, collaborative, and co-operative learning activities, many of which take students out of the classroom and into the community. Feedback from students who have previously taken the course, and input solicited from northern agency supervisors, are also taken into account.

Courses are delivered primarily in the communities of Nunavik in order to provide a more contextually rich and culturally congruent learning environment. Courses are taught in Inuktitut with on-site support for teachers and students from the program coordinator and/or course consultant who helped to prepare the course. The teaching team members frequently participate in learning activities with the students. Each day begins with a prayer followed by a "check-in" with all participants. Careful attention to language usage in the classroom provides an opportunity for teachers and students to clarify the meaning and appropriateness of mainstream concepts and to decide together on suitable forms of expression in their own language. All written pedagogical materials are available for students in Inuktitut and English, and students have the option to complete all written course work in their choice of language. Healing Circles are held throughout the course as required by students to support them with working through the powerful and often painful emotions evoked by the learning process. Students are evaluated on the basis of their participation, homework assignments, and a final written exam or alternative assignment (e.g., group projects, oral presentations). Students provide verbal and written feedback on each course. A celebration at the end of each course includes the community resource that helped to teach the course, and in some instances, when numbers permit, the entire community is invited to join in.

Reflection on the foregoing narrative reveals that at the local level (i.e., site-specific course development), the Nunavik program functions to some extent as an arena of cultural production that challenges and resists the ideological and structural constraints that arise from its institutional location. Some space is created for an Inuit discourse and practice of social work practice to begin to take shape. The use of Inuktitut language and syllabics in course delivery and preparation not only demonstrates respect, but also validates Inuktitut as a language of professional instruction, and facilitates a more culturally congruent learning experience for students by enabling transmission of the values and cultural meanings embedded in language. The use of Inuktitut also permits students to learn the dominant language of social work practice in a problematizing manner, which enables some measure of resistance to the ideologically coercive effects of their professional social-ization (Freire & Shor, 1987). Creating a space in the curriculum for Inuit knowl-edge disrupts the dominant discourse of professional social work and the privileging of expert knowledge in the mainstream canon. It also revalues personal life expe-rience and Inuit practitioner knowledge as crucial resources with which to con-struct a counter-hegemonic discourse and practice of Inuit social work.

The social relations in the classroom between teachers, students, and support staff, and between the classroom and community, further this objective by disrupt-ing the fixed identity categories of teacher and learner. The highly personalized rela-tionships between teachers and students effectively reconfigure relations of power and open up new subject positions for both to occupy. Here we find teachers and students, who make no claims to expert knowledge, working alongside one another in a mutual process of knowledge production. The emphasis on collaborative and co-operative learning, group process, and dialogue function to counter the com-petitive individualism of mainstream classrooms and to provide a more culturally sensitive approach to teaching and learning. Additionally, the attention given to both cognitive and affective elements of learning creates a safe, supportive class-room community where teachers and students can struggle together to make mean-ing of their everyday lived experiences, to develop an analysis of current practice, and to identify elements of an Inuit model of social work.

The foregoing practice narrative illustrates some of the specific ways in which processes of course preparation and delivery make space in the classroom for Inuit knowledge and ways of being and doing. We must take care, however, to further resist and challenge existing structural constraints on the curriculum, including systemic racism, so that the end result of our efforts is greater than a mere accommodation of Inuit students. My concern is that the nominal accommodations made to date within the existing program appear more Inuit than they really are. While these adjustments may change the experience of social work practice and education for particular individuals, they do not result in significant change or amelioration of the experience of oppression within students' social work practice setting or within the educational system. In the final section of this chapter, I draw upon lessons con-tained within the foregoing analysis of practice to suggest possible future directions for transformative change in the Nunavik social work education program.

Pathways toward a Decolonized Social Work Pedagogy

I want to return at this point to the tension identified earlier between academic stan-dards and community priorities as it poses an ethical challenge for mainstream edu-cators by raising the question of whose values are protected in the curriculum (Brown, 1992). The history of Aboriginal education in Canada clearly demonstrates that main-stream programs intended to benefit their communities cannot be a positive force for social change if program goals and content reflect only dominant society culture and values. As demonstrated in this essay, efforts at curriculum reform continue to privi-lege the dominant social work paradigm because they leave the core assumptions, values, and underlying logic of the curriculum itself unchanged. To function as an effective vehicle for individual and collective empowerment, the Nunavik social work education program must demonstrate genuine respect for Inuit cultural integrity by incorporating program standards that reflect Inuit values and beliefs concerning knowledge, teaching, and learning. The fundamental question is whether Inuit will be permitted to represent their values in the design and implementation of educational programs intended for their communities.

"As a profession, social work can advance its current anti-discriminatory objectives by seriously acknowledging Native people's inherent right to self-determination and in so doing problematize colonialism in all of its guises" (Waterfall, 2003, p. 62). The issues that emerge for critical social work practice and education in the neo-colonial context of contemporary Nunavik demand a focus on the deconstruction of White privilege and our ability to hear and respect Inuit voices as they reconstruct their cultural identity en route to a future as self-determined peoples. As mainstream educators working with Inuit peoples, we need to move toward greater accountability for our pedagogic practices, a process that begins with recognizing that we are implicated in systems of oppression that profoundly structure our understandings of one another. As long as we see ourselves as innocent, we cannot begin to walk the path of social justice and to thread our way through the complexity of power relations that infuse our practice.

The analysis of educational practice provided in this essay indicates several pathways toward a decolonized social work pedagogy. At the broadest level, explicit acknowledgement by the university of the effects of colonization on Canadian indigenous peoples and its role in this history is a crucial first step. Educational institutions have a pivotal role in transforming the relationship between indigenous peoples and Canadian society. Accordingly, "institutional recognition of the distinct place of Aboriginal nations in the federation of Canada and accommodation of Aboriginal cultures and identities should be regarded as a core responsibility rather than as a special project to be undertaken when other obligations have been met" (Canada, 1996c, p. 517).

A concerted effort to develop a genuine partnership between the university and the communities of Nunavik would, as Harris (2005) suggests, "clearly signal institutional recognition of Indigenous peoples' authority to participate in activities to further the development of culturally appropriate curriculum and an [Inuit] model of social work practice" (2005, p. 130). In collaboration with Inuit, there is an urgent need to develop a more supportive policy environment for the Nunavik program, including procedural and decision-making policies, as well as structures and concrete mechanisms to address program concerns as they arise. Clear definition of respective roles and responsibilities for program administration and accreditation is also needed to secure an effective partnership agreement. A firm commitment by the university to provide sustainable program funding would indicate the seriousness of its intentions. Additionally, as Harris (2005) observes, respect for Inuit cultural integrity would be demonstrated by institutional legitimating of the validity of Inuit epistemology, as well as integrating an Inuit world view into the curriculum and engaging in ongoing dialogue aimed at transforming social work education to better meet community needs.

On a final note, as mainstream educators working with indigenous peoples, we need to examine the discourses within which we are caught up, "to learn to see not only what we do but also what structures what we do, to deconstruct how ideological and institutional power play in our practices, and to recognize the partiality and open-endedness of our own efforts" (Lather, 1991, p. 20). Critical reflection on my own experience suggests that as mainstream educators we would do well to be much more humble about our knowledge claims and to abandon the stance of "one who knows." We are not in Nunavik to educate Inuit, but rather to learn with them the nature of the struggles that confront their communities and to be of service by putting our knowledge and ourselves at their disposal.

Note

1. This program is described in Chapter 1 of this book. I refer to it as the Nunavik program.

Wedding photo of Mike Stacey (Tsi iotená:to'kte—"Edge of town") and Margaret Beauvais-Stacey (Katsi'tsákwas—"Picking flowers"), paternal grandparents of Gail Stacey Moore

CHAPTER 4

Local and Global Approaches to Aboriginal Education:
A Description of the McGill Certificate Program in Aboriginal Social Work Practice

Gail Stacey Moore

I am a Mohawk woman from Kahnawake, an Aboriginal community approximately 60 kilometres from Montreal, Quebec. Throughout my life, I have experienced a full and rewarding professional and personal life immersed in the political and social issues of Aboriginal communities. One part of this includes my involvement in the Certificate Program in Aboriginal Social Work Practice (ASWCP) at McGill University.

The program began in 1995, following a number of different endeavours and developments. One of these factors included my return to McGill University in 1994 to do my master's degree in social work. The following chapter describes the program, my involvement in its development, and a discussion of the issues that emerged and their resolution. Our efforts were driven by the desire to create a program that directly and effectively addresses the needs of Aboriginal peoples with respect to social work and the social services available in their communities.

This paper will look at the following issues: First, I will identify continuing problems in Aboriginal education. Second, I will describe the development of the ASWCP at McGill. Third, I will provide an overview of key issues that evolved in the Certificate Program, pointing out models and solutions that have been put forward by Aboriginal peoples in professional positions. Models of education regarding minority groups are examined within national and international laws.[1] Finally, I will conclude by outlining the achievements and strengths of the Certificate Program.

This chapter is meant to be a "think piece," not a "blame piece." I ask readers to engage with it with an open heart and mind in order to see the hope and beauty of education and the possibilities it should hold for everyone.

Aboriginal Peoples and Education

The statistics regarding Aboriginal education are shocking. For example, in Canada, while only 9.8 percent of the total Canadian population age 15 and up have less than a grade nine education, 17.5 percent of registered Indians and 24.2 percent of First Nations people living on reserves in this age group do so. However, this is a decrease from 21.9 percent in 1996 (Canada, 2001a). For Aboriginal peoples aged 15 and over, only 3 percent have a university degree compared to 13.3 percent of the Canadian population. Between 1996 and 2001, the percentage of Aboriginal peoples in post-secondary education went from 36.6 percent to 39.9 percent while the total Canadian population enrolment increased from 50.9 percent to 54.6 percent. This means that Aboriginal student enrolment has remained at the same rate (Canada, 2001a).

Kirkness and Barnhardt (1991) question why universities continue to implement and support policies and practices that have historically produced abysmal results for First Nations students. The maintenance of such policies and practices is hard to comprehend given the ample research and documentary evidence indicating the availability of more appropriate and effective alternatives.

Castellano, Stalwick, and Wein (1986) view the same issue in the following terms:

> While the bid by Native authorities for a share in the decision-making power in University programs may be perceived as an incursion on academic freedom, institutional autonomy and legislative mandates, it could be argued that it is consistent with the influence exerted by the professionals and the interested public over the performance of other professional programs. The Native public occupies a relatively powerless position vis-à-vis post-secondary educational institutions and therefore, has very limited means, within conventional structures, of protecting itself from insensitive or incompetent practitioners who emerge from inappropriate education programs. (p. 176)

While both arguments are correct, the subsequent reasoning used to explain why the problem persists does not encompass the total picture. We must see the problem in its totality. It is not a matter of merely having more appropriate and effective alternatives (Kirkness & Barnhardt, 1991) or looking at the problem as a failure in the competency of professionals. Rather, we must reconsider the legislation mandated by the countries we live in and encourage Aboriginal leadership to press for more moral and legal commitment in America, and for the entrenchment of the existing Aboriginal right to education in Canada. At the same time there needs to be a groundswell of support from our Aboriginal communities and from universities to work together to ensure that non-Aboriginal professionals work appropriately, sensitively, and effectively in our communities.

An Aboriginal Woman's Personal Commitment to Education

One of the reasons for my solid commitment to the education of Aboriginal peoples lies in the fact that there are so few of us who are able to operate at a professional level as educators and social workers both within and outside of our communities. As an Aboriginal woman educated in the mainstream system, I know the needs Aboriginal peoples face in accessing an education. I also recognize the barriers we face in approaching the mainstream system. Because of this, I am well prepared to contribute to the resolution of the Native peoples' struggles for education.

In 1976 I began my undergraduate studies at the McGill School of Social Work. Unfortunately, I quickly became quite unhappy with the program, particularly with the absence of Aboriginal-focused readings and discussions concerning the social work needs of Aboriginal peoples. Since so many Aboriginal peoples were in such desperate need of social services, the absence of Aboriginal-centred materials was shocking to me. At that point, however, I swallowed my disappointment and continued my learning mission, choosing courses in the program that suited me and discarding everything else.

When I began the program, my approach to social work was already politicized. I was well aware of many social issues, yet much to my surprise, as my studies continued, my perspectives on many of these issues began to change, grow, and develop. In rethinking some of my strong positions and opinions on Aboriginal issues, I found they were sometimes based on rumours, prejudice, or closed-mindedness. I began to see other points of view and alternative ways of approaching the issues. Most importantly, I began to understand that change is not to be feared, but welcomed as it can improve a situation. With a conscious awareness of what was happening, I became more open to learning and thus, self-development. I completed my Bachelor of Social Work in 1979 and although my educational experience was not always positive, it equipped me to reach much that I have achieved since then.

In 1988 I became part of the founding committee of a Native women's shelter in Montreal. For the next 10 years I worked at the Native Women's Shelter with Alanis O'Bomsawin, president; Caroline Oblin, a Cree woman, board member, and a graduate of McGill's School of Social Work; and Anita Pratt, a Cree woman from Saskatchewan who was hired as the executive director. During this time, the Native Friendship Centre of Montreal was struggling with the Welfare Department to accept the centre as a home address for homeless Aboriginal peoples. The centre was eventually successful and soon after began a planning committee to establish a shelter for homeless Aboriginal women.

For five years, I was also very involved in Aboriginal politics in Ottawa. As a speaker for the Native Women's Association of Canada, I lobbied the federal government for a seat at the constitutional table for Native women and eventually took the federal government to the Supreme Court of Canada.

By this time, I had lived such an incredibly full and active life in Aboriginal politics that it was time to slow the pace, or so I thought. In 1994 I decided to go back to school to earn my master's degree. I explored a number of programs at McGill, but nothing seemed to encompass what I needed to forge ahead in my struggle in Aboriginal politics. However, I strongly believe that if we, as Aboriginal peoples, want to be self-governing, as we do, we must prepare ourselves to be the best that we can be for our nations. We must be able to fill the many roles required for self-governance. In order to do so, we must be prepared to work hard, to become educated, and to take our responsibilities seriously. I applied and in April 1994 was accepted in the Master's of Social Work Program at McGill University.

The Certificate Program in Aboriginal Social Work Practice

In 1994, when I began my master's degree at McGill University, I was immediately invited by Professor Liesel Urtnowski, associate professor in social work, to attend a meeting with the Steering Committee of what would become the ASWCP. Liesel had been coordinating the Northern Certificate Social Work Program for Inuit peoples since 1982.

Program Background

The 1993–1994 Director's Report of the Native Women's Shelter of Montreal clearly presented a significant concern within social work practice in Aboriginal communities, which became the basis of the Certificate Program at McGill. In the report, the term "training" appeared with the following explanation:

> The Shelter has also been negotiating with the McGill Department of Social Work to access training that would enable our staff to acquire the academic background they needed to function in the Shelter. This training would eventually give our employees a degree in Social Work. As such, we are looking closely at current training programs at McGill and employed by Inuit Community Workers. Liesel Urtnowski, a professor at McGill and a teacher for the Inuit program, is lending us a helping hand, acting as a resource person between the Shelter and McGill. (Native Women's Shelter of Montreal, 1993–1994, p. 4)

Because we were adamant about hiring Aboriginal peoples as counsellors at the shelter, developing a training program specifically for Aboriginal students seemed an excellent direction to take. Most of the counsellors at the shelter were untrained, but eager to become involved in a training program that also offered credits toward a university degree.

Program Development

The need for an Aboriginal centred and accessible program was also strongly articulated by a number of other Aboriginal service providers who had previously approached several faculty members of the McGill School of Social Work. As a result of extensive discussion with these individuals, the Aboriginal Steering Committee, which included representatives from the McGill and the Aboriginal communities, was established to work out the details and prospects for an accredited professional program in social work. The committee met regularly from September 1994 to the spring of 1995.

The program aimed to prepare Aboriginal peoples for social work in their communities through professional training, focusing on particular social-cultural characteristics, as well as specific social service needs in the communities, such as addictions, family violence, and sexual abuse. The 30-credit program, offered part-time over a three-year period, would be composed of students already working in social services who wished to further their training, as well as those who had little background or experience but wanted to pursue a career in social work. The program would combine classroom work and field practice. Entrance requirements for student applicants without a college diploma included being a mature student over 21, and providing two references from the community (for more information, refer to Appendix A).

Throughout the early stages of the program development, we came up against a number of hurdles. For example, the timing of the courses became an issue, with McGill bureaucracy being the primary barrier. Because of the lengthy period of time it would take to have the certificate receive faculty approval, we wanted to offer our first course before the Certificate Program was approved. Eventually we were granted a small seed grant from the office of the Dean of Graduate Studies, and were able to offer the first course in April 1995. Even though our government funding was approved by the fall of 1995, it still took a long time to navigate through the remainder of the academic procedures and bureaucracy.

Recruitment

To ensure effective recruitment, the Steering Committee members held information meetings in the places our students would come from, including Kahnawake, Kanehsatake, and Montreal. Although attendance at these meetings was surprisingly high, Native counsellors were initially hesitant to enrol in the program. Many had previously tried to gain a university degree, but had failed. Another factor in their uncertainty was the distance between Kanehsatake and Montreal. (Kanehsatake lies about one hour outside of Montreal, which, for some, is a considerable distance considering the cost of public transportation and the time involved in the commute.) Furthermore, along with their new academic workloads, most of these students would also maintain an ongoing responsibility for their families and their work outside the home. Their task was indeed arduous. Eight of the 28 students who comprised the first group of students were already employed in an agency on or off their reserves. While some were given time off or were paid to attend the course, the majority had to take pay cuts or make up for time lost by working evenings or weekends, sometimes both. Most of the students were women and ranged in age from 35–56 years. The majority of the students were living in Kahnawake and Kanehsatake, while the remainder came from other parts of Canada and were either working or trying to find employment in Montreal.

In preparation for the first course, "Introduction to Practicum," Professor Ingrid Thompson Cooper, program co-coordinator and co-instructor, and I compiled the course reader with culturally appropriate reading materials. Throughout the course I continually reminded the students that reading is an acquired skill, "so if at first you don't understand everything you read, don't give up!" A lot of effort was put into making the students feel comfortable. As the course progressed, the students were taken on a tour of the university and shown such facilities as the bank machines, and where they could obtain food both on and off campus. A tour of the libraries was arranged and there were group trips to obtain McGill identification cards. In class there was always a ready supply of coffee. At the end of nearly every class I would say, "And come back [to class] next week, I want to see you here!" They would all laugh and they would be back.

Evolving Issues and Experiences

The issues and experiences that evolved during the program included building trust in new relationships between Aboriginals and non-Aboriginals, developing writing skills, accessing student funding, dealing with personal and family crises, and approaching the application and meaning of new knowledge.

Trust Issues and the Role of the Aboriginal Instructor

It takes a particular kind of non-Aboriginal instructor to teach Aboriginal adult students. They must be flexible and open. Most of all they must not have their egos or intellects overtake their style or methods of teaching. There must be a willingness to learn from Aboriginal peoples and be able to change and adjust their teaching style to meet the needs of the students.[2] Aboriginal peoples originate from an oral tradition. Our past experiences have shown us that when we have trusted and shared our histories with others, exploitation was the result, so we are very careful when we share our lives with others.

Because I learned to trust and respect Ingrid, other Aboriginal students began to do the same. With her practical and gentle nature, Ingrid began to move among the Aboriginal students, sharing her new knowledge and experiences. We began to work in unison, trusting and respecting each other. If she had a concern or problem with what I was doing, we would talk about it and work toward a solution. The same would transpire if I had a problem with what she was doing. Because it takes time to trust others, especially after you have been misled or let down time after time, developing our relationship was a slow, purposeful process. As we built up our relationship with each other, we also developed our relationships with students. We both loved teaching our classes.

As the first course progressed, my role as the Aboriginal co-instructor[3] evolved and solidified to ensure that the program remained centred on Aboriginal concerns, needs, and strengths. As the co-instructor for all of the certificate courses, I worked on behalf of the students as a mediator between them and the instructor. Essentially, we wanted to make the students feel welcome. We focused on several key goals. For example, with respect to previous bad experiences or failures, we wanted to ensure that the students would not be afraid or reluctant to try again. We also wanted to ensure that an equal amount of course material was produced either by Aboriginal authors and/or that the curriculum and materials maintained a high degree of Aboriginal content. When this was not possible, we made sure that non-Native "theories" or materials were appropriately applied to Aboriginal culture and community.

In order to ensure that the academic language of some texts would not intimidate the students, I modelled asking questions and requesting clarification. For example, I would ask questions such as: "Could you tell us the meaning of this word? Could you explain that in some other way? Could you repeat what you just said?" I tried to show the students that they could ask questions if they didn't understand something; that asking questions does not mean you are "not very smart." In fact, I would tell them that it is "not very smart" to not ask for an explanation of something you do not understand. Furthermore, I explained that it is often the case that where one person does not understand, there are others in the same situation.

The students readily came to me with their problems, some practical and others more complicated. If I could not handle all of them, which was often the case due to the number of issues and problems, with the student's permission I would invite Ingrid's help. We also provided tutors who would be available for any problems the students had in writing their papers or in giving presentations.

Developing Writing Skills

Developing good writing skills was a problem for many of the students in the Certificate Program. For example, this sometimes resulted in the students missing assignment deadlines. Since I come from the same place as the students in the ASWCP, I understand them and what it takes to develop writing skills. I also had experienced difficulty in developing my writing skills, but I had forced myself to try, and with time and the corrections and comments of my instructors, I improved.

As a teacher, getting the students to write was a major challenge for several reasons. First, in the Aboriginal community we follow oral traditions and, second, writing is very revealing. Many of us have had to be secretive to prevent others from accessing our thought processes or inner culture. We needed to protect it because in our experience, our culture is misused and the information we give has often been used in a negative way. As a result, the students are very closed, as I was. For a long time, I could not write papers that were significant and because of this, I could not grow because I continually needed to guard parts of myself. A significant challenge I faced was balancing my need to guard myself and develop my academic writing skills.

In response to their struggles, I usually met with the students personally, encouraging them to simply write about their personal thoughts on course readings. This is why we developed the log-writing component as an assignment in most of the courses. It was a way of having the students discuss the readings and develop their own analyses, linking the material to broader themes and their personal experiences. These exercises, which are really very basic, give the students a format to follow—to read and respond. The process has become extremely helpful because it addresses both the academic and personal dynamics of education and also encourages the student to engage in classroom discussions.

One important lesson in encouraging students to develop their writing skills is to focus on content and not structure. Initially, I did not mark on punctuation or grammar. Rather, I began to do so only in the third course once the students were more comfortable with the university setting, the course and writing demands, and the instructors. It worked very well, perhaps because the students became more relaxed and less anxious, realizing that their "mistakes" in grammar and/or punctuation were not as important as their ideas and thoughts about the subject. Some instructors tell me that the writing abilities of some of our graduates are equivalent to those of third-year students in the regular program. In one instance, a student with excellent reading comprehension and oral communication skills could not write. We agreed to have an oral presentation for his final assignment. He was outstanding and was later assigned a tutor to help him improve his writing skills.

Tutorials for writing skills were filled quickly and we were continually impressed with the students' commitment to learning and to improving their reading and writing skills.

Student Funding: Scholarships and Access to Education

The students in the Certificate Program have faced many problems in accessing funds to attend school. According to the Indian Act, a federal statute, status Indians (those registered in Ottawa with the Department of Indian Affairs) are eligible for financial assistance. Many people feel that Aboriginal peoples' right to financial assistance puts them in a very fortunate situation. However, it is important to realize that we come from impoverished communities and families, and many of our students had family members—parents, siblings, and children—depending on them for some financial assistance. This is a heavy burden to carry. Native peoples tend to share money through lending and borrowing. Twenty-four percent of the non-reserve population in 2001 cited family responsibilities as an obstacle to finishing post-secondary schooling (Statistics Canada, 2003). Furthermore, many students are overwhelmed with attending university in a big city. Finding and paying for parking, babysitters, and proper attire add to the difficulty of the whole academic experience for many students and can all contribute to failure.

Lippman's research (1975)[4] finds that:

> Middle-class whites have long urged Aboriginals to partake of the education offered them, have provided scholarships to make this economically feasible and then have expected Aborigines to achieve in large number. Some have responded—many have not. (p. 18)

In Canada there is a recently established National Scholarship for Aboriginal students in social work. However, scholarship-based funding, while an important support in assisting Aboriginal peoples to have better access to higher education, has not addressed the needs of all the potential students. The requirements for sponsorships often do not take into consideration all the components and challenges to Aboriginal participation in academic programs. A case in point includes our struggle to receive scholarships or bursaries for the ASWCP students. Even though I tried very hard to gain access to Native-centred funds for our students, I was unsuccessful because our program is not a full degree program, so it did not meet the requirements of the scholarships, which required that the student complete the full degree. This was in spite of the fact that the 30 credits are equivalent to the first-year degree program and our graduates are able to apply for entry to the second year of the regular Bachelor of Social Work Program at McGill. Again, despite great need, funding and thus access to education are hampered by requirements implemented without reflecting the real needs of Aboriginal students. The 2001 Aboriginal Peoples Survey cited that 22 percent of individuals listed financial reasons for being unable to complete post-secondary education (Statistics Canada, 2003). More access must be made possible on the educational front before Aboriginal peoples can take full advantage of these scholarships.

In the ASWCP, we do a number of things to help our students financially, particularly in terms of finding money to help pay for some of the tuition fees and required books. For example, through personal contact with a former colleague of mine, I was able to access monies from a private foundation that had funds for people with educational needs. In response to the assistance we provide, several of our graduate students have told us that although they had gone to university previously, the severe financial constraints they encountered was a significant reason for their failure.

Flexibility and Awareness: Accounting for Personal and Family Crises

In the ASWCP, we make a point of maintaining a high degree of awareness of and flexibility concerning personal and community crises. This grants the students a sense of comfort and possibility, in spite of their previous experiences. Throughout the courses, while many of the students experience serious family and personal crises, they are disciplined enough to continue with their studies. Throughout the program, counselling is available to them at all times. The students are invited to speak to either me or to Ingrid Thompson Cooper. We also offer external referrals for those interested. Many of the students do need our services either in times of short-term crisis or for more long-term counselling. In addition, both of us have been consistently available for both technical and academic advice. Our students take advantage of all the services offered and they begin to blossom.

Applying the Knowledge

Overall, the students are incredibly eager to learn. They are very receptive to the knowledge we want to share with them and they quickly begin to apply their new knowledge within their communities. For example, one of our students, a shy woman who almost always walked through her reserve with her eyes on the ground, was incensed enough to talk on our community radio. She learned in an addictions class that even one drink of alcohol can cause fetal alcohol syndrome or fetal alcohol effects on unborn children. The women in the program were very alarmed; most of them were completely unaware that even small amounts of alcohol can cause developmental damage to our precious children. A number of students wrote papers and gave presentations about what they had learned. One woman, realizing that her daughter did in fact have fetal alcohol syndrome, broke down during her presentation, blaming herself for this tragedy. How heartbreaking it was to hear when she kept saying, "But I never knew." Another student, a former alcoholic who is now sober, said to me, "I thought I knew everything about addiction. Boy, was I wrong, I learned so much from this class."

Building Networks: Aboriginal Students as Agents of Change

One of the highlights in the first year of our program was when the class was invited in October to meet with other Aboriginal students in Akwesasne[5] at St. Lawrence College. The students exchanged course information, ideas, and plans for the future of these programs. They also discussed community issues and ways to prevent the serious problems of violence, sexual abuse, and suicide. The importance of confidentiality and how past experiences have made this issue a priority in Native communities remained a key focus of these discussions. Furthermore, the students discussed ways of garnering youth involvement, including striving for and promoting community awareness on Native issues and active community participation in speaking out, as a united whole, against injustice, all with the goal of acting as agents of change.

The discussions were lively and hopeful. In summary, we learned that we must be committed, trained, and dedicated to address all of these issues as they affect our daily lives. We promoted the belief that violence, sexual abuse, and suicide are interrelated problems. Overall the sessions were a great success—friendships were formed, information was exchanged, and plans for ongoing contact and discussions were made. Experiencing this meeting early on in our program helped us consolidate our ideas, and gave us the sense that together we were on the right track.

Implications of an Aboriginal Social Work Program: Some Observations

Wounds of the Past: Reclaiming Our Future

In general, Aboriginal peoples are both ambivalent *and* reluctant to embrace "outside" education, as this has never worked in the past. Residential schools, failure, punishment for the use of Native language, malnourishment, cruelty, and sexual abuse are pervasive in the Aboriginal experience of the mainstream education system. Furthermore, Lippman (1975) observes that:

> Aboriginal parents do see that higher education has not helped and in fact in many instances has isolated them from their group without White acceptance or jobs.... The education that so far has been offered has been largely irrelevant in content and inappropriate in presentation. It has been prepared for a white world, which is closed to most Aborigines. (pp. 13, 18)

Yet, as found by Armstrong, Kennedy, and Oberle (1990), higher levels of education tend to be followed by increased employment rates in both Aboriginal and non-Aboriginal populations. Lippman (1975) agrees, writing: "empirical evidence in traditional areas suggests that Aborigines are rapidly becoming aware of the power which literacy brings and therefore desire it for their children" (p. 13). Recently reported rates of education are positive. Among the Aboriginal population, people aged 30 and up account for the largest proportion of post-secondary enrolment

(Canada, 2001a). The 2001 Census notes that 9 percent of the non-reserve Aboriginal population aged 20–64 were attending school full-time, compared with 7 percent of the total Canadian non-reserve population (Statistics Canada, 2003).

Although Aboriginal parents are becoming more positive about the possibilities of higher education for their children, hesitation and fear of formal training are still evident in many Native communities and, in some communities, seeking an education within the mainstream system continues to be frowned upon. This is illustrated, for example, in the way in which Kahnawake Shakotiia'takehnhas Community Services (KSCS) has been structured, where there remains a degree of hesitation toward turning over the training of personnel to academics. When it first began, KSCS was a social service agency run by two Aboriginal peoples, which came under the jurisdiction of the provincial government for funding. Later, a band council resolution was passed giving official Mohawk recognition to the agency. This provided a foothold for the community's plan to start building self-governing structures empowered by a band council resolution.

In pursuing self-governance, and in response to some of the negative experiences with the mainstream education system, as well as the ineffective and even destructive social work practices offered by non-Native social workers, it has become the policy of some Aboriginal agencies that it is better if you are not trained because then you are a more approachable person to work with in the given population.

Today, many of the Aboriginal counsellors working at such agencies remain untrained in clinical practice. While it is also important to keep in mind that there is certainly validity in Natives' hesitation toward the mainstream education system, the maintenance of such policies can also be self-limiting. Although the mainstream education system often ignores or objects to Aboriginal requests for accommodation, claiming "interference with academic freedom, institutional autonomy and legislative mandates, performance is at issue here and, for example, the professions as well as the public would have plenty to say if engineering graduates regularly built bridges which fall down" (Castellano, Stalwick & Wein, 1986, p. 176).

Aboriginal Content and Academic Standards

One of the dilemmas at the beginning of the program was how we would ensure Aboriginal content in the course curriculum. We decided that in all the courses we would have an Aboriginal teacher with professional accreditation, extensive knowledge of the Aboriginal communities to be served, and strong curriculum development abilities. The instructor must also demonstrate an ability to review course content and teaching materials with the goal of achieving a balance between mainstream and Aboriginal teaching techniques and reading materials using quality articles either written by or about Aboriginal peoples.

An Aboriginal social worker must achieve a level of professionalism demanded by both the Aboriginal and non-Aboriginal communities. Social workers who graduate from the McGill School of Social Work's regular program are often not prepared to work with the minority populations who may make up the majority of their clientele. The ASWCP addresses such gaps by preparing its students to meet the needs of the populations they will actually work with.

A Difference of Values

While developing the Certificate Program, we found it important to clearly identify areas of difference in the values and world views of Aboriginal and non-Aboriginal populations. In a report by DuBray (1985), based on a number of empirical studies of the differences between American and Anglo-American values, it was found that there were in fact many differences between both groups. Zintz (1963) identified several key areas of difference between Aboriginal and non-Aboriginal values. Generally, while Native Americans tend to value co-operation, sharing, humility, and tradition, Anglo-Americans are more likely to prize individualism, competition, mastery, or success, and are future-time oriented.

Although the two cultures are quite distinct from one another in their world views, each carries its own strengths. In the mainstream education system, the Anglo-American perspective is the default point of departure, dominating teaching methods, curriculum content, and teacher-student relations. In a lecture given by Dr. Clare Brant (1982), he describes several ethics or principles that are considered uniquely important to Native peoples. Brant suggests that some principles can have negative impacts on Native children's educational experiences, particularly in Anglo-American school systems. First, the ethic of non-interference, which stipulates that no Aboriginal person should tell another Aboriginal person what to do, can be problematic because it includes school-age children who, in theory, can decide whether or not they wish to attend school, do their homework, follow the teacher's instructions, and so forth (Brant, 1982, p. 2). Second, Brant says that teachers may label Aboriginal children as "lazy" or "difficult" because of Aboriginals' different concept of time, which is not based on strict timetables (p. 4). Based on the results of his study, DuBray (1985) advocates that within mainstream education, there needs to be an infusion of ethnic cultural context, including that of Native populations, within academic disciplines such as nursing, psychiatry, psychology, social work, counselling, and theology.

Achieving Balance

At this point, I would like to raise an issue concerning control. In brief, I want to emphasize that there must be some control by Aboriginal peoples over the educational systems of which their populations are a part. However, from my own personal experiences, as well as having witnessed the growth in our program, I feel it is also important that curriculum setting is planned in conjunction with someone educated in the mainstream education system. Instructing students in a variety of areas allows for further growth and expansion into as many jobs, interests, and opportunities as possible.

At times during my work with the Steering Committee, I have witnessed a clash of ideals. For example, some Aboriginal agencies pushed to have the Certificate

Program train students to fit directly into positions in their agencies. This is not a good direction as it may further limit the full potential of the students as well as their access to new jobs and unique opportunities. On the other hand, sometimes community members tried to control the courses offered and their content based on the dissatisfaction of some student(s) who were unable to continue the program. Basically, we wanted to ensure that there was always a balance in the program of universal educational goals that included a body of both mainstream and Aboriginal knowledge.

Appealing to Aboriginal Diversities

The ASWCP is composed of a diverse student population, which includes Mohawks from Kahnawake and Kanehsatake and the urban Aboriginal population. The latter consists of a variety of groups, including Mohawks, who for reasons of education, employment, and marriages with non-Aboriginals have decided to move into the greater Montreal area. The others have come from Ontario, Saskatchewan, Manitoba, the Northwest Territories, and from Inuit communities in northern Quebec. The ASWCP also attracts Aboriginal students who have been adopted by non-Aboriginal families and are now looking for their roots and culture. Thus, the students in the ASWCP are representative of much of the Aboriginal population in Canada.

Urban Aboriginal peoples face many of the same problems that reserve Aboriginals face, such as unemployment, poverty, and alcohol and drug addictions, as well as discrimination, yet they face these issues without the help and support of the extended family. Furthermore, as Miller (1982) found:

Many [urban Indians] have integrated the values of the dominant society into their lives while retaining pride and identification with their Indian background, while others experience continual conflict in attempting to achieve a balance between their Indian values and those of the dominant society. (p. 157)

Aboriginal Jobs: Who Has Them?

With an ever-increasing population attending university and acquiring a bachelor's degree, it is clear that throughout much of the world, a knowledge-based society is emerging. The need for a university education is as important to Aboriginal peoples as it is to the rest of society. Unfortunately, Aboriginals do not tend to be a representative group of the population gaining a university education and thus do not compose a significant portion of the professionally trained social work staff working within their communities. One of the key problems emerging from such situations is the idea that the educated portion of our population is best able to serve as the "expertise that is lacking in the community itself" (McLaughlin, 1982, p. 272). As an Aboriginal woman having a lifetime of experience both living and working within Aboriginal communities, I can state that this is definitely a misconception. Aboriginal social workers are best qualified to work in Aboriginal communities. The failure to acknowledge this has led to serious mistakes, including past and current ineffective social work practices,[6] not to mention the risk of cultural destruction, all of which we deal with at the reserve level today. Within Aboriginal social work programs, the training of Aboriginal peoples must be the first priority. Only after this should we look at the training of non-Aboriginal people to fill any outstanding positions until other Aboriginals are trained to replace them.

While working in the program at McGill, I have met a number of non-Aboriginal people who have worked with Aboriginal populations who claim extensive experience and knowledge about Aboriginal issues. They believe themselves best able to solve the "Indian problem." In some cases, they use the information they have gathered to secure their own jobs on the reserves. To a certain extent, I regard these workers as predators taking jobs away from Aboriginal students/graduates and am therefore very cautious with the time I spend with them. There are so few jobs on the reserves; poverty prevails and there are many single-parent families and seriously troubled individuals and families. Although non-Aboriginal social workers have been beneficial for some Native communities in the past, when they continue to occupy the majority of social work positions on the reserves, they are no longer helping Aboriginal communities. Furthermore, they often do not possess the necessary experience and background required for effective and meaningful social work within Aboriginal communities.

In response, we must question why the social work agencies continue hiring non-Aboriginals, especially in light of the emerging population of professional Aboriginal social workers. I fear it is because agency directors are trained within the mainstream educational systems and are therefore skeptical of newly emerging programs, such as the Certificate Program. Ignoring both the presence and successes of such programs illustrates that the non-Aboriginal sector of social workers servicing Native communities shows no real vested interest in the community. Furthermore, non-Aboriginal social workers cannot live on the reserve and, as a result, do not maintain their contracts for long periods of time. Hiring practices that show preferences for non-Aboriginal social workers do not address some of the key issues in today's Native communities, including the high turnover of non-Native professional people working at reserve agencies. Finally, there remains the tremendous number of social, psychological (trust issues), cultural, economic, and even political problems either caused or perpetuated by the practices of non-Aboriginal social workers. Current and future generations of Aboriginal communities, both on and off the reserves, would benefit from a marked increase in Aboriginal social workers. This is well documented in Fiddler's (2000) analysis of the need for Aboriginal social workers across Canada. As such, the mainstream education system, social work agencies, and funding programs could best aid Aboriginal peoples by promoting and facilitating the presence of Native social workers within their own communities.

The field placement component of the ASWCP was implemented as an effort to encourage the development of a group of skilled Native social workers who could work in both Native and non-Native communities. Some students want to broaden their community experiences by having their field placements in the Aboriginal community, while others are interested in seeing how non-Aboriginal institutions manage their programs. It can be noted, however, that almost all the students had the goal of eventually working in an Aboriginal community or agency. What is essential is that the achievements of these students are recognized and that we give them all the space and opportunity they need to apply their knowledge and skills.

Aboriginal Education: From Local to Global Contexts

Federal and Provincial Jurisdiction in Canada

Section 93 of Canada's Constitution Act, 1867 establishes provincial jurisdiction in education on a broad basis (Canada, 1867). It reads: "In and for each Province the Legislature may exclusively make laws in relation to education." From this base we can assume that "education" is a provincial responsibility and Indians, as previously mentioned, are a federal responsibility. It is now evident why jurisdictional battles between federal and provincial governments persist.

In Canada, "federal laws will be upheld [in courts] because they are education laws," and if a federal law and a provincial law seem to cover the same area, theoretically they will both be permitted to stand because there will not be an actual conflict (MacPherson, 1991, 20). Federal jurisdiction flows from the Constitution Act, 1867 (formerly the British North American Act, 1867), which states under the Indian Act (Canada, 1985) that Parliament has jurisdiction over "Indians and lands reserved for Indians" (Section 91(24)).

The further fleshing out of this rather simplistic sentence came in a court case, *Four B Manufacturing Ltd. vs. United Garment Workers of America* (1979), wherein Justice Beetz said:

Section 91(24) of the *British North American Act, 1867* assigns jurisdiction to Parliament over two distinct subject matters: Indians *and* lands reserved for Indians, non-Indians *on* lands reserved for the Indians (339).

The interpretation of Section 91(24) concludes that, "the Federal Government, if it wanted, could enact a law or laws dealing with the education of *all* Indian children wherever they live" (MacPherson, 1991, p. 23). While interpretation is based on federal jurisprudence, I believe that Aboriginal peoples in Canada could now make a stronger case against this interpretation. Their case would be based on the deplorable experiment by the federal government at "civilizing" Aboriginal children in its residential schools.

A case in point regarding non-educational constitutional doctrine appears in MacPherson's report on *Cardinal vs. Attorney General of Alberta* (MacPherson, 1991). The case concerns the question of whether the Alberta Wildlife Act (a provincial act under provincial jurisdiction) applies to a treaty concerning Indians who sell moose meat to a non-Indian on the reserve. The Supreme Court answered affirmatively.[7] There is also the *Four B Manufacturing Ltd. vs. United Government Workers of America* (1979), where, as previously mentioned, the Supreme Court of Canada upheld that a provincial law of general application can apply to federal subject matters. Finally in the case of *Jack and Charlie vs. The Queen* (1985), the Supreme Court of Canada again upheld that a provincial wildlife law was applicable to Indians.

Despite the protective measures of the Indian Act, which is backed by the 1867 Constitution and, as such, the federal government, time and again we see instances where Canada's provincial governments are able to overrule such jurisdiction through the introduction of legislation that either negates Aboriginal rights or routinely ignores them.

Section 88 of the Indian Act reads:

> Subject to the terms of any treaty and any other Act of the Parliament of Canada, all laws of general application from time to time in force in any province are applicable to and in respect of Indians in the province except to the extent that such laws are inconsistent with this Act or any order, rule, regulation or by-law made there under and except to the extent that such laws make provision for any matter for which provision is made by or under this Act. (Canada, 1985)

Provincial laws that fall under the singling-out doctrine, for example, a provincial education act that fails to distinguish unique Indian rights and educational needs from the mainstream students population in its province, become constitutionally sound. However, if Indians were given special mention or, to use a famous Quebec language position, "prominence," it would then contravene the Constitutional Act. At this point, I have to question why the federal and provincial governments cannot "get their act(s) together."

The second area of concern is that provincial law of general application cannot in any way affect federal jurisdiction. With regard to Aboriginal peoples, this means that no provincial law can be passed if it alters or affects "Indianness," including Indian practices or status. However, education is not in the category of federal jurisdiction and responds to provincial legislation. Confusingly, federal law states that provincial laws of general application cannot affect Indian lands or their use. This means that a provincial government cannot regulate federal schools or band schools, as this would contravene federal jurisdiction. Finally, the Doctrine of Conflict in the Indian Act (sections 114–123) clearly indicates that the Indian Act, which falls under federal legislation, can supersede all or part of any provincial act that conflicts with federal jurisdiction.

These issues are not presently of any risk to Aboriginals because both federal and provincial laws and regulations contain so little in the way of Indian educational matters that no conflict exists. However, if the federal government were to establish an Aboriginal Education Act and Right to Self-Determination Act, or an Educational Assistance Act (like the one in the US), then the cleaning up of provincial education laws and regulations as they affect Aboriginals on reserves may gain greater attention.

Unfortunately, it appears that the federal government is more concerned with the scope and nature of rights as opposed to the delivery of these rights (in this case the right to education) to the broadest number of Aboriginal peoples. MacPherson (1991) writes: "Section 91(24) of the Constitution Act, 1867 would easily support a comprehensive national law dealing with Indian education" (p. 24). As such, the Constitution and legal framework for the all-inclusive Aboriginal education, which includes status and non-status Indians, Métis, and Inuit, is clearly in place. What is missing is the will on the part of the federal government to establish such a national program.

International Law

International law is a particular kind of law that is formed outside federal or national laws, but which can be adopted by individual national and state governments. Canada is a signatory to several covenants and conventions, including the recognition of Aboriginal rights to education. While these conventions and covenants are not enforceable in the Canadian courts, they are designed to politically and morally bind signatories to certain agreements.

The Native women's struggle to end the discriminatory policies of the Indian Act is documented in Section 12(1)B of the Act.[8] In response to this gender discrimination, Sandra Lovelace, a Maliseet Indian, took her case to the United Nations court. Here it was decided that Canada was in contravention of the International Covenant on Civil and Political Rights. The international court decided that on the basis of Article 27, the Indian Act was in fact depriving Sandra Lovelace of her right as a minority to enjoy her culture, practise her religion, and use the language of her community with others of her group. Due to international embarrassment, Canada repealed section 12(1)B of the Indian Act in 1985. Interestingly, the repeal coincided with the establishment of the Canadian Charter of Rights and Freedoms. This was encouraging news for the future of Aboriginal education as its concepts, relevance, and applications are positively defined in international law. Specific convention articles addressing Aboriginal education underscore that some measures are coded in international law to ensure the most reasonable protection of Aboriginal rights to education.[9]

The move by Aboriginal peoples to become involved at the international, constitutional, federal, and provincial governmental levels can be summarized by their wish to participate, consult with, and consent to the laws that affect them directly or indirectly. It also follows that this same movement must further establish and recognize educational development, application, and policy. It is the only way to make some sense out of the tangled complexity of the Aboriginal education issue in Canada. The enormous sense of failure and guilt about our education that Aboriginal peoples carry is a result of not knowing or understanding the catastrophic state of affairs regarding the laws surrounding our education. As well as marking a clearer starting point toward resolving some of the problems of our current educational system, we would be further relieved if we understood that in many instances, these far-reaching problems are largely out of control.

In February 1995, Aborigines in Australia and the Torres Strait Islanders published a report advising the minister of education that education is "the most important strategy for achieving self-determination for the Aboriginal people." However, "our mission of education is not compatible with the current education system" (Lippman, 1975, p. 26). Such reports must be received as a clear message of the unacceptable nature of educational programs with respect to the Aboriginal population. They should provoke positive responses from policy makers as they lament the absence of relevant educational programs and, subsequently, promising possibilities for the future of Aboriginal education rights.

How much clearer can their message be? Who is responsible for the absence of educational systems that incorporate models of teaching and learning that are relevant for minority populations? How can this all be resolved?

International Responses to Aboriginal Education

A review of the history of Native education in other countries where Aboriginal peoples faced European colonization indicates that "the process of forced adjustment and loss has been present in the area of education [on both a national and international scale]" (MacPherson, 1991, pp. 13–14). These countries and regions include Torres Strait Islands, New Zealand, Australia, and the United States. This section focuses on recent attempts at implementing Aboriginal-centred education programs in these countries.

The MacPherson (1991) report demonstrates that the "Kohango Reo" program in New Zealand is successful because "it incorporates Maori cultural values and community organization into the New Zealand education system" (p. 14). The program is designed for preschoolers and hands over the responsibility of education to the Maori people. It is a community-based project and all local Maori people play a role in the daily operation, design, and long-range planning of the schools. More important, MacPherson (1991) finds that this model "could well be a catalyst for parallel changes in the rest of the New Zealand education system" (p. 14).

In Australia, a National Aboriginal Education Committee was formed to advise the federal government, illustrating new directions in Aboriginal education where "Aboriginal education consultative groups work closely with the National Committee to provide advice to state governments and education agencies" (MacPherson, 1991, p. 15). Although these program initiatives appear to incorporate the Aboriginal population into mainstream society, MacPherson (1991) reports that Canada has very little to learn from this example as "Australian Aborigines are treated worse and are in poorer shape than their Canadian counterparts" (p. 15).

Although American constitutional arrangements in the field of education are quite different from those in New Zealand, Australia, and the Torres Strait region, they are similar to the extent that all their Aboriginal educational programs are disappointing. The Indian Self-Determination and Education Assistance Act is an American piece of legislation that accepts not only the notion of Native self-government, but also ties it closely to an educational concept. However, unfortunately, as MacPherson's (1991) research has shown, "the system of Indian education in the United States is very poor" (p. 15). Even while there is a move toward community-based and Aboriginal-directed education in parts of the United States, and where tribal sovereignty is judicially recognized, the sovereign authority of the federal government "allows for a considerable scope of power over Indian Affairs" (MacPherson, 1991, p. 15).

Globalizing Cultures: Accommodation, Accreditation, and Institutional Racism

It is not the intent of this paper to cast a dark shadow over McGill University's *modus operandi*, especially considering the fact that its way of being coincides with the rest of the world. However, it is up to those institutions that are now at the forefront of education in North America to start making inroads to a more universally acceptable education system wherein the rights of Aboriginals as well as other minority identities are honoured and preserved. Education must reflect society. As it currently stands, it does not. Today's educational systems cannot continue to be based on outdated models of teaching and learning. Educators and the institutions they work in must remain current and competent otherwise they become etched in the stone replicas of the very buildings they occupy.

The education systems to which Aboriginal peoples have access, both locally and internationally, tend to be based on the dominant mainstream educational philosophy and therefore preclude Aboriginal culture, vision, and world view as well as their success within that system. However, throughout the course of my master's degree, I have noted that course content by and about other minority groups, such as Blacks and Asians, also rarely appears in the academic materials provided at McGill. Unless it is given in a specific course or discipline (such as anthropology), it is usually not a part of the general materials and discourse of the university.

There are, however, some interesting events and circumstances challenging this. With globalization, the number of nationalities and countries involved in the social and economic world markets is continually increasing. As a result, there are more international students at McGill and other major universities. At the same time, there appears to be some movement toward inclusiveness at the university: a shift is in the making. It is still on the fringes, but nevertheless it is there, as witnessed by the presence of the two social work Certificate Programs at McGill, one for the Inuit and the other for First Nations.

In terms of institutional racism, the article "Is Social Work Racist?" provides a contextualized analysis of some of the literature produced within social work (McMahon & Allen-Mearers, 1992). The study, based on 117 articles on minority groups, indicates that much of social work literature is indeed naive and superficial, while failing to address minority groups in a social context. At the McGill School of Social Work, with the exception of a cross-cultural course, there is a marked absence of socially relevant literature pertaining to minorities, and in this context I include Aboriginal peoples. One then is not surprised by the findings demonstrated by McMahon and Allen-Mearers (1992). It is also evident from my own personal experience at McGill that the focus is predominantly centred on the self-development of the individual students, which precludes cultural education.

Just as mainstream curricula rarely represent and teach about other minority groups, access to education is not merely a local Aboriginal problem. Ray and Poonwassie (1992) have taught, researched, and developed curricula internationally, with a particular interest in the role of cultural differences and how this impacts access and rights to education. Their work reveals that even though international standards with respect to education do exist, they are not always respected. Often they are "used to define an ideal basis for the removal of educational barriers" (Ray & Poonwassie, 1992, p. 161). These barriers are the same as those faced by Aboriginal peoples in Canada through "individual, classroom, or systemic institutionalized bureaucracy" (p. 161).

Ray and Poonwassie (1992) also examined educationally divided societies where attempts at resolving these traditional barriers to educational access are becoming more imaginative, including the Soviet Union, China, United States, Caribbean, Colombia, the Sudan, India, and the Basques (in Spain). Among all of these nations it was found that educational opportunities "have traditionally favored the dominant members of society" (p. 161).

As noted in MacPherson's research (1991), other proposed and implemented plans within the scope of Aboriginal education movements include the development of independent Aboriginal schools and family education centres, the further development of an Aboriginal task force on Aboriginal social worker trainee schemes, and Aboriginal programs in colleges, which provide special entry and support for Aboriginal trainee teachers. Other projects could include developing outstation schools located in decentralized communities and offering bilingual programs in regular schools attended by Aboriginal children.

Ingredients for Change and Success

Political Will and Aboriginal Leadership

It is interesting to question the intention of the government concerning Aboriginal peoples. I believe that if I can figure out the complexity of regulations and recommendations, I am sure they have as well. The area of education for Aboriginal peoples has been a story of failures, dropouts, and despair. The present system is not set up for Aboriginal peoples, but rather for mainstream society. As such, failure has been built in from the beginning for Aboriginal peoples. The answers to these problems, while generally ignored, lie in research projects, reports, articles, journals, and books. The laws have been in place since the 1867 British North American Act. The models are available and they are many, varied, reasonable, and possible. What is missing is the overall will of government and its institutions, including universities, to become the heart of the movement toward the full participation of Aboriginal peoples in the education process. Without this momentum we will continue to face failure, high dropout and unemployment rates, addictions, violence, and unnecessary rates of accidental deaths and widespread despair.

The ingredient that has been slow in coming is a strong organized movement and lobby by Aboriginal peoples to urge the governments and universities to fully commit to ensuring the participation of Aboriginal peoples in the educational process. Yet, who can blame Aboriginals for being extremely reluctant toward being educated by the system of governments and educators that gave us the residential schools? Within residential schools, Aboriginals were taught by the religious orders of both Canada and the United States, especially in Quebec where English-speaking nuns were unavailable and therefore imported from the United States. The most important duty of these instructors was to impart the word, sense, and mission of Christianity to the "heathen" Aboriginal communities. Aboriginal children were separated from their parents at an early age and sent to residential schools. They were punished when they used their own language to speak to each other, and many of them died in the care of these religious institutions (Perley, 1993). Through malnutrition, brutality, sexual abuse, and separation from families and siblings, the Aboriginal culture was as assaulted as their bodies and minds. Their cores were torn apart (Canada, 1996a; Chansonneuve, 2005; Haig-Brown, 1989).

The majority of the students in the Certificate Program are the children of those who endured the residential school system. As such, current Aboriginal perceptions of education remain strongly shaped by this history, remembered through personal oral narratives. Why should we believe that mainstream culture and intellect are the best and that everyone should be trained and educated in its likeness? After all, this is also the same system that so often produces graduates who know little or nothing about other cultures besides their own. As a result, we now have professionals in the social work field who are destructive and ineffectual in their work, particularly with minority groups.

Our experience of education must change. One way to achieve this is through inclusive participation.

Participation

Learning brings progress and a review of articles, journals, and books on education shows that universities must allow for more Native and minority public participation at the level of post-secondary education. Participation in areas regarding program design and implementation is only a temporary gain. Aboriginal peoples must also be allowed to participate in the accreditation process in social work education. As researchers Castellano, Stalwick, and Wein (1986) report:

> If the goal is to broaden the perspective of social work and make available to all practitioners the knowledge, skills and attitudes appropriate to Native Social Work, the requisite change must occur at the heart of the institution not just the periphery. This will cause the re-examination of the existing social work course not only in relation to its Native relevancy, but also to the mission and effectiveness of mainstream programs. (p. 182).

It is imperative that Aboriginal peoples are no longer cut off from the extensive bodies of knowledge in social work, especially those that are relevant and applicable in a cross-cultural context (Castellano, Stalwick & Wein, 1986). There must also be an incorporation of language, spirituality, oral tradition, and local custom if Aboriginal peoples are to feel a part of the educational system. The model that Castellano and her colleagues propose implies that Native students would enrol as individuals in regular programs and Native context would be incorporated through the elective courses, field placements in Native services or communities, and Native-related research projects. If the true concept of cross-culturalism implies a healthy fusion of majority and minority populations, we must root ourselves together at universities like McGill. Furthermore, short-term experimental programs like the ASWCP must be replaced with long-term programs.

Programs in Aboriginal social work must become a recognized specialty within regular programs. In order to achieve this goal, Indian people must be trained and educated as professionals in order to do the work that is needed in their communities. Many Aboriginal peoples feel that if they were unsuccessful at the high school level, university is out of the question. This is not so and I am living proof of this. I failed two grades in high school, but I hung on until I received my high school leaving certificate. I married in my early twenties, had two children, and then decided to *try* to apply to a university. I applied as a mature student at the age of 31, and entered the McGill School of Social Work when my youngest child started grade one. When he finished grade three, I had a bachelor's degree in social work. I completed my master's degree in social work when I was 55. It is never too late. You are never too old and if you can handle life with any degree of competency, which Aboriginal peoples as survivors do, you can get a degree.

Strong Cultural Content

The mainstream educational systems do not generally teach multiculturalism or prejudice reduction, which are some of the most important elements to enable people to live peacefully in the continuing globalization of our world, wherein Whites are no longer the majority. As such, the mainstream system must adapt to current trends or they will not survive globalization. Rather, they will be swallowed up into a world totally foreign to them.

As such, it is very important that the mainstream system incorporates academia produced by and about other cultures, such as African, African American, Middle Eastern, Asian, etc. Having been through the mainstream system from elementary and post-secondary school through to my graduate studies I believe that I understand White culture well. Now I wish to expand my knowledge of the other peoples of the world. Canadians continue to allow many nationalities into Canada with the majority of the population having no understanding of these cultures; what a shame to lose a tremendous learning experience.

Making Education Successful

In spite of its struggles, the Certificate Program has been successful in helping Aboriginal peoples access post-secondary education. The success is tied to a number of factors, including mature student admissions, having the Aboriginal co-instructor, emphasizing Aboriginal content, the establishment of community support networks, tutorials, and the high degree of flexibility in the program. These indicators of "success" could continue to be built upon to create a more mainstream Aboriginal program or developed into the mainstream programming as a part of the regular curriculum of the entire education system.

Rather than supporting reserve-based post-secondary education, I support harmonizing programs into the mainstream body of education that presently exists in universities, while establishing both cultural relevancy in curriculum development and strong professional, Aboriginal-focused leadership, therefore allowing for further community control and user involvement (Lippitt & Romero, 1992). "Strong partnerships between school staff, students, parents, community residents and other partners in education, such as local businesses, are essential to building on effective school systems" (Jewison, 1995, p. 9). Instead of remaining on the periphery, Aboriginals need to be included in significant decision-making bodies and comprise a significant voice in the system.

Through my research, it has become clearer as to why Aboriginal education is not becoming a more significant part of the mainstream education system. First, although it is clear that education is necessary to reach self-determination, the present educational systems do not accommodate Aboriginal peoples. Second, Aboriginal peoples are not a majority population and therefore are not part of the decision-making educational body, which is formed and shaped by the dominant majority. Third, there are no clear constitutional guarantees to accessible and relevant education programs for Aboriginal peoples. In fact, even if one were hammered out, it would probably not cover all Aboriginal peoples, but would more than likely cover only status Indians. The federal government can, however, broaden this coverage to all as has been in the scope of its power since the 1876 Indian Act. Fourth, with the exception of British Columbia and Quebec, in particular, provincially there is little or no interest in broadening the educational system. In Quebec, the Education Act could become a battleground over territorial integrity rather than a genuine interest in the betterment of Aboriginal education. Fifth, currently international law seems to be the best venue for Aboriginal leadership to take their quest for educational access, decision making, language, culture, and values. Even if we look at the history of failures regarding Aboriginal education in countries around the world, it is evident that Canada is presently treating this issue better than some (for example, Australia), but less well than others with a similar colonial history. The best example of a well-developed, culturally sensitive approach is probably New Zealand (Cairns, Fulcher, Kereopa, Nia Nia, & Tait-Rolleston, 1998).

Overall there must be a three-pronged approach to tackle the problems. First, there must be a constitutional and international entrenchment of relevant and accessible educational programs for all members of society, including Aboriginals. Second, we need to see a genuine movement of educators to include the Aboriginal population in decision making, curriculum development, and participation on committees and boards. Third, we must develop an organized movement by the

Aboriginal population to press for participation at every turn in the educational systems that impact their children.

Summary and Conclusions

The McGill Certificate Program was designed to address the complex needs of Aboriginal peoples from diverse backgrounds and has been largely successful with many Aboriginal peoples. Of the 28 students initially registered in the program, 25 students completed our first course (89 percent). This achievement was really an academic breakthrough compared to the usual high dropout rates of Aboriginal peoples. When I reflect on these students, I see such beautiful people in the face of incredible adversity, poverty, and tragedy, who are happy to be learning, even if it means looking at ourselves, our shortcomings, and our struggles. To me this is what learning is about. We also believe that the program has achieved the professional methods, approaches, and results reflective of the high academic standards of the university setting.

The program is promising because it is comprehensive. It is long enough to train a core group of social workers who can then support each other, start up their own jobs, and make the long needed and necessary changes and improvements within their communities. The course content in the Certificate Program focuses explicitly on the issues we face in our communities (addictions, family violence, sexual abuse, and mental illness), and evokes extensive discussions and efforts on how these things can be changed in order to achieve a better place for our children to inherit.

In conclusion, this paper is possibly the most difficult piece I have ever written, not due to the content, but because of the anger I have felt regarding the subject of education for Aboriginal peoples. It is in such an abominable state, not only in Canada, but also in other countries around the world. Given my lifetime of experiences living and working both within and outside of Aboriginal communities and my unfortunately rare professional qualifications, I have often felt as though I had to come up with some sort of answer to the problem single-handedly. I had no solution, nor did Aboriginal parents, the Native community, the Canadian or provincial laws, or the international communities. How was I to have some magical answer to this perpetual problem in Aboriginal education?

After having explored this issue by identifying the problems in terms of how they have been defined by others and the solutions that have been recommended, I now realize that no one person has all the answers. The problem is as complex as its solutions. A solid foundation for Aboriginal education in Canada must first of all be built upon and solidly rooted in coordinated federal and provincial laws. Jurisdictional issues between provincial and federal governments must be worked out to expedite the framework for a constitutional entrenchment of the existing rights of all Aboriginal peoples, including status and non-status Aboriginals, Métis, and Inuit. The rights of all Aboriginal peoples must extend to full participation, support, and financial aid in the educational processes of this country. Failing to do so condemns Aboriginal peoples to the periphery of the educational systems, where they now stand.

It is evident that there are no easy solutions to our quest for Aboriginal inclusion in the educational system. However, as an educator from the Mohawk nation who has explored the topic extensively, I am beginning to breathe easier as I see the full scope of the complexity of the problems. I realize that neither I alone, nor programs like the McGill Certificate Program in Aboriginal Social Work, can address the myriad of changes, legislation, and needs that Aboriginal education demands. Within Aboriginal communities there is some movement and reason for hope. We must not suffocate this spark emanating from the communities, but treat it very carefully and tenderly so as to rebuild our communities on a foundation of solid commitment at every level. We want to succeed, to excel, and to have fair and equal access to relevant and applicable educational programs in Canada. The Certificate Program in Aboriginal Social Work and similar programs are only a small piece of the solution, but I am certainly proud of the steps we have taken and will continue to take as we move forward through the millennium. One small step at a time!

Notes

1. In this context *only* do I include Aboriginal peoples as minorities; in fact, we are the first and original inhabitants of this land, which entitles us to special rights.
2. The process of establishing a positive and functional dynamic between Aboriginal and non-Aboriginal instructors is further explored in Chapter 5, "Building Bridges: The Development of an Aboriginal Program from the Viewpoints of the Native and Non-Native Teachers."
3. I was the Aboriginal co-instructor in every class, assisting the main instructor. Eventually I was the main instructor in two courses.
4. While Lippman's important work is based on the Aboriginal peoples in Australia, her observations are equally applicable to Canada's indigenous populations.
5. A Mohawk reserve that straddles the Quebec/Ontario border and also the Canadian–American border.
6. An example of this is placing an Aboriginal child at risk in his or her own home with a non-Native family when there is a suitable Aboriginal home for the child in the community.
7. Justice Marthland said on pp. 559–560 of the court ruling:

> But it is also well-established that provincial legislation enacted under the heading of s.92 does not necessarily become invalid because it affects something which is subject to federal legislation. A provincial legislature could not enact legislation in relation to Indians, or in relation to Indian reserves, but this is far from saying that the effect of s.91(24) of the British North American Act 1867 was to create enclaves within a province within the boundaries of which provincial legislation could have no application. In my opinion, the test as to the application of provincial legislation within a reserve is the same as with respect to its application within the province and that is that it must be within the authority of s.92 and must not be in relation to a subject matter assigned exclusively to the Canadian under s.91. Two of these subjects are Indians and Indian reserves, but if provincial legislation within the limits of s.92 is not construed as being legislation in relation to those classes of subjects (or any other subject under s.91) it is applicable anywhere in the province including Indian reserves, even though Indians or Indian reserves might be affected by it. My point is that s.91(24) enumerates classes of subjects over which the federal parliament has the exclusive power to legislate, but it does not purport to define areas within a province within which the power of a province to enact legislation, otherwise within its powers, is to be excluded. (MacPherson, 1991, p. 25)

8. The Act previously denied Indian women their status when marrying a non-Indian man, while allowing men to maintain their status regardless of whom they married, and in turn also pass this status on to their non-Indian wives.
9. The Indigenous and Tribal Peoples Convention, 1978 (Convention 169), was adopted by the General Conference of the International Labour Organization (ILO) in 1991. It states that "Canada is not yet a signatory of the convention, however, it is a member of the ILO and … Canada has played a major role in the drafting of the convention" (MacPherson, 1991, p. 36). Since we can expect that Canada will soon sign the Convention, I am including Part VI of the Convention, Article 26 and Article 27:

Article 26
Measures shall be taken to ensure that members of the peoples concerned have the opportunity to acquire education at all levels on at least an equal footing with the rest of the national community.

Article 27
1. Education programs and services for the peoples concerned shall be developed and implemented in co-operation with and to address their special needs, and shall incorporate their histories, their knowledge and technologies, their value systems and their further social economic and cultural aspirations.
2. The competent authority shall ensure the training of members of these peoples and their involvement in the formulation and implementation of educational programs, with a view to the progressive transfer of responsibility for the conduct of these programs to these peoples as appropriate.
3. In addition, governments shall recognize the right of these peoples to establish their own educational institutions and facilities, provided that such institutions meet minimum standards established by the competent authority in consultation with these peoples. Appropriate resources shall be provided for this purpose. (McPherson, 1991, p. 36)

Appendix A:

Certificate Program in Aboriginal Social Work Practice

The McGill School of Social Work and the Aboriginal community are in the process of developing a professional Certificate Program in Aboriginal social work practice. This is the result of extensive discussion with a number of Aboriginal human service providers who have been working with the McGill School of Social Work faculty since September 1993.

The three-year, 30-credit certificate program will be equal to one year of the Bachelor of Social Work program (BSW) and therefore will qualify graduates to enter the second year of the three-year, 90-credit BSW program.

The program will have a strong Aboriginal content and the curriculum will be developed and taught by Aboriginal social work practitioners working collaboratively with teaching staff of the School of Social Work. As well, there will be an emphasis on practice courses that will involve Aboriginal practitioners taking into consideration the well-being of potential students who are working. This will enable students to develop practice skills to assist them in providing better services for the greater Aboriginal communities.

Program Objectives

The overall purpose of the program is to prepare Aboriginal peoples in the Montreal area for social work practice within their communities. The program is intended to train:

- those Aboriginal peoples already working in community agencies who wish to further their training
- those Aboriginal peoples who want to develop a future career in social work but are not currently working in the field

Program Structure

The program will be offered over a three-year period. Students will take one 39-hour course per term for three terms a year. These credit courses of three hours will be offered once a week during the day.

Program Description

The courses are planned to reflect the socio-cultural characteristics of Aboriginal societies as well as the specific social service needs of their communities. The proposed program will provide professional training in assessment and counselling skills for a range of social problems, such as addictions, family violence, child abuse, mental health problems, and offenders.

1. The courses included in the program focus on different aspects of social problems and social work practice. Within this framework, particular attention will be given to specific problems facing the Aboriginal families and communities, in particular family violence and child sexual abuse as well as worker wellness and healing.
2. Courses will reflect the following themes: identification and analysis of social problems; welfare policy and legislation; methods of social work practice, including traditional treatment models, with individuals, groups, and organizations; community organizing and community-based research.
3. Format will include a combination of classroom work and field practice in a variety of clinical and traditional settings in the Montreal area.

NICKI GARWOOD

A rainbow over Payne River, Nunavik

CHAPTER 5

Building Bridges:
The Development of an Aboriginal Program from the Viewpoints of the Native and Non-Native Teachers

Ingrid Thompson Cooper, Gail Stacey Moore, Alisha Schotsman-Apale, and Florence Dobson

Introduction

The history of Aboriginal communities around the world is replete with experiences of colonization, oppression, cultural assimilation, and relocation. While Canada's Aboriginal communities, like many others, have long been the recipients of social outreach programs, more and more Aboriginal communities and social work agencies were revealing their frustration with the absence of long-term, accessible, and Aboriginal-centred educational programs.

In Montreal, a team of Aboriginal and non-Aboriginal social workers responded to the frustrations expressed by various local Aboriginal groups by developing the Certificate Program in Aboriginal Social Work Practice at McGill University (ASWCP). Details of the early days of the program's development and the ensuing challenges and tensions are described in the previous chapter (Chapter 4) by Gail Stacey Moore, a Mohawk social worker and co-founder of the program with Ingrid Thompson Cooper, a social work professor at the university. "Establishing a program for Indigenous people in a mainstream academic institution with a strong emphasis on academic excellence represented a real challenge for the Social Work department, for the University as a whole, and for us as individuals" (Thompson Cooper, 2004, p. 89). As depicted by Stacey Moore, the path to developing the ASWCP was a process of overcoming barriers and building bridges. As Gail and Ingrid met the various challenges and hurdles, sometimes with difficulty, they developed a relationship, which they now perceive as a major component of the eventual successful establishment of the program. It was out of that relationship that other vital relationships developed—between the teachers and the students, between the School of Social Work and the Aboriginal agencies, and between the community and the students. Another major player in the success of the program was one of the instructors, Florence Dobson, who ultimately taught three of the 10 courses in the Certificate Program, two on addictions and one on mental health.

This chapter chronicles the development of the Certificate Program in Aboriginal Social Work at McGill University from the perspectives and experiences of the three main contributors: Ingrid Thompson Cooper and Gail Stacey Moore, program co-coordinators and instructors; and Florence Dobson, a principal instructor.

While the three women are social workers, their professional backgrounds are markedly different. Ingrid has extensive clinical experience as a forensic social worker, working with complex and highly sensitive issues such as sexual abuse. Gail, a Mohawk woman from Kahnawake, has been working with Aboriginal communities as a social worker, community organizer, and political activist since the late 1970s. As described in Chapter 4, in the fall of 1994 Gail returned to McGill University to do her master's degree in social work. Florence Dobson held a clinical practice at the addictions unit of the Montreal General Hospital and was a faculty lecturer at the McGill School of Social Work for a number of years.

Alisha Schotsman-Apale, a research assistant, interviewed the three women using a questionnaire developed in consultation with Gail and Ingrid. While the information on program development has been already described in Chapter 4, the focus here is on the differing perspectives of the three teachers and how these came together and ultimately shaped the program. Their insights and experiences offer an instructive narrative of the trials and achievements in establishing a meaningful program for Aboriginal peoples in a mainstream academic institution.

Developing an Aboriginal Certificate Program

Inception of the Program

In response to the question "Whose idea was the Aboriginal Program?" Ingrid replied:

> … it was a combination of factors that came together. Gail says there is no such thing as coincidence and I tend to agree with her. There were four things: First, my workshop experience at Kanehsatake; secondly, a development at the School in continuing education; thirdly, the discovery that the director of the Native Women's Shelter in Montreal had been asking for training for her workers; and finally, Gail's return to McGill to do her MSW degree.

After the 1990 Oka crisis[1] Ingrid conducted a series of workshops on sexual abuse at Onento:ken Treatment Center in Kanehsatake. At the end, while they said they had enjoyed the sessions, they were "sick to death" of workshops and what they really needed and wanted was a solid, more in-depth professional training program. Ingrid recalled this when, in the spring/summer of 1994, she was asked by a colleague, Lieba Aronoff, if she had any ideas for needs for a continuing education program. At the same time, Liesel Urtnowski had spoken to Ingrid about the fact that Anita Pratt, a Cree woman and director of the Native Women's Shelter, had been asking Liesel for some time to start a training program for her workers, similar to the one Liesel was operating in the North with the Inuit. These ideas became more focused with the news that Gail Stacey Moore, a co-founder with Anita of the Native Women's Shelter, was returning to McGill. Ingrid recalls:

> I remember Liesel saying to me, "Boy, are you ever lucky! Gail is coming back to McGill this fall to do her master's." I had never heard of her. However, I phoned her and invited her to an initial meeting.

During the initial planning meeting, Ingrid recalls that Gail remained non-committal.

> She was hesitant, choosing instead to sit back and listen. She knew she could be very helpful, but wasn't sure if the committee would be willing or able to learn to be flexible and to take the time and initiative required to make this program work.

Gail agrees:

> I admit that I was cautious. I had to be because I recognized the enormity of the challenges that lay ahead; here were three competent women, who were very capable of working in the mainstream academic system. What they lacked, however, was an in-depth understanding of the Aboriginal educational experience. They were going at a rapid pace and had full confidence in themselves, but I was hesitant because I didn't think they really understood what they were taking on. So I thought I am going to observe for awhile and not jump in head first. I knew I could be helpful, but I wasn't sure if they were willing to learn to be flexible, to learn....

Following the first meeting, however, Gail recognized that intention-wise, their hearts were very open, and she saw in them the potential and willingness for flexibility and openness. Yet since she had just returned from four years in a demanding project at the NWAC (Native Women's Association of Canada), she needed a break from that kind of stress and pressure. As such, she did not want to be at the forefront of this project. At the same time, however, she recognized that if the project were to succeed, Aboriginal leadership was paramount: She would need to be deeply involved in the planning and development of the program.

Early on an Advisory Committee was set up to plan for the development of the program. Ingrid recalls that, although she did not understand all of the dynamics, she recognized there were sensitive issues that needed to be addressed correctly.

> I was really a novice in understanding Aboriginal issues, but I recall at an early meeting when we were trying to come up with ideas for more members on the committee, the name of an Aboriginal woman was suggested. She was an employee of one of the Native organizations that was supportive of the program; as well she was also going to attend courses. While the two Native committee members supported the potential candidate, a non-Native committee member who worked at the same organization was opposed to this because of a conflict of interests. As I listened I realized that while this view made sense in the hierarchical world of the university, somehow, from an Aboriginal perspective, it was wrong. If the program was to succeed, we would have to get it right. I voted to have the Aboriginal woman on our committee; of course it was the right decision but at the time, I was unaware of how right it was.

Over the course of the year, the Advisory Committee continued to meet. Gail and Ingrid held information meetings in the two communities of Kahnewake and

Kahnesetake and also one at McGill for the urban Natives. Although there was no confirmed funding source and with no idea of how many students would actually attend, Ingrid and Gail put on the first course in the spring of 1995.

Ingrid recalled that, during this period, amidst the uncertainties, "I often felt as though we were sailing in the wind. We had no clear road map to guide us. We knew what we wanted to do, but were not sure how to do it."

Confronting Barriers

The Administration Barrier

One of the most difficult barriers in developing the program lay in tackling the administration system at McGill, which was incredibly cumbersome.[2] In order to get funding, rooms, supplies, and accreditation, the ASWCP had to be recognized by the Faculty of Arts, a process that took nearly a year and a half. As the program began to take shape, Gail was often taken aback at the seemingly effortless pace with which the project progressed. This was very different from the battles Gail had been involved in while fighting for Aboriginal rights and recognition. She recalls that:

> As we moved along, I realized that for them it looked almost effortless to move into the system at McGill. There was some resistance, but it was manageable. If it had been an Aboriginal person leading this, we would have met with too much resistance because it would have been too foreign an experience. So having people already in the system introduce it made a big difference. I was always amazed that they never hit a wall that wasn't manageable.

From Ingrid's perspective, however, the struggle to negotiate the university system was much more pronounced:

> The most difficult barrier for me, particularly because I'm not very good at it, was that we had to tackle the McGill administration [Faculty of Arts] to have the program approved.

In retrospect, Ingrid recalls that initially her approach at the faculty meeting was very naive. At the first meeting, the faculty accused the program of reverse racism because it strictly excluded all non-Natives from admission.

> The faculties and administrative systems couldn't understand why we only wanted it for Aboriginal students and the reason for that is very clear: They need to have a chance—to have a safe space to talk and learn and they need to take those jobs in their communities which were held by non-Natives. We had quite a fight on our hands.

Refusing to buckle under the outcomes of the first meeting, Ingrid and Bill Rowe, director of the School of Social Work, prepared for a second meeting.

The second time we went in armed. Bill brought the 1996 Royal Commission Report on Aboriginal People (Canada, 1996a) and gave the faculty members a brief review of the history of Aboriginal experiences in Canada. Gail has said to me a number of times how appreciative she was that for once she didn't have to be at the forefront of administrative battles. I found that very interesting as I knew that throughout her career, she, as with so many Aboriginals, had fought an endless number of administrative battles, and was consequently very good at it. At this point, however, what she really wanted was to focus her energies on developing the program and obtaining her master's degree. Because Bill and I fought the majority of these initial battles, Gail was free to study and teach.

Barriers between the University and Students

While administrative barriers present challenges to those working within the system, navigating McGill administration would have been a completely overwhelming barrier for most of the Aboriginal students. For Ingrid, the more she listened and learned about the Aboriginal community, the more evident it became that those First Nation students who had gone through the regular program at the School of Social Work had experienced a very hard struggle and often felt lost. Ingrid emphasizes that:

> Even flexibility with respect to registration deadlines was crucial if these students were to stay in the program. Their struggles are not a result of any personal inadequacies, but rather, are a reflection of their lives, which are often so fraught with crisis that the complexity and inflexibility of highly bureaucratic systems gravely impede the students' ability to complete educational programs.

Gail's involvement in the program greatly facilitated this process. She continually offered her experiences as insight for the program developers and instructors in order to explain the challenges students had that otherwise would not have been fully understood or appreciated. For example, Gail describes that even the decision to go back to school is a difficult one for both her and the students because it has an enormous impact not only on the students' own lives, but also on the lives of those around them:

> The decision to go back was difficult because I couldn't afford to finance both my education and my family and so I had to try to go when everyone was doing a little better. When you make a decision to go back to school, it doesn't just affect yourself. It affects the collectivity. This is very different from the White world. Nothing here happens without consultation, whereas in the non-Native communities this seems to be very different.

Establishing a Native–Non-Native Collaboration

With the help of Gail and other Native members of the Advisory Committee, in order for the ASWCP to be an accessible program, the realities and obligations of the students' daily lives would have to recognized, validated, and accounted for. Thus, a great deal of effort needed to be devoted to breaking down many of the barriers between the community and the school in order to make the university a more welcoming and accessible place. Most of the students in the first year of the program were middle-aged women, many of whom worked and had children, as well as strong extended family ties, and thus responsibilities. Often these students were responsible for providing a significant source of financial support for their families and relatives, either through social service jobs, taxi driving, cleaning, or welfare revenues. Many of them had also experienced difficulties in their lives such as drug and/or alcohol addiction, sexual and physical abuse, and other types of family violence. Approximately half of the students in the first group had attended college, but none had been able to complete their program (Thompson Cooper, 2004).

Getting Started: First Course

Ingrid and Gail knew that developing a trusting and open relationship with the students was paramount to success and chose a practicum course as the first course. Ingrid sensed that if she was to be the type of instructor who could teach Aboriginal students effectively and understand their needs, due to her lack of experience with the Native population, she had to make significant efforts to get to know the Aboriginal students. Beginning with a course that Ingrid could teach would help this. Furthermore, had the program begun with an emotionally intense topic or an especially academically challenging course, it would have run the risk of overwhelming and alienating the students.

In April 1995, the Aboriginal Certificate Program offered its first course with the help of a small seed grant. With the program underway, new challenges presented themselves, including the absence of secure funds. Further interviews illustrated that despite seemingly relentless administrative barriers, the persistence of each contributor toward establishing and delivering the program paid off. Throughout the program, from day-to-day experiences to more long-term developments and outcomes, there would be a continuous stream of tests and rewards.

On the first day of class, Ingrid remembers feeling uneasy, and her uncertainties about what had begun and particularly her ability to meet the needs of the students quickly surfaced. Before the first day of classes, Gail and Ingrid had no idea how many students would show up. Thirty-five people came in—far more than were expected. According to Ingrid:

> It was chaotic and crowded. At one point, I left to get more copies. A student turned to Gail and asked why the teacher was so "nervous and agitated." They didn't see the need for me to run around, just because there weren't enough papers. Right away, I was struck by this different value system about what is important for Aboriginal peoples. In retrospect, I often laugh at this and have to acknowledge the degree to which the program has changed me and my approach to teaching and social work.

Coming in with a background in the mainstream system, Ingrid found the shift toward an Aboriginal-focused program challenging, but also refreshing and inspiring. When asked to describe the aspect of teaching she had the most difficulty with, Ingrid responded by turning what is one of the most strongly admired aspects of being a university professor on its head:

> One of the most striking challenges I immediately faced was learning not to be the expert. Throughout all our lives as professionals and educators we are groomed to be experts. Our whole careers are spent building our "expertise." Yet throughout the Certificate Program, I very quickly realized that I needed to unlearn my role as the expert, which requires a considerable degree of humility along with an ongoing willingness to learn. I had to learn not to always have an answer, to learn to hold back, which was hard for me. With my clinical experience as a social worker, I was good at finding creative answers. But "unlearning" this was essential because at the end of the day, it is the Aboriginal person who has to decide if the material is applicable or not. It was an interesting and difficult switch, but an important one. The more I held back, the more I learned from them.

Choosing Instructors

In developing the ASWCP, it quickly became evident that selecting teachers to work in the program was an important and difficult task. While instructors were chosen based on their experience as social workers and social work educators, their openness and flexibility were essential. Both Gail and Ingrid can attest to the fact that for some people this is easier than for others. Working with social work educators who had been involved in the university for many years was one of the toughest challenges in the co-teaching dynamic. As Ingrid points out:

> It was often hard to get them to adapt to a teaching style that worked well with the Aboriginal community as opposed to one that was developed to address the mainstream student population. Social work takes on a particular form within Aboriginal communities and non-Aboriginal instructors needed to respond to this. We [non-Native teachers] all had a lot to learn and unlearn.

Early on in the program, Florence was asked to teach and she became central to the program, teaching three important courses on addictions and mental health.

For Florence, like others, teaching in the ASWCP has been an experience of growth and learning. From the beginning, Florence recognized that in order to teach about addictions effectively, she needed to incorporate the problems of addictions within her growing awareness of the issues in the community at large.

> Although my previous experiences with Aboriginals did not give me a deep insight into the Aboriginal communities, it did make the extent of the problems more clear. Because of this, and due to my training in alcohol and drug abuse, which is certainly a big problem in Native communities, I was asked to teach in the program.

One of the most important tasks for the instructors was to learn to adapt to the realities of the students' lives. Florence's previous experience in adult education and the demands adult learners have to meet while studying, such as maintaining jobs and caring for children and extended families, helped her adapt to the specific needs of the certificate students. She still had further adjustments to make as she explains:

> I would often go to class with all the material that I wanted to cover and often could-n't get through it because other issues would come up. I had to learn that the transi-tion from teaching in the mainstream system to teaching in the ASWCP lies in a shift of priorities. The priority was no longer pushing through as much material as possi-ble. I had to make sure that what I taught was very clear because a lot of the material I taught was very technical and many of the students had not been in school for a long time. I also had some students who had been studying for a long time, so I had to find a balance and accommodate all of them.

Co-teaching: From Daily Experience to a Teaching Model

The practice of having an Aboriginal–non-Aboriginal teaching team was not the result of a conscious decision based on a theoretical premise. Rather, it happened almost by instinct and developed in a natural way from the beginning of the program—first with Aboriginals and non-Aboriginals working together on the Advisory Committee and then with Gail and Ingrid coordinating the program together (see Zapf, 1999a for an excellent description of this co-operative teaching). As Ingrid recalls:

> It was very clear to me that without Gail, or someone like her, there was no way we could move forward because she was our connection to the Aboriginal community. The more I listened, the clearer it became that those students who had gone through the regular program at the School of Social Work had a very hard struggle. They felt lost. What became quite evident—and I did not have to be convinced—was that we had to break down the barriers between the community and the school, and make McGill a welcoming place. One way to do this was by maintaining the Native–non-Native teaching approach.

Initially, Gail worked as a cultural mediator between Ingrid and Florence and the students, which proved to be essential.

> I know that with all the struggles there is a lot of mistrust in the Aboriginal commu-nity, and I came in with some of it myself. I needed to make the Aboriginal students feel comfortable, to tone down their defences, or reinterpret material that offended them. I would always have to choose who I would address—the teacher or the students—as well as what to address and what to let go of. I made a point of addressing the issues head on as they came up in class. I did this not in an effort to attack but because I needed to circumvent the perpetual racisms that were sometimes held onto too tenaciously. These forms of racism are not always conscious … or, rather, intentional. It is more a part of

who we each are as a people and even after I tried to explain the differences, or reinterpret a message gone awry, sometimes the two groups just could not understand each other, but these are the differences of culture. As much as we try, we cannot expect to fully understand one another. Because I had been so involved with Aboriginal women and communities for just about all my adult life, I believe and teach that we need to know both worlds. I have been successful in both worlds and so I am able to explain to both sides how the other functions. I can use this to reconcile them to each other. Perhaps, most importantly, having a strong Aboriginal presence in the program effectively tells the students that it is safe enough to check out and that this may be a place of openness and opportunity.

In response, Ingrid stresses that:

Gail's initial role as facilitator was fundamental. The program was demanding and we did get tired. Gail and I learned to recognize when the other was tired and we would fill in for each other, shouldering a bit more of the effort for a time. Without her, the program would have had no relevance. It would not have worked … at least, not as it did. We needed her and succeeded due to her presence.

Florence agrees:

In response to the technical nature of the course material, Gail was an advocate for the students, asking a lot of questions that the students perhaps would not have asked. I knew from Gail whether or not the material was reaching the students. Her strengths as a mediator particularly came through while discussing symptoms, diagnoses, and treatment options [for mental illness].

I am a sensitive person, but when it comes to the ASWCP and developing a relationship with Gail and the students, it is mostly just about being aware that they are different from the mainstream student population, and that I need to be open to that. And even further, I've learned that what works for one group of Aboriginal students does not work for another—they have diversity within themselves.

Gail's presence and direct involvement in the program continually reinforced a strong and very valuable role model for the students. When asked if the students responded differently to Gail than to Ingrid or Florence, Ingrid thinks that at times they were harder on Gail. She suggests that this should not really be a surprise because it was clear that they felt safer with Gail.

Gail is an Aboriginal woman and therefore it is easier for students to open up to her and respond more honestly to her. Also, she is more of a challenge to them because she represents the image of a successful Aboriginal woman. They really looked to her as a role model, someone who has been really open about her life, including her struggles and her achievements.

Bridging the Gaps

In bridging the gaps between Aboriginal and non-Aboriginal instructors and students, Gail explains that the co-teaching approach is a twofold effort. The success of the program does not lie solely in the presence of the Aboriginal voice, but also on the demeanour, intentions, and capabilities of the non-Aboriginal counterpart. As she explains:

> It takes a special non-Aboriginal person to be able to teach Aboriginal adult students. They must be flexible and open. Most of all, they cannot have their egos or intellects overtake their style or methods of teaching. There must be a willingness to learn from Aboriginal peoples and the instructors have to be able to adjust their teaching styles to best meet the needs of their students. In working closely with Ingrid, I was aware of all her goodness as well as the insensitivity that she and many other non-Native persons carry unknowingly. She was often not even aware of the misconceptions she carried. I have a great deal of admiration and respect for Ingrid, which she has earned over the years that I have known her, and so approaching her to correct a misconception was indeed daunting and had to be handled carefully. When I did confront her, she apologized for the insensitivity, and I do give her every credit for the confident, assertive way in which she went ahead, expecting everything we planned together or through our committee of students and professors to fall into place.

Ingrid realizes this, commenting:

> We should never have a non-Aboriginal instructor as the sole educator in the classroom because no matter how sensitive we are, as a non-Native instructor, with all the best intention and experience in the world, we just can't get it exactly right.

In narrating their co-teaching experiences, Ingrid, Gail, and Florence came to fully recognize and appreciate the importance and strength of a collaborative effort, which greatly enhanced their ability to approach some of the key and highly sensitive issues within Aboriginal communities. According to Ingrid:

> We each brought different strengths and approaches to the courses. The reason it worked is because we had respect for each other, which was further built up over time. Our dynamic was one of respect and listening.

Similarly, Gail maintains that while teaching a course, the instructors work with each other, not against each other.

> This is especially the case with Ingrid's course on sexual abuse. She treats it [clinically], and has resolved it and reconciled it within herself, whereas many of us have not done that. The students also respond very well to this. Having both of us there makes a big difference, especially during a tough subject because I can quietly leave for a while with an upset student. It is definitely a learning and healing process, but

to do this successfully really depends on the manner and approach of the teacher. Because Ingrid demonstrates understanding and a level of comfort with the issue, she can help the students immensely.

The co-teaching approach remains an indispensable point of departure in the Aboriginal Social Work Certificate Program. In working with Ingrid, Gail, and Florence, it was clear that each of them had a lot to learn and "unlearn" about each other and about their approaches to education. Gail explains that she often had to remember that despite their commitment to build the program with respect to the Aboriginal world view, Ingrid, Florence, and the other instructors are not Aboriginal.

> I often had to reconcile in my own mind that I didn't have to make them Aboriginal, which I think I tried to do because I valued our relationship and their contributions to what we needed to do. With Ingrid, I wanted her to be able to move as she thought she could, even though I knew that she was missing some things. But I had to realize that I cannot make people what they are not—this is too overwhelming.

The unwavering effort of the non-Native instructors remains one of the main reasons for Gail's continued commitment to the program. Here she has found people who are willing to listen, which lends possibility to the prospect of building constructive and sustainable bridges.

Overcoming Tensions

Throughout the various efforts spent on bridging Aboriginal and non-Aboriginal perspectives on healing, teaching, and learning, there were certainly times when tensions developed. When asked how they dealt with this, the three women responded with an honesty that is refreshingly instructive.

Confrontation for Gail could be difficult:

> Sometimes my inner anger was triggered by a casual remark about some sacred belief or an offhanded response to issues that are close to Aboriginal hearts. When this came up, I had to take the time to think it over, debating what should be addressed. This largely depended on what kind of impact it could have on their teaching abilities and how it might negatively affect the rapport they held with the students. I would also have to determine if it was a significant misunderstanding of the culture, or if this was just a minor issue that the students could forgivingly overlook. In our culture, there are things we do not do with older people and with those in superior positions, although I do recognize that this may be both cultural and learned through White domination over Natives.

Likewise, for Ingrid, addressing conflict could be hurtful:

> Of course, at times I did become defensive and emotional. But I would recognize this and try to overcome it, addressing my insensitivity so that I could learn from it. I

remember one presentation where I had brought in a speaker. I thought it went well, but the topic was difficult and heavy. Later Gail told me she felt he'd been racist and I thought: "If this is racism, I've really got to work on it." The confrontation from Gail hurt. I had to respect Gail's feelings, as well as the students, yet I couldn't avoid what I thought. I didn't recognize the racism in it and by implication that was really hurtful and painful for me. We kept discussing it and eventually came to some sort of resolution, but it was painful.

While much of the information Florence teaches on drug therapy is considered neutral, the symptoms, diagnoses, and treatment approaches are often strongly bound in cultural knowledge and experience. Florence recalls one instance in particular where Gail approached her about being culturally insensitive.

It was on the definition of psychosis, which I explained according to the Western scientific view. However, what would be considered psychotic in our culture was not considered psychotic in theirs. For example, within Aboriginal cultures, hearing voices is not necessarily considered psychotic or symptomatic of any mental illness, whereas in our culture, it often is. In fact, as Gail informs us, hearing voices is often a significant spiritual experience. Failing to recognize this seriously undermines the value and experience of spirituality among many Aboriginals. While teaching, I also had to be aware that psychotherapy is not a common approach in Aboriginal methods of therapy. I encouraged the students to explore and employ healing methods that they could import into their own communities. In our classes, we taught about treatment by having the students give class presentations. Some of them brought in traditional healers, while others employed more Western-based models of healing. So they really taught each other about the treatment aspect.

Despite the discomfort that accompanies confrontation, throughout it all, the instructors focused on the success of the program and the discussions around disagreements actually solidified the relationships of the three women.

Teaching and Healing: Striking a Balance

As the program progressed, it became abundantly clear that for many students, learning involves a process of healing. A new challenge for the instructors and students lay in achieving a balance between teaching and healing. From the outset, Florence, Gail, and Ingrid were aware that the course content would address specific issues that many of the students had personally encountered. Clearly, students in the mainstream social work program experience problems, but not to the same extent as the Aboriginal students. This is where the immediate challenge of teaching in the ASWCP differs significantly from teaching in the mainstream system. Gail explains that since the course material so often reflected students' life experiences, the program often became an outlet for the students and the instructors needed to deal sensitively with these topics. At the same time, they needed to maintain their focus on teaching. As she explains:

The program material becomes very personal because many of the issues, including sexual assault, drug abuse, and suicide, are what they deal with daily in their communities, so what I have tried to do is develop a program that is reflective of community issues and then to help them build skills to address this. We want to show the students that there is hope and that people can change. The students come in with many questions, many whys: Why can't they drop drugs? Be better parents?, etc. This is precisely what education, especially social work education, is all about. It is a process of personal growth and there are things you have to approach personally.

Achieving this balance also demanded sensitivity, patience, and support among the students. As Gail recalls:

When one student became upset, they were all very helpful and supportive of each other. We would certainly talk about it for some time in class, but I would also meet with the student after the class and talk more about the issue. I would also often refer the student to the proper resources. But sometimes, it was just incredibly overwhelming. At these times, I'm not sure how much teaching got done. It is important to keep in mind, however, that this is also cathartic for the student in terms of personal healing, which is essential in equipping them to be more effective social workers. If they will work well as social workers, they must first experience personal healing.

Not only were the needs of the Aboriginal students different from those in the regular social work program, but they also varied from one student to another. Many of the students were at different stages in their personal development and healing. Most of the students, Florence notes, "are very shy and often lacking confidence. The majority of them have experienced one or more serious problems in their lives, including suicide, mental illness, sexual assault, violence, and addiction."

For Florence, one of the biggest adjustments in working in the ASWCP came with the experience of students using the classroom as a catharsis. Her sentiments resonate strongly with what Ingrid experienced in her courses on sexual abuse, where the boundaries between teaching, learning, and healing become fused.

When talking about problems in the mainstream program there are students with problems, but not with the same magnitude as in the ASWCP. I needed to adapt to this. Sometimes it would mean not being able to cover all the material, which was hard for me initially because I thought I wasn't achieving my mandate. I had to learn that learning was healing for many of the students. This was very new for me and very different from the mainstream system. In fact, the students often felt comfortable enough to approach me about their feelings and experiences. Some of the students have actually said to me that I made them aware that what was happening to them and what they were feeling did not mean they were "crazy."

In the chapter on "Education as Healing," Ingrid, Gail, and Florence elaborate on the teaching-healing approach and the importance of keeping a balance. Upon reflection, they believe that the healing aspect is absolutely necessary for the students in order for them to work effectively as social workers in their communities. This confirms that at the basis of the teaching-healing experience lies their belief that one cannot teach about empathy without modelling it. Through such experiences, the value and relevance of the ASWCP deepened significantly.

Resilience

The three women agree that while it is necessary to acknowledge the history of oppression among Native communities, it is also important to recognize the degree of strength, resilience, and persistence that accompany this.

In discussing resilience, Florence responds:

> The resilience of the students was often astounding. I don't know how to explain it, but it was powerful. I have not experienced it in the mainstream system. Many of the Aboriginal students have experienced brutal and traumatic events, both as children and as adults, but their eagerness to learn was remarkable. At the beginning, many of the students were dubious about their ability to survive in an academic setting, but the program was successful in giving them hope and confidence. In spite of the devastating losses and trauma that they have experienced, the majority were not bitter and this surprised me. I think the non-Aboriginal community could learn much about courage and resilience from them. On a personal level, teaching in the program has opened my eyes and made me more aware of and interested in the Aboriginal population and their history. Working with the students has been truly inspirational. I would like to see expansion beyond the Certificate Program because there really is a need for more programs like this to equip Aboriginal peoples to work as professionals in their own community.

Ingrid explains that the resilience we witness is a mark of their determination and motivation and, of course, their history.

> As Gail has explained, as a community, Natives are generally very ambivalent about education in the outside world because of their previous negative and destructive experiences. But I agree with what Gail says: Education is the most powerful tool to free ourselves from whatever we are suffering from—from whatever has disempowered us. In terms of their persistence, I cannot explain it. These students go through such difficult personal crises, yet they persevere. And they would continue to come to class where most of us would take three weeks off. Of course, sometimes they would have to withdraw temporarily and return later. We had to be flexible with this, and it has been a major reason for the success of the program.

Gail's response to the complexities of their persistence brings in a more personal narrative:

First of all, in seeking to understand all that accounts for the students' persistence, we have to consider the ground rules at work—that is, all that they have to deal with that the mainstream student populations don't. We are very resilient because this is what we have always lived … and community certainly gives strength. We carry a lot because we carry our personal trials, but also we bear the burdens of our extended families. Yet this is also what gives incredible resilience and because of the value of community, it doesn't matter what I have to go through to help these students. I will stand by them. The thing that has made me realize the importance of the program both professionally and personally is that I see the growth in the graduates. What I am finding is that it becomes a lifeline for them. I see people who have been given the greatest amount of hope to continue their education, even though historically, education has been a horrendous experience. But in this program, education is being redefined as an experience of possibility and opportunity. The possibility gives immense hope. It gives them a goal of regaining their self-esteem and dignity as a person. It shows them that they are able to achieve and that they contain within themselves the essence of self-reliance, development, and education.

Reflections and Conclusions

The Aboriginal Certificate Program responds directly to a clearly identified need in Native communities, namely, the lack of trained Aboriginal social workers. Employing Aboriginal peoples to staff the social service sector in their communities has been a huge challenge primarily because there are not enough Aboriginal peoples trained to do this type of work. As such the true relevance of the ASWCP at McGill is measured in terms of its ability to equip Aboriginal students with the skills required to deliver social services in their communities.

In reflecting upon the past 10 years, Ingrid recognizes the extent to which the program has changed her, both in her theoretical perspective on education and in the classroom. "I think we are far too hierarchical in regular courses. We put students through far too many unnecessary hoops." She continues by sharing that even her course work and exams in the regular program have changed. In reviewing her course material, she now thinks about the user-friendliness of the course, questioning the intentions and motivations behind all the barriers and the jargon. "Now I always ask myself: What is the point of this? What language am I using? Why is so much of it so alienating?"

An important part of building a truly comprehensive educational program means acknowledging that, in general, education has not had many positive results for the Aboriginal communities. Gail explains that this is further complicated by the fact that when someone is successful, they are considered "White."

Often, in Native communities, there is not a big ambition to be educated. It is not a priority because it makes you think White and act White, and we know that we have to maintain our differences in order to maintain our identity. It is not just about people standing in the way of our success, it is also the law and the funding that prohibits us.

The "right" for "all" to education does not necessarily include everyone, as Aboriginals are generally not part of the university population.

Given all of this, how could it have worked without a strong Aboriginal presence? The Certificate Program developed through a bridging of capacities, ideas, and willpower from both the Aboriginal and non-Aboriginal communities. At the basis of this program lies the belief that social work practice within Native communities can be a profession that is practised, directed, and owned by Aboriginals themselves. The sense of community that developed between the students, Gail, and the non-Aboriginal instructors created a space where these tensions could be better understood and addressed, and where both healing and learning could occur. The Certificate Program continues as a work in progress, creating a space where the skills and achievements of both Natives and non-Natives are woven together and, hopefully, where the strength and healing of Aboriginal peoples and communities are moving forward.

The positive impact of the program, built on the relationships that were formed, can perhaps best be expressed in an unsolicited letter that a graduate of the program recently wrote to the three instructors.

To Gail, Ingrid, and Florence,

I understand now what this program truly offers. You have educated me through a process of healing and education. You have taken my personal beliefs, experiences, and insights to a higher level of understanding. I can now work with different systems, understand these systems, and use the holistic approach to keep myself grounded.

I believe that your approach to my education can help me to remain focused on my clients no matter what chaos I observe or become a part of.

You have made me stronger. You have also done what you said you would do ... given me a base to work from ... general knowledge and an understanding of what holistic means in the communities and systems we work in. (T. Lizotte, personal communication, April 2005)

Notes

1. The crisis was initiated when some non-Native people from Oka, the village near Kanehsetake, attempted to extend their golf course onto Aboriginal sacred land. The Mohawks rallied and men, women, and children formed a human barrier to protect the area. This resulted in a full-scale confrontation and an armed standoff between the Mohawk warriors on one side and the police, tanks, and the Canadian army on the other. A provincial police officer was killed; no inquiry has proven from which direction the shots were fired. Mohawks from Kahnawake blocked a bridge to Montreal, and Kahnawake was also surrounded by tanks and the military. Food and medical supplies had to be smuggled into the community by Native peoples (Obomsawin, 1993). An effort to evacuate the elderly and some women and their children from Kahnawake, with the support of the police, was disastrous. Individuals from a nearby non-Native community, seemingly unstopped by the police, stoned the cars. Children and babies cut by the shattered glass were taken to the hospital and several elderly people died shortly after from the stress (Obomsawin, 2000). The standoff lasted for 78 days and many abuses of the Mohawk people occurred during that time.

   This event, which has had a profound effect on all Canadians, "was a crisis that paralyzed an entire province, and forever transformed the politics of Aboriginal People in Canada," (York & Pindera, 1991, frontispiece). For a full account, see Ciaccia (2000) and York and Pindera (1991). Eventually, the federal government purchased the disputed land and handed it over to the community of Kahnesatake. Four Mohawks were convicted on firearms charges.

2. These institutional barriers and ways to overcome them have been well described in the literature. See, for example, Canada (1996b), Dominelli (1997), Haig-Brown (1995), Pinderhughes (1994), and Young (1999).

Inclusion, by Michael Loft, with technical assistance by Lydia El-Cherif

CHAPTER 6

Strengths and Weaknesses of a Specialized Program:
Learning from Students in Aboriginal Social Work Education in Canada

Amanda Grenier

Aboriginal Social Work Education in Canada: Learning from Student Feedback

Providing Aboriginal social work education in Canada and abroad raises several challenges at the institutional, professional, and personal levels. The historical context of the colonization of Aboriginal peoples in Canada (Canada, 1996a),[1] the subsequent particular social issues facing Aboriginal communities (i.e., high unemployment rates, poverty, addiction, and critical housing shortages), the inadequacies of mainstream social services in responding to related needs (Castellano, Stalwick & Wein, 1986), the structural barriers to participation in post-secondary education or professional training, and the shortage in the provision of professional training required to work with these communities (Fiddler, 2000) are all reasons why conventional teaching approaches in social work must be adapted for cultural relevance and implementation in diverse Aboriginal communities (see Rosenman, 1980, for a discussion of social work education in the Australian context and Cairns, Fulcher, Kereopa, Nia Nia, & Tait-Rolleston, 1998, for New Zealand). Aboriginal leaders and educational institutions agree that mainstream non-Aboriginal social work practices cannot be simply transplanted into an Aboriginal educational context (Brown, 1992; Ruttan, 2000).

A variety of models for Aboriginal social work education programs have been developed across Canadian schools of social work, including the autonomous, affiliated autonomous, special Native, and conventional. Each of these models offers particular strengths and contains inherent weaknesses (for a full discussion of these models, see Castellano, Stalwick & Wein, 1986). Despite the advantages and disadvantages of each model, however, Kirkness and Barnhardt (1991) state that all of these programs and institutions make a commitment to "culturally appropriate, readily accessible, quality post-secondary education for First Nations people" (p. 12). This chapter presents student feedback from an evaluation of the McGill Certificate Program in Aboriginal Social Work, a "special native model" (Castellano, Stalwick & Wein, 1986), wherein courses are offered to Aboriginal students in a non-degree-granting Certificate Program separate from the mainstream undergraduate degree program (BSW). The following discussion focuses on selected issues facing the McGill program, situating these within the larger context of Aboriginal social work education in Canada and abroad.[2]

Evaluation of the Program

The Certificate Program in Aboriginal Social Work Practice (hereafter referred to as ASWCP) is intended to provide professional training for two groups: Aboriginal peoples wishing to further their training who are already working in community agencies, and Aboriginal peoples who want to develop a future career in social work but who are not currently working in the field (see Stacey Moore in Chapter 4 of this book and Thompson Cooper, 2004, on the development of the ASWCP). While the overall demographic portrait of the students has shifted over the years from that of middle-aged women with families to the inclusion of younger and less experienced students seeking a specifically Aboriginal learning environment, the program's structure remains centred on strong Aboriginal content designed to foster the development of practice skills that will assist students in better providing services to their respective communities. After five years in operation (1995–2000), the program staff and faculty were interested in conducting an appraisal of the program in order to build on its strengths, detect weaknesses, and adapt content in keeping with the ever-changing realities of Aboriginal peoples in Canada. Conducting an evaluation of an Aboriginal education program posed a unique challenge, however, as conventional measurements of program success that tend to focus on institutional priorities of student retention and post-graduate employment fail to incorporate student perspectives, experiences, and meanings given to and derived from participation (McKenzie & Mitchinson, 1989). This is especially the case in relation to many Aboriginal students whose success involves "more than simply obtaining a university degree to get a better job" (Kirkness & Barnhardt, 1991, p. 2). The authors emphasize the need for "a higher educational system that *respects* them for who they are, that is *relevant* to their view of the world, that offers reciprocity in the relationships with others, and that helps them exercise *responsibility* over their own lives" (Kirkness & Barnhardt, 1991, p. 2).

In order to honour the voices of students, it was decided that a fundamentally qualitative analytical approach should provide the backbone for a methodology incorporating the use of questionnaires with an account of student reflections and evaluations gathered during focus groups. Although consultations did take place with program directors regarding their interests and needs pertaining to the evaluation, I conducted the process with assistance from the student advisory board, research assistants, and student participants. Participants were invited to identify the strengths and weaknesses of the program; share their thoughts about what the program represents to them both on a personal and professional level; and make suggestions as to how the program could be modified to better suit their needs, goals, and the changing needs of their communities. Guiding questions for the study and the focus groups themselves pertained to the accessibility, cultural relevance, significance, transferability, and overall level of success represented by the content, instruction, and classroom community (Grenier, 2001).

The potential sample population for the evaluation included all current and former ASWCP students. Five focus groups, each containing four to six people, were conducted both at McGill and in one nearby Aboriginal community. In the focus groups, broadly stated questions served as guidelines for discussion, which, in turn, allowed participants to raise new questions and themes. As is standard, all identifying information has been removed from the focus group transcripts in order to protect the students' identities.

This paper presents an overview of the students' reflections on the Aboriginal-specific program from the standpoint that members of marginalized groups are in the best position to comment on their own success in the educational process. What follows is a thematic overview of the focus group discussions that intentionally centres on the extent to which the program achieved an acceptable level of cultural relevance and created community within the larger institution of McGill. The paper will take account of the weaknesses inherent within a "special Native" model (Castellano, Stalwick & Wein, 1986) for Aboriginal education in the context of the ASWCP, including marginalization within the larger university context, while showcasing the strategies that students used in negotiating their position within this environment. A primary objective of this paper is to give space to student voices in the hope that some of the challenges that Aboriginal students face within professional and university communities can be acknowledged. For this reason the students often have the last word throughout. My goal is to ensure that their insights find a home in the larger planning efforts and theoretical work on the content and delivery of Aboriginal social work education in Canada.

Strengths of the Program

A unifying factor among students was the ASWCP being chosen largely for its Aboriginal specificity, meaning that students indicated an initial attraction to the Aboriginal content of the program and not necessarily to its social work focus. This reflects the importance of cultural relevancy reported by Ruttan (2000). Secondary was the desire for social work training, yet, more importantly, how this would need to be met within an Aboriginal-specific program. ASWCP students with past experience of mainstream educational programs and environments indicated how Aboriginal content had been absent therein. The following accounts illustrate this issue:

> This ... is something that was completely absent in the courses that I've taken.... That's why ... it's interesting.... It shows a lot of the history and having other Native people ... getting to understand their issues ... what they're going through and sharing the experiences and maybe helping each other.
>
> No, my God, the stuff we covered, the meat and potatoes of it ... you just don't even get that in the bachelor's. I thought to myself, oh God, even if I wanted to go and get the bachelor, it would probably be so generic and boring and antiseptic.... You just don't get to know anything. You're stuck.

This is similar to the Aboriginal education students interviewed by Friesen and Orr (1998), who were "dismayed that Aboriginal content had been withheld from them during their [mainstream] schooling and consistently identified Aboriginal courses as the best ones taken at [the school in question]" (p. 193). Fundamentally, the Aboriginal specificity of the ASWCP addressed an unmet need for Aboriginal specificity within a social work program and opened doors for those students with little former experience in social work.

Diversity within and among Aboriginal students in the program (e.g., Mohawk, Inuit, rural, urban, etc.) was also identified as a strength of the ASWCP. Students highlighted the differences as a positive aspect of the program and felt that, for the most part, their differences were recognized within the program content and instruction. Students contrasted this experience to popular and homogenizing assumptions that all Aboriginals are the same and share common beliefs, values, needs, and ancestries. Interestingly, however, students admitted that until their involvement in the program, they did not possess a great deal of knowledge about each other's communities and were therefore concerned as to whether all Aboriginal diversity was accounted for in the material. Students discussed issues related to intergroup diversity:

> We have ... diversity in the sense that we don't just have people who live on reserve. We've got urban ... people coming in ... they have their own history.... There's a real mixture ... people come in who are adopted and they don't have roots to go to.... I wouldn't hear from someone who is a Cree, who is adopted.... We all have different perspectives too.... We [speaking of those in one of the focus groups] come from the same community, but I'm sure each one of us has a different angle ... in terms of traditional things.
>
> Because people think that all Indians are the same, but we're not the same because we all have different cultures, and we don't have the opportunity to actually ... meet and work with the others.

Challenging outside perceptions of homogeneity within the program, students illustrated questions of inclusiveness, representation, and recognition often raised by the presence of intergroup diversity and variations among students or groups of students within such programs (McKenzie & Mitchinson, 1989). Diversity within the group raises questions about how to approach issues of representation and recognition in the classroom; there was some concern for "Mohawk dominance" within the group and the ways in which different groups were represented. There was a particular concern that urban Aboriginal or Inuit lives had been misrepresented and/or not adequately addressed. Students' concerns regarding the presence of extensive intergroup differences (e.g., background, geographic location, traditions, cultural or non-cultural, etc.) are indicative of the need for instructors and students alike to acknowledge the potential for homogenization and subjugation to occur even in the context of an Aboriginal-specific program. Therefore, a major challenge arising from student feedback is how to maintain a balance between the Aboriginal specificity of the program (i.e., being an Aboriginal-specific program by design) and the intergroup diversity of student members, which demands and merits recognition.

Linked with discussions of Aboriginal specificity and intergroup diversity were students' observations on the importance of having Aboriginal mediators (i.e.,

Aboriginal co-facilitators for non-Aboriginal instructors and/or guest speakers) to bridge the gap between the mode of instruction and Aboriginal lived realities, as well as to enhance the relevance of the material for the students.[3] One student discusses the potential for disrespect in the absence of a mediator:

> If you're not going to do it right, don't do it at all. I figure … to do otherwise would be a disrespect … for me to sit down and … comment on … Mohawk culture is an insult…. I'm totally ignorant of the Mohawk culture…. What gives me the right? I know nothing….

Chief Dan George (Salish) has referred to Aboriginal teachers as the "new warriors" who have to "understand both worlds, learn how to integrate them, to use this knowledge [these 'weapons'] effectively, and how to model this ability for their students" (quoted in McAlpine, Cross, Whiteduck & Wolforth, 1990, p. 82). In this sense of understanding "both worlds," students viewed the mediator for the program as a Mohawk mediator, and the guest speakers as mediating particular Aboriginal lives and traditions in the context of social work practice in the field. Gail Stacey Moore, the Aboriginal co-instructor in all of the courses, helped clarify issues for non-Aboriginal instructors and worked toward bridging the daunting and multifaceted divide of privilege, oppression, culture, tradition, context, and experience that existed and is always necessarily present between Aboriginal students and non-Aboriginal instructors. According to the students, the presence of mediators helps to keep the lines of communication open for dissent and discomfort when they arise. Consider the following quote:

> Everyone had enough strength and understanding to know what was going on and … it's interesting how… [the instructor] mentioned she didn't even see that perspective … but … she had [the mediator] to say … hello, did you get that angle?

In addition to bridging the gap, mediators helped to verify the accuracy of particular writings and diffuse misrepresentations or misunderstandings. For example, students related an experience of a non-Aboriginal guest speaker who spoke inappropriately; in this situation, the mediator fulfilled an essential role in terms of debriefing with the students after the fact and facilitating a discussion on the issues that arose for the students throughout the lecture.

Cultural relevance was identified as another major strength of the ASWCP. Students discussed how material resonated with personal and community experiences, using the word "real" to describe course content. This is expressed in the following quote: "… it's … real stuff what's in that program … real things that are happening every day in Native communities. I'm sure it's happening elsewhere but … it *does* happen in our communities [emphasis of student]…." Another student commented that "it gives you ownership when you're talking about people that you know." When speaking of the cultural relevance of the program content, students gave examples of specific courses (i.e., Legal Problems of the Poor,[4] Addictions, and Adult/Child Sexual Abuse), invited Aboriginal speakers (i.e., on issues such as residential schools), and community members who could address specific topics (i.e., suicide) from their perspective. Students requested speakers who could lead discussions on cultural ways of learning as well as those who could speak to their experience as clients. Students felt that the courses assisted them in filling gaps in their knowledge about the dangers, implications, and effects of social problems facing many Aboriginal peoples, as well as imparting an overall understanding of the needs of certain communities. Such responses on the cultural relevance of the program echo the general literature on adapted curricula; in a discussion on Aboriginal education, Battiste (1998) insists that "We cannot continue to allow Aboriginal students to be given a fragmented existence in a curriculum that does not mirror them, nor should they be denied understanding the historical context that has created the fragmentation" (p. 24).

With regard to instructors, there is a need for them to feel that they are properly interpreting and honouring the diverse cultural and linguistic backgrounds of their students in the choice, design, and delivery of content. The mediator thus takes a measure of responsibility for the creation of a respectful dynamic among all members of the classroom community in this regard by adding a third level of understanding. Without a mediator, subjects are discussed with no explicit regard for the difficulties inherent in fostering open communication among non-Aboriginal instructors of privilege and students who are subject to marginalization on many different fronts. Students felt that the potential for instructors to "trespass" upon the values, beliefs, or experiences of students and for students to struggle with feelings of disempowerment, frustration, or helplessness as a result (i.e., at the thought of critiquing or correcting the words of a professor in a university classroom) was reduced by the presence of a mediator. It is clear that the person filling that role is working to mediate not only a cultural disparity but also the intersection of race and class, and a history of colonialism and exclusion. Ultimately, the subject of mediation is a deeply rooted historical power imbalance that must be particularly railed against in the context of an Aboriginal-specific education program at a prestigious university. (See Zapf, 1997, for a discussion on issues of authority and communication between non-Aboriginal instructors and Aboriginal students, as well as Bodor & Zapf, 2002, on experimenting with alternative teaching models in such a setting.)

Student discussions about bringing course material "back to the community" indicated that the knowledge gained though the program helped students to develop the understanding and insight needed to make changes on a variety of levels (e.g., self, family, community, society, etc.). For example, the program had enabled them to acquire a deeper understanding of family members' actions situated within the context of total community health. Students indicated that the courses taught them to negotiate, communicate their needs, and make changes such as redefining family roles, changing patterns of interaction with friends and neighbours, as well as integrating course concepts into their daily lives. Mothers, in particular, talked about noticing a transformation in day-to-day interactions with their children. This recognition of change provided a sense of hope for future generations that students might break negative cycles by politicizing and ultimately empowering their children to take charge of their own future and that of their community.

Weaknesses of the Program

Students discussed feeling marginalized from the School of Social Work and the McGill community as a result of belonging to a segregated program. The extant division between ASWCP students and those in the conventional BSW was a source of great discomfort for the former as they wondered if they were being unfavourably situated in a value-laden dichotomy differentiating between "normal" social work and "Aboriginal" social work. Students in the ASWCP were not included in many social work activities such as orientation and graduation,[5] and had little interaction with students in the BSW program. Students also felt marginalized by staff and faculty who did not know them, were unable to answer their questions, and did not seem to accept that they were "really in social work." A few interpreted the constant room changes in one semester as a sign of their "low priority" status within the school. These sources of discomfort and feelings of alienation from the school community were also likely informed by students' awareness of the way in which they were perceived by others and of how this perception is informed by racism and other systemic oppressions. They felt that their involvement was based on their status as members of a disadvantaged group and not on their own merit; a major concern was that admission was being viewed by people outside the program as a type of "affirmative action" on the part of the university. When students within the program were not perceived as taking the program seriously, there was a reported loss of confidence in the program from both within and outside of its ranks. Students stressed the need to strike a balance between the pressures of deadlines and life circumstances, as any lack of motivation on the part of a particular student was linked to conflict during group work wherein different levels of commitment affected the overall group cohesion.[6] Such conflicts within the ASWCP are directly indicative of its status as a site of reconciliation and difference within an environment generally devoted to one sole marker of educational or professional attainment: a university degree.

To students, adaptations such as flexible assignment deadlines set in the spirit of educational accessibility sometimes led to feelings of marginalization. An awareness of the perception that the program was "easier" or that the Aboriginal students were not as intelligent nor as qualified as their counterparts in the BSW program permeated student commentary on their relationship to the School of Social Work as a whole. Comparisons made between the programs and references to the BSW as the "regular program" seemed to reveal how students felt separate and marginalized in the context of McGill and the BSW program. Consider the following quotes, one of which is connected directly to experiences of systemic and internalized racism:

> What it means, what it means for me? It's not as hard as mainstream, okay? I don't think it is. I don't think if I'm gonna get a grade here, it's gonna be so clear-cut.... My tendency is to think that ... it's not as hard.

I have a friend…. She's talked to people who have been through it and who say … people who aren't in it who are mainstream look at it as like, you know … Indians need to get it, so it must be so easy…. That's a friend who [is] … a practising social worker.

Throughout the focus groups several observations were made regarding how McGill and the mainstream social work community tended to value bachelor's degrees over certificates and would likely question the credibility and standards of the ASWCP. Students discussed professional mechanisms of standardization in relation to the separate program, the emergence of negative feelings related to holding "lesser" qualifications (e.g., a certificate and not a "professional" degree), and the effects of these feelings and observations upon their motivation to succeed. Students felt that their efforts were somewhat minimized due to their certificate status. According to a report by Castellano et al. (1986), standards and credibility have long been an issue relative to Aboriginal social work education in Canada. The authors echo concerns that "academic institutions tend to equate 'different' with 'inferior' and Native students voiced that the designation 'Native' may imply lower standards in a program" (p. 177). Pace and Smith (1990) have also focused on the tensions between adapted curriculum and the perception of "relaxed" academic standards.

In addition to feeling ostracized as a result of their enrolment in a separate Certificate Program within Social Work, students discussed how, by the same token, Aboriginal communities are generally skeptical of McGill as an institution and of social work as a profession. This means that students must negotiate the skepticism of both their Aboriginal community and the academic institution of McGill. In general, the certificate is valuable in attaining a job in their communities—for the most part, Aboriginal communities do not differentiate between the two levels of training (e.g., a certificate or a bachelor's degree) and one may find stable employment without a degree. Many applicants have not completed a formal high school diploma and the program, offered through the Department of Continuing Education but delivered through the School of Social Work, is consequently structured to recognize and value students' lived experiences.[7] However, there is a tension here between the honouring of students' lived experiences within the Aboriginal-specific program and the external scrutinizing influence of agencies, standards, and credentials:

I never got a chance to finish school, I only had elementary…. I had younger siblings to raise, so my past experiences were negative. Scholastically I was lacking, so that played into when I was applying to the course. Was I the right material? Did I have what it took? … Will I make myself look stupid because I lacked what the other students had? Scholastically I'm not at the same level as the rest…. But after being in the group after two years, I realize that what I lacked education-wise I bring in life skills, so there's a balance…. You do a three-sixty because now I'm beginning to realize that my life experience is just as worthy. Although it's not a high school diploma … it's just as important….

In addition to personal feelings associated with being involved in the program, students discussed receiving mixed messages about their role in relation to professional standards; they were not sure of their title or their qualifications, nor of how these would operate within the larger context of social work in an agency. Students were unsure as to whether the jobs they would be performing would be those of a case-worker or a social worker.[8] Although they believed they were qualified for the position of caseworker, many were confused in relation to the role performed in their field placement and part-time jobs. In the experience of many students, their title of "caseworker" denoted a position of lesser responsibility than the title of "social worker," although at times they felt they were being asked to perform as social workers. The following quote, extracted from a focus group discussion in relation to the question "What do you expect to be doing after you graduate?" demonstrates students' uncertainty about their qualifications:

Student 1: What are you capable to do with the certificate? ... I don't even know what I'm capable of doing. What can I do with the certificate?

Student 2: It's generally thought that you can fit in any social work milieu. That's my impression.

Student 3: It's not a BSW. I get mixed messages from the people at work. They call you a caseworker, not a social worker. Some say I should go back to work while others say I should go back to school.

Distrust of either McGill as an institution or of the field of social work in general meant that some community members did not support the certificate. Students often walk the line in terms of the need for acceptance and validation from the social service bureaucracy on the one hand, and the approval and support of their own communities on the other. Such skepticism from the community was particularly difficult for those students who required workplace support in order to attend the classes and complete their certificates. Lack thereof was considered a major obstacle to completion. For example:

I've seen some other people who worked, or ... who have dropped out of the course when they got jobs because often, employers weren't very flexible on scheduling. But the other thing is maybe it's just too much for them.... There's not that many organizations who have that clause where they allow for training and development and things like that so they say, well you know, that's three hours off my time, sorry.

With regard to employment, more than one student reported that they had difficulties securing a position after graduation. In contrast, the report produced by CASSW (Canadian Association of Schools of Social Work) (Fiddler, 2000) expresses a difficulty in recruiting and retaining equally qualified social workers and indicates that there is a need for Aboriginal social work training. Difficulty securing employment even in the face of severe community need may be related to students' desires to return solely to their own community upon completion of the certificate, an overall lack of funding available for social work positions, or agencies' need to hire BSW graduates to fill these positions. Students expressed concern about whether the program will provide a relatively small community with an overabundance of people and thus limit graduates' employment opportunities. Some students raised the issue that not every Aboriginal client would want an Aboriginal social worker, particularly one from their own community with whom they may come into contact on an informal basis. This could possibly require graduates to obtain employment in another community, although, as previously stated, many graduates were reluctant to do so. Such potential hurdles raise questions about whether students will be able to return to their communities upon graduation.[9]

Issue: Healing of Individual, Family, and Community

According to students, an important function of the ASWCP was its role as an intermediary between themselves and educational institutions, especially as this applies to the healing of scars left by exclusion, oppression, and the wielding of education as a tool of assimilation. Nabigon, Hagey, Webster, and MacKay (1999) highlight the interconnection between healing, learning, and community process. A supportive and participative approach to student learning is also documented by Young (1999). In the evaluation of the ASWCP, students repeatedly reported previous negative experiences with "school" and were intimidated by the prospect of enrolling in a post-secondary program. The prevalence of such negative associations with formal education reinforces the injunction that such Aboriginal-specific programs must be deliberately structured so as to best support the particular learning needs of students while respecting the place occupied by imposed education in the consciousness of many First Nations. Haig-Brown (1995) has made the following observation regarding a centre for Aboriginal education: "The programs within the Native Education Centre are established to address the students' previous educational experiences, not to recreate them" (p. 194). Students who had acquired negative experiences of formal education highlighted differences between these and their time in the ASWCP—specifically how the sense of community and supportive teaching style helped them to continue with the program, allowing them to develop a positive association with school. According to the students, the course structure and instructors' teaching style helped to raise their self-esteem; some students reported that they realized the value of their life experiences and learned that they were capable of doing well in school. As a result of participation in the ASWCP, some were even inspired to continue on with their schooling, this being perhaps one of the most significant, long-lasting, and notable successes of the program.

Despite the many positive accounts, however, the classroom is not a neutral domain but remains a space wherein confrontation and conflict both operate. Some students felt that this space had its limits and that positive accounts of the classroom environment must be balanced with difficulty and hardship. Participation in the ASWCP regularly involved tackling issues that were both systemic and incredibly personal, and students stressed the importance of taking these risks and becoming more comfortable in the process. An example was given of a student who "blew up" in class and the consequent issues raised for the students in attendance. Alongside such recognition of the limitations of the classroom space, however, students reported that the intergroup solidarity could assist them in "making things different." Nevertheless, it must be noted that students experienced varying levels of safety and openness and had arrived at different places in relation to their personal healing both within the program and upon completion:

> For some of them it was like new stuff and [they] hadn't probably worked on themselves personally, personal growth stuff ... for some of them if was ... [sigh] traumatic ... because of the sexual abuse and that, which is prevalent on Native land and, you know, getting triggered and all that stuff. For some it was their first time....

Such variation in students' needs raises questions about how to best support students who are coping with abuse, addiction, or trauma while simultaneously meeting the needs of students who are unaffected or at a different point in their healing process. A balance must be struck between allocating space wherein students can heal and designating time for the development of students' practical and academic skills; students who gained a lot from personal introspection during class time ran the risk of having their behaviour interpreted by others as a withdrawal from the class. Whether a balance was indeed successfully negotiated between personal growth and academics, many reflected on how the instruction and course material fostered individual development at each student's own pace. (See Nabigon et al., 1999, on the use of the Learning Circle in research and teaching.)

A common theme in responses pertained to how a smaller accessible community within the impersonal institutional context of McGill and a space in which to speak facilitated access to the university. Consider the following quote, which speaks to the student's fear and lack of confidence in relation to McGill: "I had ... a mindset ... about McGill.... It's way out off there somewhere ... but now it's attainable.... I know even I can do it." Students also stressed the role that such a supportive community played in their personal healing processes:

> It was like we were a big family.... We started off with 40 or 30 right at the beginning, but because we come from small communities, most people knew each other already, so it's not as if I was one student going into McGill and I didn't know anybody. I thought it was made simple.

Some students mentioned that they would phone each other at many times throughout the year to check in and help each other through the learning process:

> Everybody in our class, the group that started out and the group that's still there today ... there's phone calls among us.... Somebody is having a hard time outside of class will phone me and somebody else will phone me....
>
> I think there is something that I don't think you could ever get ... in other programs—[it] is that therapeutic element.... Everyone was there for each other and you could make calls at 11, you know, when you're hitting some heated topics that, you

know, we're all on the phone thinking, okay say the right thing, what should I say? Okay … and now those techniques at talking to one another, which seemed so artificial, script-like, now they become second nature…. I guess maybe we're getting some of those skills, you know, when we don't just see those skills behind social work. You use it in your day to day.

A significant amount of time was spent discussing how the program community went beyond enabling access and offering support to establishing what students refer to as a "safe space." In this space students felt able to let down their guard and discuss difficult personal experiences as well as challenge particular ideas and resolve conflicts among themselves or with instructors. Dulac (1996) has discussed how students in Aboriginal education programs face many personal challenges (e.g., addictions, sexual abuse, abuse within residential schools, etc.) in addition to those documented for mature students (e.g., juggling family responsibilities and employment, etc.). Students discussed how such traumatic memories or experiences were often triggered by their participation and how they felt safe discussing the course material in relation to their lives:

The sexual abuse course … was the most difficult course for everybody in our class because … everybody had it somewhere…. I don't care, aunt, uncle … there were very deep things and to have to go back to deal with some of the things you've awakened … you were … in the heart of courses, reading about … alcohol or drug or … oh, that's why….

Although there were admittedly varying levels of personal comfort within class discussions, most felt that the class environment within the program was generally safe. In students' accounts this space was often connected with personal development, the use of voice, and the act of claiming space. This is not surprising considering that the primary way to take space in a classroom environment is through the active use of voice. While claiming space represents the various ways, either spoken or not, that students used to make themselves heard, they could only do so within a safe environment:

Yeah. Safe space … I never used to talk. [laughter]
She was a very quiet girl.
And then after only one course now, you can't shut me up.
I keep encouraging her. [laughter]

Apart from being a demonstrated prerequisite for student success, the "safe space" was viewed by most as a site in which to practise the positive models of conflict resolution that they had learned. Students were able to work through conflicts in class while increasing their own assertiveness and empowering each other: "*It* teaches us that we don't have to sit on what we are feeling because we're afraid to step on somebody else's toes [student emphasis]." In this sense, the classroom offers more than a safe space—it offers a challenging and transformative space to engage in productive and restorative conflict. The demonstrated need for a "safe space" justifies the need to maintain the ASWCP as an Aboriginal-specific program offered only to Aboriginal students. This is consistent with observations made by Haig-Brown (1995): "As adults, students have chosen to be in a place where all the other students are of First Nations ancestry" (p. 197).

Conclusion: The Personal and the Political

Similar to the findings of Friesen and Orr (1998), the ASWCP students held the concerns of their communities close to heart and desired to give back what they had learned. Many highlighted how they would pick and choose what holds meaning for themselves and cultural relevance for their community (e.g., what can be integrated within their particular traditions and way of life). Despite the potentially positive repercussions of community knowledge transfer, however, students felt pressure to be role models for others. They voiced fears that, as graduates, they would be held up within their communities, and that being placed in this position would expose them to increased scrutiny and added expectations. Some experienced anger at the prospect of having to take on such a role and surmised that this would change the way their community viewed, interacted with, and judged them. Students also felt this change to be unfair despite understanding that attending the program contained the implicit acknowledgement that graduation could entail becoming a role model. This form of reluctance may stem from systemic racism that forces members of certain communities to redeem their people by becoming exemplary members of the dominant society. Many ASWCP students struggled as follows:

> I think you have to be strong enough in your sense of self to understand … when this hits you.… I don't want it … you don't want to be put up on a pedestal for the rest of the community and say, "Look, she can do it, you can do it." Just so that they can either (1) see you fail; (2) fall flat on your face; or (3) be the ones that pull you off your pedestal.

In the spirit of Freirean notions of critical literacy (Freire, 2000), the teachings of the program enabled students to better recognize systemic injustices such as racism and classism in Canadian society. Students who came to learn how they could work against the injustices of the system from within (i.e., in a major Canadian academic institution) felt that the program equipped them with tools to use "inside" with an eye to fomenting change and transformation on the "outside." While the tools learned can and should also be problematized as those of the master's (Lorde, 1983), students used these to negotiate between the "two worlds," a process that Bruyere (1998) has commented on as "living in another man's house." Students, however, discussed how despite some of the differences in approaches, they felt they could be more assertive and gave concrete examples of this change in their lives and personalities. Through shared experiences and understandings students could identify common goals and share insights with respect to planning, future directions, and political issues such as self-determination and self-government. Take the following quote as an example of the combination of knowledge and confidence, which had a large impact:

> I thought I would hate … [the course on legal problems] because I would be so angry from the reading I just didn't want to get involved in it because of all the injustice that has happened to our people … so I went to that course really with my mindset already that I'm doing it under duress. I don't want to go there because of the Indian Act that was imposed upon us and all that. But then I did read the stuff and I was a little bit happy with some of the people that were fighting for rights in British Columbia and then I thought I can just do this for my own self. So I wrote the papers just to get out all my frustrations and irritations and I got very good marks on them [laugh] and it was just like … it was therapy for me, so it turned up to be a very positive thing.… Just thinking about it makes my blood pressure go up, you know, because of all the injustice and the things that happened to our people. But then I was able to write it down and just let it go … you know, write it down and just let it go. It was good for me.

Evaluation findings related to this specific program highlight several key issues and challenges within the larger context of Aboriginal social work education in Canada. First, this evaluation brought up the tension between admissions policies facilitating initial access and institutional structures providing necessary student support after admission. Another tension that emerged in students' responses was that of the creation of a space that is safe and the creation or maintenance of feelings of marginalization from other students and "mainstream" programs. This is especially the case where students may have little opportunity to interact with the larger school and institution due largely to a lack of access and/or to feelings of exclusion. Significantly, students expressed a desire for a critical appraisal of the role that the social work profession has played in their communities and, in particular, of how social workers have been implicated in the dissolution and separation of Aboriginal families through assimilation policies and organizational practices. Student feedback also raised a major challenge regarding the relationship between historical cycles of socio-cultural marginalization and targeted education programs such as the ASWCP. The question now is, how can programs such as the ASWCP encourage access to meaningful and relevant educational and employment opportunities and encourage full participation in a leadership capacity without reinforcing existing social hierarchies?

Notes

1. See Long (1992) for a history of the social movements and militancy of Aboriginal peoples against colonization and marginality.
2. For discussions of different models, see Zapf, Bastien, Bodor, Carriere, and Pelech (2000) on the BSW program for Alberta's rural, remote, and Aboriginal communities; Urtnowski (1996) on the McGill Certificate Program in Northern Social Work Practice; and Pace and Smith (1990) on Dalhousie University's Nation-specific approach.
3. The involvement of elders in teaching has also been elaborated by Nabigon, Hagey, Webster, and MacKay (1999).
4. The content of the course was on the historical relations of Aboriginal peoples and the Euro-Canadians. The Certificate Program had to use course titles from the mainstream program, so they did not necessarily reflect the content.
5. While all the social work students, including the certificate students, received their diploma at the same ceremony, graduates of the Certificate Program graduated as a special group in the Department of Continuing Education rather than with those receiving their BSW degree within the Faculty of Arts.
6. While we recognized the students' perception that sometimes we were "easier" on some students in terms of lateness and deadlines, this was usually due to privileged information we had about the students' circumstances—information we could not share. However, if students missed too many classes due to lateness or absenteeism, the student was required to repeat the course (The Editors).
7. Administration of training without degree or certification is not uncommon. Pace and Smith (1990) have commented on this lack of formal recognition in Nova Scotia.
8. Under the regulations of the Professional Association of Social Workers of Quebec, all workers must have a BSW and belong to the association in order to use the title "social worker." Workers who do not meet these criteria may work under the category of "agent des relations humaines" (ARH translates roughly as "caseworker"). It is not surprising, therefore, that in most communities the social work positions are held by non-Aboriginal workers and the casework positions by Aboriginal workers.
9. A follow-up study of 20 graduates of the program showed that 19 obtained employment in Native organizations, the majority in their community. Some were hired at a managerial level (Thompson Cooper, Stacey Moore & Priestley, 2002). What we observed was that some students were approached by agencies before they finished their certificate, therefore sometimes prolonging the amount of time it took them to complete the program (The Editors).

A tipi erected by students and a Cree elder from Hobbema for a weekend course in southern Alberta

CHAPTER 7

Aboriginal BSW Education in Rural and Remote Communities:

The University of Calgary's Learning Circle Model

Michael Kim Zapf

There are many ways to tell a story. The storyteller can choose where to begin and then select various combinations of the events and people for emphasis, according to the context and the intentions of the listener/reader. Following the overall intent of this book to explore experiences with Aboriginal social work education in Canada, Australia, and New Zealand, I attempt in this chapter to tell the story of the University of Calgary's Learning Circle model of BSW education for Aboriginal students in Alberta. Grounded in the expressed needs of local Aboriginal communities across the province of Alberta in western Canada, the Learning Circle model was also informed by experiences reported from similar social work education efforts elsewhere in Canada, Australia, and New Zealand.

Since the first courses were offered in 2000, the Learning Circle model has continued to evolve. Its story is ongoing. I have chosen here to relate the original vision, curriculum design, and delivery approach, with an emphasis on local and international connections.

Context

When the University of Calgary was created in 1968, the provincial government of Alberta did not want to fund duplicate professional schools in Calgary and Edmonton (where the long-established University of Alberta is located). Professional schools were allocated between the two universities. The University of Calgary was given a provincial mandate for all university-level social work education in Alberta. The Faculty of Social Work at the University of Calgary has been teaching and graduating students for 40 years now, with courses available primarily at three urban campus locations: Calgary, Edmonton, and Lethbridge. Throughout much of this period, Aboriginal students relocating from rural and remote communities to urban campus locations for their BSW education had voiced concerns about the accessibility and relevance of coursework grounded in western European assumptions that did not fit well with the world views and helping practices back home.

During the mid-1990s, the University of Calgary experienced severe budget cuts from the Klein government. The Faculty of Social Work staff complement dropped from 43 to 27 faculty members with an overall increase in student numbers. Survival of the urban-based programs became the priority during this time; there were no resources to allocate toward outreach or different models of curriculum and delivery to meet the needs of Aboriginal students. By the late 1990s, the cuts eased and the provincial government began to reinvest in education, but this was not done by restoring previous levels of funding for operations. Instead, the government held out "funding envelopes," packages of program monies that reflected government priorities. Universities and departments were invited to submit proposals to compete for these funding envelopes. One of the declared priority areas was "access." With a power base in rural Alberta, the provincial government wanted to improve accessibility to university education outside of urban areas.

BSW Access Vision

In 1998, a consortium of interest groups came together to develop a proposal for social work Access funding from the Government of Alberta. Their vision of a BSW Access program represented the collaborative work of diverse stakeholder groups, including the Northern BSW Stakeholders' Council (representatives from Children's Services Regions, Métis settlements, Métis zones, First Nations and tribal organizations, northern regions of Family & Social Services, private northern service agencies, post-secondary institutions under the Alberta North umbrella); First Nations Adult & Higher Education Consortium, with member colleges and education boards from the Treaty 6 and Treaty 7 areas plus the North Peace Tribal Council; the Alberta College of Social Workers; and the University of Calgary Faculty of Social Work. The collaborative proposal was successful and funding was received in early 1999.

While the government viewed "access" from the narrow perspective of additional non-urban bodies in seats for credit courses, the collaborative BSW Access Proposal (Rogers, 1998) put forward a much broader and innovative notion of accessibility in terms of a curriculum that would be accessible geographically and culturally. Excerpts from the proposal illustrate this vision of accessibility. Overall, the new effort would be dedicated to "increasing accessibility, responsiveness, and affordability of University of Calgary accredited social work degrees" (Rogers, 1998, p. 1). Recognizing the unique needs of potential students in rural, remote, and Aboriginal communities, "changes in traditional BSW delivery methods" were declared to be "a central component of the proposed program expansion" (p. 3). Specific guidelines then called for "innovative course content" (p. 9) that would be "culturally and geographically relevant" (p. 6). BSW curriculum content and delivery modes were to be "adapted" (p. 6) and "re-designed" (p. 10) to be "sensitive to First Nations and Métis peoples" (p. 6) and "aligned with traditional philosophies and knowledge systems" (p. 11). Course delivery methods were to be "flexible in time, place, and mode" (p. 5), with course scheduling "based on a flexible entry model and home community placements" (p. 11). This new model was to feature a "mutually designed infrastructure" with content "of the same quality as the programs currently delivered on-site by the Faculty" (pp. 1–2), leading to the accredited University of Calgary BSW degree.

Lessons from Other Places

The first step toward realizing the BSW Access vision was to examine the results and issues reported by similar Aboriginal outreach efforts in other places. Through this process, an appreciation developed for the work done in New Zealand, Australia, and other regions of Canada.

In the 1980s, a New Zealand report critical of social service delivery to rural communities led to government initiatives to increase the number of Maori social work graduates (Rangihau, 1986). In taking on this challenge, the School of Social Work at Victoria University of Wellington discovered that meaningful reform "involved establishing a new curriculum structure, new teaching material, and adult learning methods, plus recruitment of appropriate staff" (Cairns, Fulcher, Kereopa, Nia Nia, & Tait-Rolleston, 1998, p. 161). In particular, this group found that modular teaching approaches worked well in the New Zealand context, with courses designed and delivered in partnership with local resource persons. Working in collaboration with regional social service agencies and tribal groups, the university developed a program that could be "portable" through the use of a "modular teaching format" (Cairns et al., 1998, p. 158) with 27–30-hour modules focused around specific themes. Some of these modules were "taught in partnership with Maori people" (Cairns et al., 1998, p. 159).

Work in Australia in the 1980s warned of dangers arising from the dominance of American models and teaching materials in Australian schools of social work. With particular attention to remote Aboriginal communities, Rosenman (1980) was concerned that isolated regions in Australia could become simply the setting for application of American theory to American-defined problems. In order to build a truly Australian social work practice, Rosenman (1980) asserted that:

> Social work educators must understand the local culture along with the social, political, and economic forces that have shaped it, and analyze the degree to which social work is related to the local environment and acts as a force in shaping society. (p. 118)

An influential Australian report in the 1990s highlighted a need for accessible social work education in hinterland regions to offer local people careers in social work (Sturmey, 1992). Resulting social work education outreach efforts would have to feature curricula developed around themes and frameworks with meaning in the local context connected to community life and current issues (Cheers, 1998; Green, 2000; Sturmey, 1992). This material had to be core to the program rather than optional or peripheral, leading to what Lonne and Cheers (2000) called "generalist and community-embedded practice" (p. 52).

The University of Calgary also found work from other regions of Canada that supported the lessons from New Zealand and Australia. In the late 1980s, the Canadian Association of Schools of Social Work (CASSW) had established a task force to explore how social work education could respond in a meaningful way to Canada's multicultural reality. Their report, *Social Work Education at the Crossroads: The Challenge of Diversity* contained recommendations related to organizational structures and policies, relevant curriculum content, recruitment of minority students and faculty, field practice with minority populations, and partnerships with community groups (Christenson, 1991).

Social work distance education efforts in Canada had found that potential students tended to be mature individuals already employed in the human services field (Callahan & Wharf, 1989). They would require part-time evening and weekend classes that would not force a choice between employment and school. Educational institutions were challenged to be flexible in meeting the needs of these students. Rigidly sequenced courses and prerequisites could impose barriers for outreach Aboriginal social work students (Zapf, 1998). An outreach program in Saskatchewan found it necessary "to subordinate sequencing to accessibility" (Martinez-Brawley, 1986, p. 60) and offered part-time courses "not as a second class alternative but as the main programmatic thrust" (p. 56). Without flexible course offerings designed to accommodate local students who are also employed, educational institutions might actually contribute to perpetuation of the familiar pattern of urban-trained graduates moving to outlying regions to gain experience before returning to the city while local workers are relegated to low-status paraprofessional positions.

Canadian experiences also spoke to issues of administration and staffing for outreach Aboriginal social work education efforts. Both the Native Human Services Project at Laurentian University (Alcoze & Mawhiney, 1988) and the Northern BSW Program in Thompson, Manitoba (Paziuk, 1992) developed program advisory committees with representation from regional Aboriginal groups, the university, students and faculty, and local employing social agencies. Formal mechanisms for ongoing collaboration between the educational institutions and the regions were important to ensure a continuing voice for the communities as well as relevance and accountability of the programs.

Another crucial administrative requirement necessary for the success of Aboriginal outreach education efforts was identified as "ongoing, as opposed to temporary, financial commitment" (Alcoze & Mawhiney, 1988, p. 50) from the funding sources and the home university. Communities had to have confidence in the future of a program before they would commit their own resources or send their students.

The literature also spoke to staffing issues for such programs. An overview of the Northern Human Service Worker/BSW program offered through Yukon College in Whitehorse (Senkpiel, 1997) concluded that instructors had to be flexible and committed to cultural relevance. How material is taught may be as important as the content itself. From his experiences with a satellite program in northern Manitoba, De Montigny (1992) cautioned that urban campus expectations of workload may not be appropriate for outreach faculty, who must travel extensively, work through spring/summer sessions, and spend time with students and community members who have special needs.

Anecdotal accounts in the literature described overwhelming pressures on Aboriginal social work students. Issues included family demands, parenting obligations, financial crises and uncertainty, personal healing, fears of returning to school after many years away, and confirmation of the tremendous importance of staying in the home community (Beaulieu, 1993; Grieves, 1992; Lalonde, 1993; Peacock, 1993). Considering the alternative of moving to an urban non-Aboriginal academic setting, German (1997) described such a move as a "spiritual challenge" (p. 34). Beyond the demands of the education process itself, the student has to deal with transition needs related to the social, physical, emotional, and spiritual transition as well. Griffin-Pierce (1997) used the stronger terms "spiritual dislocation" and "emotional desolation" to describe the impact of such a move to the urban centre for educational purposes. "Far from mere homesickness, such feelings are based on an unconscious sense of having violated the natural and moral order in a culture which reifies order. Such stress is profound and unrelenting" (Griffin-Pierce, 1997, p. 5).

Lessons from these earlier Aboriginal social work education activities in New Zealand, Australia, and Canada provided strong direction for development of the University of Calgary's BSW Access program. It was clear that new social work education programs intended to reach Aboriginal students would have to go far beyond simply increasing student numbers. Every aspect of program funding, recruitment, location, content, delivery, organization, and community connections must be part of the change effort. Staff recruited for the BSW Access work would have to be flexible, committed to cultural relevance, and willing to assume unconventional teaching schedules and practices that challenged conventional university workload patterns. Courses would have to be offered in the students' home communities or regions. New curriculum structures would have to consider part-time, modular, weekend, and evening course offerings without rigid sequencing. New teaching materials would have to be developed around themes relevant to the local context; this content should be core rather than optional. The local community must be a collaborative partner in the design, delivery, and ongoing monitoring of the program. Stable funding would be necessary to inspire trust in the communities.

Staffing and Recruitment

At the outset, the Faculty of Social Work had to hire the right team to develop and bring the BSW Access vision to life. For the first time in the university's history, an Academic Selection Committee included Aboriginal peoples from community stakeholder groups as full voting members. A Métis elder from Grande Prairie and a Blackfoot education counsellor from Old Sun College participated in the formal selection process along with representatives from the Faculty of Social Work and an Aboriginal faculty member from sociology. The original BSW Access division team consisted of two male and two female assistant professors, all new to the University of Calgary (with no baggage as to how things had been done before!). A fifth person, a full professor with extensive teaching and administration experience, was appointed as BSW Access division head. This team of five represented diverse cultural backgrounds: First Nations, Métis, and non-Native. Such diversity meant that curriculum and delivery design work would be challenging and intense, requiring mutual trust, respect, and shared commitment to the overall Access vision.

Many potential Access students had a long history of negative experiences dealing with large bureaucracies. English was not a first language for many. Considerable academic and administrative support would be necessary. The Faculty of Social Work also recruited an Access Student Services staff person who spent a great deal of time on the telephone with applicants and potential students advising them on program requirements and details, and helping them assess their own situations relative to these requirements. The Student Services staff person would also travel to potential Access delivery sites for information workshops and direct assistance at crucial times of the year for application and registration deadlines.

The Learning Circle

Working in collaboration with community stakeholders over the summer of 1999, the new BSW Access team developed an innovative model for BSW curriculum and delivery. The community consultation process had made clear that the new program could not involve full-time study because most students in rural areas would be employed throughout their Access course experience. (In fact, Access students actually formed the backbone of the local social service network in many of the communities where the BSW would be delivered. Local agencies and the community could not afford to have all these people leave their jobs to attend school full-time even if classes were available locally.) A basic Access delivery pattern of nine-hour modules every two weeks was developed as a direct response to the needs expressed by both potential students and community agencies. Typically, this would involve three hours on Friday evening followed by six hours on Saturday.

Access division faculty members began with the vision from the BSW Access proposal and content from the existing accredited on-campus BSW program in their work to develop a variation of the curriculum with geographic and cultural relevance for students outside urban centres. Core BSW academic content was grouped into four general theme areas with meaning for social work in rural, remote, and Aboriginal communities: Generalist Practice in Context; Communication and Information; Diversity and Oppression; and Social Work Methods. These four general theme areas were then developed into theme courses with core curriculum material specifically adapted for application in rural, remote, and Aboriginal contexts. Each theme course consisted of eight nine-hour modules:

Generalist Practice in Context Theme Course

- Orientation/Seminar
- Generalist Social Work Practice (History, Assumptions, Components)
- Rural Context Considerations
- Northern Context Considerations
- Aboriginal Context Considerations
- Values and Ethics Considerations
- Local Applications
- Integration/Summary

Communication and Information Theme Course

- Orientation/Seminar
- Research and Generalist Practice
- Knowledge Building in Context
- Interviewing in Generalist Practice
- Interviewing in Context
- Documentation
- Local Applications
- Integration/Summary

Diversity and Oppression Theme Course

- Orientation/Seminar
- Diversity and Generalist Practice
- Colonization and Decolonization
- Canadian Social Policy
- Human Development and Environments
- Program Evaluation
- Local Applications
- Integration/Summary

Social Work Methods Theme Course

- Methods within Generalist Practice
- Approaches and Contexts with Individuals (two modules)
- Approaches and Contexts with Groups and Families (two modules)
- Approaches and Contexts with Communities and Organizations (two modules)
- Integration/Summary

The basic structure of this BSW curriculum variation could be represented in circular form based on a Medicine Wheel framework that was affirmed in Aboriginal communities during the collaborative developmental work. This non-sequential and non-hierarchical model for curriculum and delivery came to be known as the Learning Circle (as represented in Figure 7.1).

Within each of the four theme areas of the Learning Circle, students would also take a portfolio project course where they would be challenged to integrate their professional and lived experiences (including learning from the theme course) into a reflective project through supported independent study. Once all four theme courses and related portfolio projects were complete, BSW Access students could move on to a practicum placement in their own region with a flexible schedule negotiated between student, agency, and faculty. Accompanying the practicum was an integrative practice seminar to promote the integration of theory and practice within the local context.

FIGURE 7.1

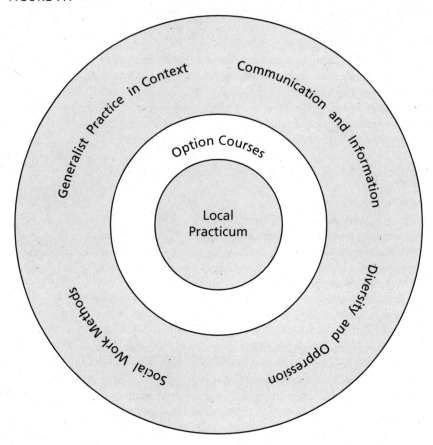

Once the new Learning Circle model had gone back to the communities for feedback and revisions, it was approved by the faculty in time to offer BSW Access courses in January 2000 to 73 students in six communities: Standoff (227 km from Calgary), Hobbema (216 km), Slave Lake (545 km), Grande Prairie (720 km), Peace River (749 km), and High Level (1029 km). Approximately half of the students identified themselves as Aboriginal. The Access funding had been designated to address social work education in "rural, remote, and Aboriginal communities." Some delivery sites were primarily or exclusively Aboriginal; others were non-Aboriginal. Some sites were mixed.

Aboriginal Content

Readings from the developing literature on Aboriginal social work were required for each theme course. Many of these readings came from the Canadian *Native Social Work Journal* (for example: Carriere-Laboucane, 1997; German, 1997; Stevenson,

1999) and the *Northern Social Work Series* published by the Lakehead University Centre for Northern Studies (for example: Borg, Delaney & Sellick, 1997; Bruyere, 1999; Meawasige, 1995). Other required readings explored Aboriginal approaches to knowledge building that emphasized processes of coming-to-know rather than an end state of knowledge-as-product (for example, Barden & Boyer, 1993; Colorado, 1991; Gilchrist, 1997; Nabigon, Hagey, Webster & MacKay, 1999; Webster & Reyno, 1999). At least one module in each theme course was devoted to "Local Applications," allowing local healers, elders, agency workers, and community resource people to present information and lead discussion with students to connect course content in a meaningful way with the history, current practices, and visions for the local region.

Community Connections

The original BSW Access proposal declared that "a Distance Planning Circle will be created, consisting of representatives from all participating and stakeholder groups" (Rogers, 1998, p. 3). CASSW standards similarly called for schools to provide opportunities for participation in planning and evaluation of programs by "stakeholders" (2.12), "Aboriginal communities" (2.13), and "professionals and professional associations" (2.14). Terms of reference were drafted and approved in June 2000 for a Northern BSW Distance Planning Circle representing regions and stakeholder groups to serve an ongoing advisory function and provide a forum for identification of critical issues facing social workers and communities in northern Alberta. Meeting at least once each academic term, this group reviews BSW Access division activities and makes recommendations to the faculty regarding curriculum, delivery, and relationship with the community.

Funding

Funding for the BSW Access initiative was secure for the first four years, after which time it would become part of the faculty's core operating budget when the target student numbers were achieved. This commitment allowed the Faculty of Social Work and the outlying regions to proceed with confidence in the continuance of Access delivery in outlying regions. Goals in term of access (student numbers) were achieved to the government's satisfaction and the funding is now part of the faculty's core operational budget.

International Connections

I have described earlier in this chapter the process of collaboration between the University of Calgary and communities across Alberta in development of the Learning Circle model. A decision was made early in that development process to disseminate the model to the wider social work community for discussion and feedback. In addition to presentations at conferences of the Alberta College of Social Workers and the CASSW, the University of Calgary's BSW Learning Circle model has been presented and discussed internationally at the International Federation of Social Workers Conference; the International Rural Communities Conference; the Australian Association of Social Workers Conference; the International Conference on Diversity in Organizations, Communities, and Nations; and the International Learning Conference. These presentations led to subsequent publication of two book chapters and four refereed journal articles (appearing in *Rural Social Work; The Tribal College Journal; The International Journal of Diversity in Organizations, Communities, and Nations;* and *The International Journal of Learning*). As well, the BSW Access division has responded to specific enquiries and requests for material about the Learning Circle model from across Canada and from social work educators in such diverse settings as Israel, Taipei, Bangkok, and Belize. There seems to be international interest in the model because of its ability to incorporate local history, issues, and healing practices in the delivery of a mainstream accredited social work degree.

Ongoing connections with Australia have been particularly strong. The current president of the Australian Association of Social Workers, Dr. Bob Lonne, has visited the BSW Access program on several occasions, most recently in the summer of 2006. Another senior social work educator from Australia and editor of *Rural Social Work*, Dr. Brian Cheers, spent six weeks with Calgary's BSW Access division in the spring of 2001 to learn more about the Learning Circle curriculum and delivery model. He visited many Access delivery sites across Alberta, attended community meetings, and taught in Access spring block courses. Upon his return to Australia, he wrote:

> I am convinced that the BSW Access Program is the most advanced of its kind in the world. Since returning to Australia I have encouraged my own university to start work on developing a similar program for delivery in rural and remote areas of Australia and I know that at least one other Australian university is thinking along the same lines. Both of these universities are using the University of Calgary Program as a guide. (Dr. Brian Cheers, personal correspondence, December 2001)

Evolution of the Learning Circle

The first courses were offered in six delivery sites in January 2000. Some additional sites have been added since that time. Other sites have been phased out as local needs were met. Still other sites have paused to allow for preparation of a new cohort of admissible Access students. Some sites, particularly those featuring active community colleges in the community, have continued with continuous new admissions. From a high of nine delivery sites in 2002, an average of five or six appears to be the norm. Nearly 400 students in rural, remote, and Aboriginal communities across Alberta have graduated from the Learning Circle route to the University of Calgary BSW degree. Half of those are Aboriginal students. Retention rates within the Learning Circle model are very high, averaging 90 percent (Ayala & Weiden, 2003).

The Learning Circle model is not static. For the purposes of this chapter, I chose to tell the story of the Learning Circle at its original design and implementation stage, but that was only one point in its evolution. The model is dynamic and has been modified and adapted to meet changing needs. Resources are constantly updated. The readings mentioned earlier in this chapter were those selected from sources available at the time the initial Learning Circle was developed. There have been many important publications since that time that have given rise to new required readings, including *Seeking Mino-Pimatisiwin: An Aboriginal Approach to Helping* (Hart, 2002), *Blackfoot Ways of Knowing: The Worldview of the Siksikaitsitapi* (Bastien, 2004), and *Protecting Aboriginal Children* (Walmsley, 2005).

In 2003, a Métis cohort was initiated. Although Métis world view, traditions, and healing practices are often subsumed under the general label "Aboriginal," there are distinct features that have a direct bearing on the provision of effective services within that community. Following the faculty's Access model, active collaborative planning (involving the Faculty of Social Work, the Métis Nation of Alberta, the Métis Settlements General Council, Métis Child and Family Services, and the Métis Bursary Program) resulted in a funded cohort of Métis BSW students with Métis instruction and materials relevant to Métis history and healing practices following the Learning Circle curriculum and delivery model. This was a first in Canadian social work education.

The social work education environment in Alberta is also changing and the future is hard to predict. Community colleges are lobbying government for degree-granting status and the BSW is a priority for them. The First Nations Adult and Higher Education Consortium (FNAHEC) has been working on an Aboriginal BSW curriculum for some years and may soon be ready to put their program forward. Technology progresses, and a Virtual Learning Circle of Web-based courses has been developed by the Faculty of Social Work to reach students in outlying areas where a cohort face-to-face approach may not be possible. The original Learning Circle model continues to grow and adapt in this environment.

In closing, I return to the early days of the Learning Circle and an elder from Grande Prairie named Donna Lajeunesse. Donna was an active member of the group who participated in the writing of the original BSW Access proposal, and she was a member of the Academic Selection Committee that did the initial BSW Access recruiting. Once she saw the resulting Learning Circle model and its implications for social work education, she wrote:

> An institution where people go to become more knowledgeable and gain wisdom should be sharing the knowledge of the world. The place of learning should never be restricted to "Western/Eastern" or any other specific identifiable area. Knowledge should be attainable through our learning institutions without the biases of where the knowledge comes from. This concept, it is my belief, has not existed in Canada since colonization. With open minds and open hearts perhaps we, as Canadians, can welcome and respect the values and beliefs of all people and continue to introduce the world's collective knowledge to students, and the public at large. It is with this thought in mind that I equate your introduction of the rural, remote, and Aboriginal BSW with the discovery that the world is not flat. (D. Lajeunesse, personal communication, November 1999)

ARTHUR WILLIAM ANSCOMBE

Coming Together, a painting by the children of the Holy Trinity Primary School, at Ashmount, in Wagga Wagga, Australia. They placed their hands on the artwork as a sign of unity showing Aboriginal and non-Aboriginal peoples coming together to unite as one.

CHAPTER 8

Aboriginal Social Work Education in Australia

Arthur William Anscombe

Indigenous Social Work Education at Charles Sturt University, Australia

A number of factors have mitigated against the indigenous peoples in Australia being successful in social work studies. These include historical, systemic issues, the nature of professional social work education, and community influences. The following is a description of one university's co-operative response to the issue.

Foley (2003) is critical of the academic discourse in Australia, which constructs a Western perspective of indigenous reality and presents a racially biased construction of the "truth." It needs to be acknowledged that this chapter has been written by a non-indigenous person and needs to be viewed with that "bias" taken into account. However, Professor Mick Dodson (2003) says that he is "unable to give comfort to the view that a non-Indigenous person should leave public statements on these questions to Indigenous people alone. The tragic circumstances ... are not alone the business of those who suffer them" (p. 8). It is in the spirit of this observation that this chapter has been written.

Indigenous Peoples in Australia

While less than 3 percent of the Australian population, indigenous peoples are almost 22 percent of the growing prison population, have more hospital admissions, higher infant mortality, more overcrowding, lower income levels, and much poorer educational outcomes as well as a host of other social and health factors. However, the macro-statistics can mask the real and human elements.

According to the data quoted in the Wilcannia Community Working Party Summit (Wilcannia Community Working Party Workshop, 2001), the average life expectancy is 36.7 years for indigenous men living in Wilcannia (a small, mostly indigenous town of about 1,000 people) and 42.5 years for indigenous women. The average age of the population at Brewarrina (another small town and 60 percent indigenous) is less than 20 years as there is a birth rate of 4.3 per female compared to a national average of 1.7 per female. Many of the communities of western New South Wales (NSW) with significant indigenous populations are characterized by low life expectancy, high rates of disease, low school retention rates, high unemployment, serious domestic violence, and heightened levels of child abuse and children at risk.

Social work as a profession is committed to the concepts of social justice, empowerment, and considering the person in his or her environment. Notwithstanding these noteworthy ambitions, social work as a profession has failed to attract significant numbers of indigenous peoples, or significantly alter the life circumstances of many of the profession's clients. Quite simply, there are few indigenous peoples entering the social work profession through formal university courses and fewer still completing those degrees. Due to high birth rates and to the non-indigenous population withdrawing from the indigenous areas, parts of western NSW are becoming increasingly "re-indigenized."

One possible scenario in the future is that significant areas of western NSW with predominantly indigenous populations will be served by predominantly "White" services. An alternative scenario involves services being delivered by poorly trained indigenous peoples and therefore may continue the social disadvantage and injustice that already exist. A third scenario involves investing in indigenous peoples in terms of university education with the understanding that they will provide culturally appropriate and significant services in the medium to long-term future.

Notwithstanding the very real overrepresentation of indigenous Australians in health and welfare client statistics, anecdotal and other evidence suggests that indigenous peoples are very substantially underrepresented in social work education programs and as professional social workers.

Charles Sturt University (CSU)

Charles Sturt University (CSU) is a national university based in inland Australia with a network of campuses in five of Australia's fastest-growing inland cities: Albury-Wodonga, Bathurst, Dubbo, Orange, and Wagga Wagga. In addition there are specialist centres in Canberra, Goulburn, Manly, and Ontario (Canada), and study centres in Brisbane, Melbourne, and Sydney. CSU has over 38,000 students and is the leading provider of distance education university studies in Australia. The regional area where CSU has a natural affinity has many indigenous peoples, with the largest grouping being Wiradjuri on whose land a number of the campuses are built.

Programs at Charles Sturt University for Indigenous Social Workers

To redress the underrepresentation of Indigenous people as social workers, CSU has made two attempts at developing an indigenous-focused pathway through the social work degree. Critical to the development of this program was an assessment of why indigenous peoples have a low participation rate in formal tertiary social work education. An intensive community consultation identified four main categories of causes for the low participation rate: history/systemic issues, family/community issues, university issues, and social work issues. These are, of course, neither mutually exclusive nor exhaustive.

A. Historic/Systemic Issues

1. It is arguable that there are historic legacies that mitigate against indigenous peoples becoming involved in the social work profession.
2. There are few satisfactory Australian cross-cultural education packages, especially those that give significant weight to local issues rather than regional or national issues.
3. Much of social work appears to concentrate on the individual rather than on the community and is focused upon Western individualism rather than indigenous communalism.
4. Academic studies tend to reward the individual and are highly competitive whereas indigenous communities may value community contribution and the role of co-operation.
5. There are systemic issues that relate to the lack of cultural capacity, including the fact that there are few role models and the effects of the destruction of cultural values and associations.
6. There are significant pressures on indigenous peoples who perceive themselves to be "a first" in the communities and are often perceived by others as compromising with White values and aspirations at the cost of their own community values and aspirations.
7. Where indigenous teachers exist in university faculties, rather than being able to teach across all areas, thereby bringing an indigenous perspective, they are frequently limited to indigenous areas.
8. There are good models for conflict resolution between indigenous and non-indigenous people.
9. Some indigenous students are made to feel responsible for teaching about indigenous issues by both their lecturers and other students.

B. Family/Community Issues

10. The rigours of academic life are seen by some indigenous peoples to be meaningless and of little practical value to family and community issues.
11. Isolation from family and kin, and of not knowing others at the university, are major factors in the continuing disempowerment and non-participation of indigenous peoples.
12. The lack of family support is a significant problem for a number of students who are interested in social work.
13. Some indigenous communities lack a sustained energy or changing capacity that would support indigenous peoples to continue educational programs over a significant period of time.
14. In some communities there is simply no pro-social modelling or family role models that indigenous students can follow.
15. There are frequently few, if any, academic staff who provide indigenous role models.

16. In some indigenous communities there are very high levels of trauma, which make the continuation of study difficult and/or chaotic. There is a level of grief and dispossession that is significantly greater than in most non-indigenous communities.
17. In some communities there are low levels of self-worth and low levels of optimism as to how things may be different. This is consistent with the communities where there are high levels of disadvantage.
18. The unstable social and economic circumstances of many students and communities mitigate against successful completion of social work and other professional studies.

To redress a number of these issues that mitigate against social welfare education being attractive to both individuals and communities, a number of attitudinal changes will need to occur at a number of levels, including the social work professional university level and the family/community level.

C. University Issues

19. Within many indigenous communities there is a lack of knowledge of and expectations about universities. To some extent, the increasing concentration of universities as businesses and concepts such as user-pays have further distanced universities from their local and regional communities.
20. Many academic staff in universities have no training in indigenous matters.
21. There are few indigenous academic staff in many universities.
22. The very nature of the academic world itself can be alienating for indigenous peoples. The nature of academic discourse, the focus on critical thinking, and the multiplicity of viewpoints can often alienate them. In addition, the focus on academic prestige and tradition in a university may also be distancing for indigenous peoples.
23. Universities that take a very strong ideological line disempower indigenous peoples whose world view may be quite different.
24. Cultural differences in learning styles for indigenous peoples are frequently not addressed. For example, much of the distance education material, which is based on writing and literacy, is inherently disempowering for indigenous peoples whose learning style might be more oral and visual.
25. The nature of teaching at universities is a further factor that can be alienating. Some teaching approaches are inclusive while other teaching approaches are exclusive.
26. University itself is constructed as a concept, which seems to be too distant from the realities of many indigenous families and communities.

27. The whole notion of a professional identity, upon which much of social work is built, seems to mitigate against indigenous peoples taking part in both the social work profession and in other professions. The professional identity is both individualistically focused and distancing from kin.
28. Social work is perceived as having no impact. Some of this perception relates to its historic legacy with indigenous peoples, but some also relates to the continuing and abiding problems in indigenous communities to which social work has had few answers.
29. Social work has negative connotations for indigenous peoples and within some indigenous communities.
30. Social work is viewed by some as a White construct based on White values.

Charles Sturt University Program

After indigenous consultation, extensive reading on indigenous education, recognition of current policy directions and aspirations, and of professional accreditation requirements for social work and the experience of working with indigenous peoples, the Charles Sturt University Social Work Program was built on six key principles and three intersecting dreams.

The six key principles are:

- recognition and respect for indigenous identity
- encouragement of self-determination
- emphasis on self-awareness and personal development
- encouragement of responsibility and self-esteem
- radical concentration on prevention and change
- insistence on similar academic quality in indigenous social work to that expected of non-indigenous degrees.

The three intersecting dreams are:

- The dream of indigenous peoples (and some non-indigenous people) to restore pride and self-determination.
- The dream of indigenous individuals to develop their individual potential to the maximum in the areas of helpers, healers, activists, and community builders.
- The dream of university academics to deliver relevant, culturally appropriate, regionally specific education that empowers indigenous peoples through knowledge and processes that integrate different traditions of learning and knowledge acquisition.

There was a recognition that "imperialism frames the Indigenous experience" (Smith, 1999, p. 19). This imperialism can be academic and/or knowledge-based imperialism.

There was a recognition that the sources of knowledge (generally understood as traditional, experimental, common sense, and scientific—see, for example, Monette, Sullivan & DeJong, 1998) had to also recognize the spiritual knowledge of indigenous communities and their holistic and integrated world view. There was recognition that learning would be a shared activity—a two-way process. The educational philosophy involved using Freirian (Freire, 2000) concepts (including "conscientization") and working from the known to the unknown, from practice to theory, from concrete to abstract, from visual and verbal to literate, from micro to macro, from family to community, from example to principle, and from specific to general.

Building on these principles and dreams, the Charles Sturt University program was developed with the following elements:

- intensive face to face teaching, around five days per subject spread across a two-week residential school shared with other subjects
- some assessment undertaken during the intensive program
- pre-intensive residential school reading and post-residential school assessment if appropriate
- close collaboration with the Indigenous Education Centre of the university to ensure that appropriate learning and other support, including evening homework help groups, are provided to students
- the employment of indigenous lecturing staff
- Aboriginal Tutorial Assistance Scheme (ATAS) support for the student when she or he returns to the community and continues studying by distance education
- attempts to attract and develop two or more indigenous students from each community in order that they would be mutually supported

Two programs were attempted. The first effort was the following:

First Attempt

The structure and entry requirements for full-time equivalent study were:

FIGURE 8.1: STRUCTURE AND ENTRY REQUIREMENTS
(FULL-TIME EQUIVALENT)

Year 1

| No prior tertiary education |
| Indigenous mode |
| Exit possible with a certificate |
| Support from employer or community |

Year 2

| Prior tertiary relevant education |
| Indigenous mode |
| Exit possible with a diploma |
| Support from employer or community |

Choice

Year 3	Two-year block credit Two placements (400 hours) Exit with degree (Bachelor of Social Welfare)

OR

	Two-year block credit Two placements (980 hours)

Year 4	Exit at year 4 with Bachelor of Social Work

The outline was as follows:

The University Certificate in Human Services Program (Working with Indigenous Communities) was developed with five core subjects:

- indigenous peoples in their environment (a large subject developed for indigenous peoples and written to reflect the generic skills required for tertiary study, indigenous social policy, and sociology relevant to indigenous students)
- substance abuse assessment and management
- working with families
- child and adolescent psychology
- social dimensions of disability

As it was possible that students would exit after one year, it was considered that these areas provided the opportunity for students to learn and also to return knowledge to the community at least at a beginning level.

The Diploma of Human Services (Working with Indigenous Communities) consisted of a range of courses on social work practice with different populations and indigenous issues (see Appendix A for the list of courses). The structure allows for multiple entry and exit points for each program to increase at least some practical knowledge skills.

This program has been suspended pending a review. The block teaching worked well and the students were enthusiastic and responsive. However, the attrition rate was very high with a number of relevant factors:

1. The university has a policy that requires all students to have computer access. This was difficult for some students living in remote areas without economical access to computer facilities and broadband, who were not able to access either academic or administrative data. For town-based students, access to Rural Transaction Centres is often limited in hours of access and costly.
2. Finances were a concern. At one point, because the university applied its normal

administrative policy, the whole cohort of students was withdrawn from the course for non-payment of a small compulsory fee.

3. A number of students could not complete enrolment, which requires a passport-size photograph for the student card. Many locations did not have the facilities for taking the photograph.

4. In post-attrition discussions, some students found that the language that was used and the level of reading required made them feel inadequate.

5. Some course material was inappropriate. For example, one subject required the development of a personal genogram (a graphic way of diagramming a client's family by diagramming the family). In many families with multiple relationships, this proved to be very difficult, while for others from different language groups it was offensive to cite the name of a dead relative.

6. Part of the attrition rate was related to family issues and family obligations (especially the death of a relative), which meant that indigenous students were unable to attend the predetermined blocks or had to leave early to fulfill family obligations.

7. Students did well in courses taught by staff with whom they related easily and did poorly in subjects where they perceived the academic staff to be detached.

8. Some subjects involved concepts that were well understood but were explained in abstract ways that reinforced the student's perceived inadequacies.

Second Attempt

The above program was suspended when the indigenous staff member appointed to facilitate the program applied for and obtained a position outside the university. Without appropriate indigenous staff and the high attrition rate, the university suspended the program pending the attraction of a suitable indigenous person to teach and mentor into the degree. Following the suspension of the program and the inability of the university to attract a suitable indigenous person and in recognition of the need for indigenous social workers, CSU joined in partnership with the Western Institute of Technical and Further Education (TAFE) in a joint program for indigenous peoples. The TAFE has a network of colleges in larger locations within the region and has a well-established infrastructure support from indigenous TAFE teachers and advisers. This program continued the dreams and principles and utilized the teaching expertise of indigenous peoples in the TAFE. To overcome some of the concerns highlighted above, the TAFE undertook a six-month bridging course for all prospective students prior to entering the joint CSU/TAFE program. The connection with TAFE overcomes some of the issues highlighted above, including computer access, on-the-spot support, local mentoring, and giving visible embodiment to the experience of education.

The course structure for the new program is:

FIGURE 8.2

	SESSION 1	SESSION 2
Year 1	2006 Entry Only—TAFE	HCS102 Communication and Human Services
		TAFE studies (three CSU subjects equivalent)
Year 2	HCS206 Social Work Theory and Practice 1 (16)	HCS207 Social Work Theory and Practice 2 (16)
		SPE201 Politics and Social Policy in Australia
	TAFE Studies (two CSU subjects equivalent)	TAFE Studies (one CSU subject equivalent)
Year 3	SOC101 Introductory Sociology / PSY113 Child and Adolescent Psychology / TAFE Studies (two CSU subjects equivalent)	PSY216 Psychology of Aging / SPE301 Critical Issues in Social Policy / SWK423 Ethics and Social Work Practice
	←———— HCS303 Professional Field Education 1 (16) ————→	
Year 4	HCS304 Social Work Theory and Practice 3 (16) / HCS204 Research Methods	HCS405 Social Work Theory and Practice 4 (16) / SOC308 Community Analysis
	←———— HCS402 Professional Field Education 2 (16) ————→	
Year 5	SPE401 Social Work and Social Policy Practice / HCS406 Social Work and Human Rights / LAW211 Law for the Human Services 1	

The program is operated on a block-release basis with Commonwealth support. It is a co-operative venture that would not have been possible without the support and encouragement of the TAFE. Early results, while not without difficulties, are promising. Some of the administrative, staffing, and institutional issues continue to be difficult. The university's inability to attract a suitable indigenous professorial appointment has created further difficulties. The distance of the program from the Faculty of Social Work (five hours from Wagga Wagga to Dubbo) has been problematic and there are concerns about the travel cost to faculty members and budget costs to the university. University-provided accommodation has had difficulties.

Students continue to struggle with access to computing and other facilities and academic language, and content continues to be a matter that is constantly reviewed.

Discussion and Conclusions

Institutional racism has its origins in the manner in which institutional arrangements and the distribution of assets and resources in the society reinforce the advantage of some and continue the disadvantage of others. It frequently refers to long-established practices built into the fabric of organizations, law, and government that continue to disadvantage minority members on racial and/or ethnic grounds. In Australia, the Commonwealth government has replaced the policies of indigenous self-determination by adopting a process of integration in relation to indigenous affairs with policies that include the abolition of the elected indigenous body (the Aboriginal and Torres Strait Islander Commission), the government appointment of an Indigenous Advisory Council, the mainstreaming of indigenous programs to government departments, the formation of local Shared Responsibility Agreements, and the replacement of reconciliation with "practical reconciliation." The future presents many challenges for tertiary educators in social work programs that are built upon the recognition of diversity within the indigenous community and an appreciation of differences between indigenous and non-indigenous people.

The failure of the university and the social work profession to attract and retain significant numbers of indigenous Australians in social work degrees has its origins in historic/systemic, family/community, university, and social work professional concerns. There continues to be a need for culturally appropriate, relevant, and empowering services provided with, for, and by indigenous peoples.

Social work education and the social work profession, in co-operation and collaboration with the indigenous community, need to develop a quadruple bottom-line approach to the issues facing indigenous communities. This quadruple bottom line must involve economic, social, spiritual, and environmental considerations. True community empowerment through education and professional social work may occur with the use of culturally appropriate, participatory, and other community-based approaches that encourage and develop local communities, local resources, and local empowerment.

Appendix A

Diploma of Human Services

Indigenous Peoples in Their Environment
Substance Abuse: Assessment and Management
Working with Families
Child and Adolescent Psychology
Social Dimensions of Disability
Justice and Indigenous Communities
Law for Human Services
Child Welfare
Introduction to Managing Indigenous Community Organizations
Psychology of Aging
Case Management
Community Analysis

One elective, to be chosen freely, but recommended from:
Child and Adolescent Mental Health
Children's Fiction
Indigenous Australian Studies

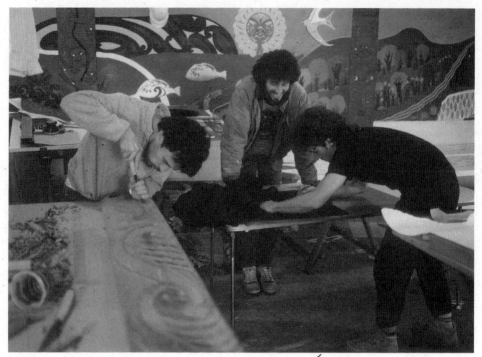

J. NAUTA

Students at the Manu Kopere Arts Centre at Hongoeka, Plimmerton

CHAPTER 9

Some Observations on Social Work Education and Indigeneity in New Zealand

Jim Anglem

Historical Background

The Treaty of Waitangi, signed on February 6, 1840, between the indigenous peoples of New Zealand (the Maori) and the British Crown, enabled people to come to New Zealand under an agreed set of circumstances known as Articles. The Articles were clear in their intent, although there would later be arguments about the different interpretations arising from the versions written in English and Maori. One of the main intentions of the treaty was to develop some semblance of control over the lawless 2,000 British settlers living among the more than 140,000 Maori, who lived in tribal communities. Each tribe considered itself to be a nation-state, so each had its own systems of administration and law. The White immigrants, however, were not subject to any law or controls and while from time to time such people fell foul of various tribes' structures, Maori felt uncomfortable about administering systems of law to people who did not belong to their tribes. Tribal chiefs felt that the British should be responsible for British people, not them.

The treaty therefore stressed several things:

- Maori would retain all of their lands, forests, waterways, fisheries, and things they regarded as intrinsically or extrinsically valuable.
- Maori would retain ownership of the land.
- The British would develop a system of government/administration for the entire country.
- Maori would enjoy all of the rights and privileges of the British people.
- Land could not be bought and sold unless by agreement of the owners and for a "fair" price and only through the agencies of the Crown.

Such a treaty obviated reasons for Maori to be concerned about an invasion and allowed for a peaceful, organized immigration process. When the first influx of British settlers arrived in New Zealand, they brought with them hopes and dreams of a better life, a life that would be free of the class oppression that many had suffered from. They believed too, that the land that they were about to call home was empty and that soon they would be able to establish themselves as landowners and help develop a society that would reflect the cultural norms that dominated the world they had recently left. The fact that the country the settlers had arrived in was not empty was something of a shock to new migrants. That there was not very much land available for them to purchase or settle on was even more disappointing. This disappointment later translated into anger and frustration as settlers were unable to convert their dreams into realities and instead, their ensuing poverty led to a need for the development of welfare programs.

At the time of the signing of the Treaty of Waitangi, Maori people enjoyed the advantages of a relatively healthy society. Early visitors such as Captain James Cook (Cook, 1900), Joseph Banks, John Savage (Savage, 1807), John Boultbee, and others (Begg & Begg, 1980) described Maori as being taller, healthier, and more family oriented than their European counterparts. Food was in plentiful supply, systems of justice and law were well defined, and welfare was a tribal and family responsibility based on the fact that children were treasured as the future strength of the tribe and old people revered for their wisdom and knowledge. From the last decade of the 18th century Maori had learned the value of overseas trade. New agricultural methods and technologies derived from the many visits from whalers, sealers, adventurers, and other Europeans were taken advantage of. While some of these technologies had allowed some tribes to settle old scores with new weaponry, old tribal values were largely complemented with increasing wealth and education via the many missionaries who had arrived. A curious anomaly soon developed: Maori were often literate whereas most of the early White settlers were not. Maori monopolized the resources from which fishing and forestry emanated, and by 1850 were clearly in a better position to forge a bicultural union than their immigrant "partner."

Fifty years later, by the end of the 19th century, all of this had changed. While social welfare had become an integral part of the government policies of New Zealand, Maori numbers had declined to less than 40,000 (compared with the 772,000 White population) and were barely acknowledged by the government as New Zealanders. Indeed, at this time government welfare assistance, if provided for Maori, was at a rate considerably less than that available for non-Maori (two-thirds).

The prevailing attitude of government can be observed in the comments on pensions by two officials, who stated that "the inclusion of Aboriginal natives, on equal terms is however, regarded as undesirable...." and "The amount of 18 pounds (NZ$36.00) which is mere subsistence to an aged European is far too large a revenue for an aged Maori" (McClure, 1998, p. 26).

It is not surprising that within the first few years of the 20th century, the government passed several pieces of legislation that gave effect to the sentiments expressed by the aforementioned officials. Two of these Acts seriously affected the Maori's ability to care for their vulnerable people and continue to provide traditional familial support. One such Act, the Tohunga Suppression Act 1907, denied the Maori's ability to use traditional healers (known as *tohunga*) as a source of counselling, wisdom, spirituality, and medicine. Such people remained at the core of Maori society and were revered for their knowledge and status, but were described variously as witch doctors and charlatans by non-Maori. A further Act denied Maori the ability to arrange interfamily adoption. These adoption arrangements (*matua whangai*) were carried out within families where a childless couple could be given a gift of a nephew or niece by other kin who had several children. The nature of Maori families, who lived together within close-knit communities, meant that such adoption practices were of little consequence to children as they were nurtured by all of their relatives.

It was this tendency of Maori to live lives that were family centred and tribally connected that was used as a reason to dismantle traditional Maori society. What little land Maori now owned had always been owned collectively. Consequently, it was difficult to get agreement on selling or a price and thus was frustrating for the ambitions of non-Maori land developers. To ensure that the vast majority of New Zealanders (White people) felt a sense of hostility toward the native inhabitants, politicians such as Sir Francis Dillon Bell trumpeted, "The first plank of public policy must be to stamp out the beastly communism of the Maori" (Rangihau, 1986, p. 584)

Yet another determination that was to add to the disastrous impact on the culture and society of Maori was the insistence that breastfeeding by Maori mothers was to cease. The reasoning behind this was the view that many of the diseases that were feared at this time—such as the bubonic plague, military tuberculosis, pneumonia, and typhoid fever—might be passed on by a breastfeeding mother, especially one who may also supply babies other than her own with milk.

The combined effect of such government interventions, as well as the discriminatory nature of much legislation, meant that not only were Maori social structures systematically dismantled but the land upon which the basis of their society was founded was removed in a series of cynical and greedy pieces of legislation, the like of which colonized peoples all over the world have witnessed.

It was of little comfort for the indigenous peoples of New Zealand that the discrimination that so severely affected them and had taken them from being culturally wealthy landowners in their own country to marginalized aliens squatting on the periphery of rich, White agricultural pastoralists within 50 years also impacted upon people of Asian extraction. Legislation "treated Asiatics in quite a different way, from the native born white subjects of His Majesty" (McClure, 1998, p. 29). The aim was to ensure that New Zealand would not be attractive to the Chinese and Japanese as a place to live. There was an overriding fear that New Zealand would be overrun by the "yellow barbarians" (McClure, 1998, p. 19).

This brief summary describes how a people and their culture were transformed from being vibrant and economically sound, with increasing trade and new technologies, and with strong social caring structures where the future of the people appeared assured, to one where Maori society would appear to be in disarray. The dreadful statistics suggest this. For example, despite representing a mere 15 percent of the population, Child Youth and Family, the primary agency for statutory care, deals with client numbers of about 45 percent Maori (New Zealand, 2000). It is not surprising, therefore, to find that their educational achievements are markedly lower than for non-Maori, as are health statistics, life expectancy, employment rates, income, and housing.

There is a clear need to create social work strategies that are both relevant and culturally appropriate for a population of Maori that is no longer homogeneous.

It is, however, a difficult challenge, which the social work profession in New Zealand acknowledges and with which social work teaching programs constantly wrestle. It is not the cultural mores that cause the difficulties but the fact that we live within an increasingly diverse society and Maori are as different from each other in their cultural beliefs and philosophies as are all other people. Some are significantly linked to their culture via their language and way of life, while others are connected to their culture through tribal or intertribal meetings and events. Others have little or no connection with their culture and may not think of themselves as being Maori even though their appearance clearly suggests that they are.

The Day Break Report and Social Work

That such matters are of considerable concern can be attributed to the worldwide emphasis in teaching on respecting human rights. The 1960s and 1970s, especially in Western society, was a time when university students and their teachers challenged existing paradigms, creating an upsurge in intolerance of sexism and racism in particular. In 1984, after allegations of racism were made by employees of the Department of Social Welfare about the nature and administration of the country's welfare agency, a seminal report was written called *Puao te Ata Tu* (Rangihau, 1986). This report acknowledged the institutional racism alleged by the brave employees who risked opprobrium and possible dismissal, and identified a range of strategies that should be established to deal with the criticisms that were raised. The report was written after the committee charged with investigating the allegations met with communities in open meetings throughout the country. They also received reports from individuals and groups.

Ultimately they were left in no doubt about what most New Zealanders, and especially Maori, thought about the government department. This resonating response was called *Ngeri* (a litany of sound), and was deeply critical of the monocultural, sexist, and impersonal processes employed by the Department of Welfare, including staff composition and training. Both government and management accepted the criticisms and attempted to employ the many strategies that were recommended.

The Report and Schools of Social Work

Although released in 1986, the *Puao te Ata Tu* Report remains an enduring guide for schools of social work. It made quite simple observations about the nature of this country that are compelling:

1. The Treaty of Waitangi in 1840 was a binding contract between two peoples.
2. The treaty therefore created a bicultural rather than monocultural country.
3. Understanding biculturalism is a precursor to developing multiculturalism.
4. The basis of welfare is respect.
5. Racism (personal, institutional, cultural) is the antithesis of welfare.

The *Puao te Ata Tu* Report was credible as it reflected widely what people wrote and said and the historical context from which the recommendations sprang was difficult to deny. Furthermore, for schools of social work and professional organizations to ignore this report is to risk repeating the faults of the past. One of these faults may have been that the theories of social work teaching employed prior to the mid-1980s tended to be Eurocentric. Such ideas possibly created social workers whose training reflected theories of practice appropriate in downtown New York or London, but were far distant from the realities of living in urban New Zealand where the predominant culture was more likely to be Maori or Pacific Island than White and Western. Indeed, it is likely that this Eurocentric reflection ignored the populations of Black, Hispanic, and Asian communities whose numbers were significant in London and New York 20 years ago.

It is argued in *Puao te Ata Tu* that the realities of diversity within New Zealand can be taught, and that dignity and respect for people can be understood within such contexts. If these things are done, it is possible to see the global picture. "Biculturalism is a precursor to developing multiculturalism" (Rangihau, 1986, p. 19).

The message from Maori communities about what social work students should know about working with Maori clients was very clear: that students should know about the history of *Aotearoa* (New Zealand); that Maori were not always at the wrong end of social indicator scales; and that there has been a logical if unpleasant series of reasons why Maori have gone from wealth and prosperity to relative impoverishment and reliance on welfare today.

Maori communities also felt that students should know about how Maori society operated in the past (education and health, sanitation, law, and justice), and should compare these systems with what has replaced them. They believed that having knowledge of such things would militate against the common view that the current parlous social status of many Maori today occurs "because they have always been like that."

Such thinking may not allow social workers to interact with clients in a helpful or non-discriminatory way. Beliefs, such as those described here, are unlikely to be carried into interactions with non-Maori clients, particularly by non-Maori social workers. This could be considered ironic, given that the deficit model sometimes ascribed to ethnic minority groups such as Maori may, in fact, properly reflect historical New Zealand when many poverty-stricken early White settlers were taken in and cared for by Maori.

The Maori Model of Welfare

Traditional Maori models of welfare are a contradiction. Traditional Maori did not have a system of welfare. Instead they had a fully inclusive society where all had designated roles based on the extended family (*whanau*), the sub-tribe (*hapu*), and the tribe (*iwi*). The role of the leader/chief (*rangatira*) was to ensure the health and wealth of the tribe. If a leader did not provide the appropriate means to assure the tribe's future, he was replaced. Tribal history through genealogy (*whakapapa*) had to be protected so that the status (*mana*) of the tribe could be maintained through its entire history. A lack of knowledge of history—of knowing who your ancestors were—is to have little knowledge of yourself as a person, which suggests a lack of in-depth meaning in your life. It might also means that you are without status.

The extended family was the basis of the tribal structure and continuance was the basis of the family. The rules to follow were simple. Children were treasured (*taonga*) as they provided for the continuation of the tribe. They were indulged, protected, and educated. They were never struck. Early missionaries found such behaviour untenable (spare the rod and spoil the child). Old people (*matua*) were revered for their knowledge and wisdom. One important role for the grandparents was the parenting of children, a task too important to leave to parents! Parents had an important role, which was to provide for and protect the children and old people.

If tribal lands were respected and protected from enemy intentions, the social structures remained strong. Social structures were strong and emotive sentiments were based on ideas of caring and sharing. These sentiments include the following:

- Friendship, hospitality (*manaaki*)
- Love, affection, warmth (*aroha*)
- Support (*tautoko*)
- Kindness (*atawhai*)
- Help, assistance (*awhina*)

These sentiments, which lie at the heart of Maori attitudes to their communities and their visiting guests, are some of the qualities that determine that most important of all Maori qualities, *mana* (status/authority). The quality of a person's hospitality or caring can be equated to his or her *mana*. Thus, a community that did not care for its elderly or children would be disdained and scorned by other communities. Such shame (*whakamaa*) would be considered intolerable. The impact on the Maori people of New Zealand of owning 64 million acres of land in 1840 but being reduced to owning a mere 3 million acres by 1975 (much of it uninhabitable) effectively reduced them to servility, and that most important human emotion, *mana*, was long forgotten as a descriptor of most Maori communities.

Maori Models of Health

Maori models of health, like social structures, were integrated into the fabric of society and were based on the concepts of caring and sharing. Water (*wai*) was a key element in health, and water supplies were categorized according to tribal needs. Drinking water was distinct from water for bathing, and rules related to sanitation were strictly adhered to. However, it was the philosophies of health that were more interesting, and it is pleasing to note that health authorities in New Zealand are taking heed of the typically First Nations attitudes toward health and treatments.

Former psychiatrist and now Maori academic, Professor Mason Durie (a member of the Ngati Kauwhata and Rangitane tribes) has written widely on a traditional concept that he called "*Te Whare Tapa Wha*," the "four walls model" of health. In assessing health, Durie suggests there must be a balance among four domains (or walls of a house) and to select one without taking account of the others is to ignore some vital ingredients necessary for rehabilitation. By using the concept of a house (*whare*) with four (*wha*) walls, he clearly demonstrates the possibility that if one of the walls collapses, then the whole house could potentially topple (Durie, 1998, 2003).

A spinal unit in Christchurch in New Zealand has strongly accepted this model as part of its approach to treatment of all patients. It was acknowledged that to treat a patient with damaged vertebrae (physical injuries, *tinana*) without taking into account their mental state and their spiritual and familial support was to risk wasting a considerable amount of energy and resources and, of course, failure in the healing process. The four domains he selected are:

1. *taha wairua* (the spiritual side)
2. *taha hinengaro* (knowledge, thoughts, emotions, feelings—behaviour)
3. *taha tinana* (the physical side)
4. *taha whanau* (family)

FIGURE 9.1

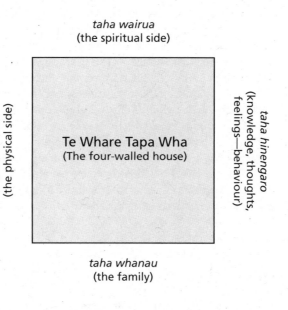

Such a model suggests that to treat a patient for a mental health problem without taking account of what family support is available, matters relating to cultural identity, or physical maladies that may be affecting the patient is likely to be ineffective.

This attempt at a holistic approach to health treatment is receiving greater acceptance nationally and is focused on in schools of social work in New Zealand as a sound approach to working with all cultures.

The Future

The profile of Maori in New Zealand has not been higher since the early years of the 19th century, which has lulled many into thinking that Maori are not only succeeding within present structures, but there have been statements made by some politicians, especially those from the right, claiming that Maori enjoy a privileged position. In 2004, Donald Brash, the leader of the National Party (the main opposition party), made it clear to the nation that he felt that Maori had undue influence over development projects. "There can be no basis for special privileges for any race, no basis for government funding based on race ... no basis for local governments to consult Maori in preference to other New Zealanders" (as cited in Slack, 2005, p. 21).

The indigenous peoples of New Zealand, who are largely poorly educated and have poor health and unemployment, with high rates of imprisonment, do not enjoy a very participative position in the larger society. Although there are clear improvements in the social indicators, these improvements are slow.

In the meantime there is much work to be done to ensure that social work students are armed with information that allows them to be forces for empowerment rather than part of the mode of grievance that so pervades much of modern Maori society. If students succeed in understanding the issues relating to the place of Maori within New Zealand, then they should possess the means to assess the significance of culture and ethnicity in their interactions with all clients. This does not suggest that they will be able to understand all cross-cultural encounters, but at least it should signal that without knowledge of historical context, it is dangerous to ascribe judgments about any groups of people whose characteristics are unfamiliar.

There is much to commend Laird's (1998) view, supported by Dean (2003) and others, that acknowledges one's ignorance ("the informed not knower") and the idea that every time one engages with a client, one should unpack one's own cultural baggage and leave it at the door so that the interactions with a client can occur without one's own judgments affecting the ability to listen effectively.

Na te mahi a muri, The work behind the scenes
Ka ora mai a mua, Makes for success in the front

MIKE PATTEN

A self-portrait of artist Mike Patten contemplating a frame from his *Lost Thoughts* series (2006). Patten's work shows the remains of a partially erased written thought. The photograph seems to depict a moment of contemplation by the artist of his erased sense of self and his sense of uncertainty about ownership of the thoughts and half-truths before him. Ironically, part of the projected image appears on the artist's back, where it is impossible for him to see it, while his own shadow blocks out even more of the message. The image more than adequately expresses the frustrations and uncertainties of many Aboriginal students caught between their own world views and those of the establishment. More of Patten's work appears in Chapter 12.

CHAPTER 10

Education as Healing:
A Central Part of Aboriginal Social Work Professional Training

Ingrid Thompson Cooper, Gail Stacey Moore, and Florence Dobson

Introduction

The main theme of this chapter is that the social work education of Aboriginal peoples involves a process of psychological healing as a major component and, furthermore, that this healing alters and enriches both the teaching process and the professional development of the students. While non-Native social work students have clearly experienced problems in their personal lives, it can probably be safely stated that it is nowhere near to the extent or severity that exists in a population of Aboriginal students. This, of course, is the result of the many years and generations of oppression and abuse to which Native peoples in this country have been subjected since the time of first contact by the policies and practices of the government (see, for example, Canada, 1996a; Dickason, 2002; Trigger, 1987; Wesley-Esquimaux & Smolewski, 2004). A major part of this in recent history is the 1876 Indian Act, which deprived Native peoples of a substantial land base and legislated every aspect of their lives from birth to death. As well, there has been the more recent practice of taking Aboriginal children away from their families and placing them in residential schools where they were subjected to physical, sexual, emotional, spiritual, and cultural abuse. While all of these schools are now closed, Aboriginal peoples and communities are still suffering and recovering from the excessive trauma of this experience (see, for example, Assembly of First Nations, 1994; Chansonneuve, 2005; Fournier & Crey, 1997; Miller, 1996). Thus, in a class of Aboriginal students, it is likely that the majority have experienced one or more serious problems in their lives, either directly themselves, or indirectly in their family. These problems include drug and alcohol addiction, sexual abuse, family violence, mental illness and suicide attempts, among others.[1] Social work education involves developing knowledge and skills in dealing with these problems. Correspondingly, students' own life experiences with these issues are inevitably raised when the topics are examined in the various courses. This paper describes how the students' experiences, often traumatic, affect both the teaching and learning processes and how this can impact positively on the students' learning and personal healing.

Background

The paper is largely based on the authors' experience during the first five years (1995–2000) of coordinating and teaching in the Aboriginal Social Work Certificate Program (ASWCP) at McGill University, described extensively in chapters 4, 5, and 6 of this book. During these early years, with the exception of our students, our experiences with them, and our own intuition, we had few resources to guide us.

We were aware of the vital importance of self-development and personal healing contained in much of the Native social work education material that is available, particularly in the material on addictions, sexual abuse, and family violence (see, for example, Hodgson, 1992; National Native Association of Treatment Directors, 1992). These papers stress the necessity for human service providers of healing themselves before they can help others and suggest ways that such healing can occur, such as in Healing Circles, sweats, and personal counselling (Antone & Hill, 1990; Nelson, Kelley & McPherson, 1985; Stevenson, 1999). Alternatively, however, little had been written about how the personal issues that are inevitably raised in Native social work courses can be dealt with in the classroom. This is not surprising given that Native social work programs are relatively new. An exception was the landmark book, *From Strength to Strength: Social Work Education and Aboriginal People* (Feehan & Hannis, 1993), which describes the Aboriginal social work program at Grant MacEwan Community College in Alberta, which has been operating since 1978. We were heartened to read about their experiences, which are compellingly described.[2] Fortunately, there is now much more material on the incorporation of Aboriginal healing models into the classroom.

During the course of the program we have changed as teachers and, we believe, as individuals; we have learned a lot and are still learning. Our ideas and thoughts on the importance of healing as a major component in Aboriginal social work training programs are in no way conclusive, but exploratory. One thing we are certain of, however, is that the topic is an important one, worthy of much further discussion and research, which will enrich both Native and non-Native social work training.

What Did We Experience?

The Experience in the Classroom

Briefly and quite simply, in response to the topic of the class and to readings prepared for a particular class, one or more students would reveal their personal experience with the subject under discussion. Some would speak out directly in the class, while others, more reticent, would share their stories in a written log that was part of the course assignment. (We should add here that sharing personal material in the log was not required, yet many students used the log as a way to dialogue with the instructor.) These revelations would always be very personal, reflecting painful and often traumatic events in their lives. It is safe to say that everyone in the classroom, teachers and students alike, would be affected by the personal accounts, in turn moving others to speak about their own background. At these times the experience of speaking and listening was both painful and touching for all, stimulating an intense atmosphere in the classroom.

Several factors created a teaching situation where the students' own personal issues and traumas, and the revelation of those issues, became part of the teaching and learning experience and ultimately part of the healing process for the students. These factors included the subject of the courses, the students' personal backgrounds and experiences, the organization of the program, and the teachers' responses to the students' revelations.

1. The Courses

While all courses in a social work program have the potential to raise personal issues for the students, because of their content, some courses are more likely to initiate reactions to painful feelings and memories. Five of our 10 courses are such courses, covering the subjects of alcoholism, drug addiction, child sexual abuse, family violence, and mental illness (including suicide). The courses deal with the nature and causes of these problems, as well as treatment options and alternatives, including both Native and non-Native materials. The material on sexual abuse, alcohol and drug addiction, and suicide seem to provoke the most responses.

2. Students' Personal Background and Experiences

Most, if not all, of our students have experienced one or more of the problems previously mentioned, either directly themselves—for example, as a victim of sexual abuse or as a former drug or alcohol abuser—or indirectly in their family. The intensity and severity of the problems vary from student to student, but generally recovery is a lengthy process for all and the students are at different stages in their healing. While some have already started to deal with their experiences and the courses represent an opportunity to further their healing process, for others, the course material provides the first opportunity to learn about and face their issues. While most of the problems are from the students' pasts, a number of students also experience various personal crises while they are in the program, such as serious health problems, loss of a relative from suicide, or physical abuse from a partner. This too can become part of the class discussions.

3. Program Organization

We realize now that the way we organized the program facilitated the process whereby the students have been able to openly share the sensitive and painful issues in their lives. The classes are small (eight to 15 students) and most of the students start the program together, taking the same courses with the same classmates until they graduate. Also, the fact that two of us, Gail and Ingrid,[3] are present in every class, and that Florence teaches three of the courses and is well known by the students, seems to give the students a sense of continuity and safety. This feeling of trust and intimacy builds over time with each successive course so that by the end of the three years, the bonds between the students and teachers are very strong. As described in chapters 4 and 5, we became aware that we were very careful in selecting our teachers, choosing those who could be flexible in their response to the students and not adhere rigidly to the lesson plan of the day.

The sequencing of the courses has also helped. The first course, "Introduction to Social Work," is a relatively neutral topic that allows students to become comfortable with each other, the teachers, the School of Social Work, and the Certificate Program itself. By the time the more sensitive topics are introduced, the students have developed a deeper level of trust with each other and also have a better understanding of the nature of social work as a profession, including the nature of change, the importance of self-development, and the role of confidentiality.

4. Teachers' Responses to the Students

In the classroom a circular process was set in place. The course information initiated the students' sharing of personal problems and the opportunity to express themselves in a safe and caring environment. This dynamic not only facilitated self-development for the students but also contributed to the mastery of the course material. As teachers, we felt a tremendous sense of responsibility to respond appropriately to the students' sharing of their personal issues and traumas. Our goals were twofold: first, we aimed to help the students develop the necessary knowledge and skills to deal with the various social and personal problems they would meet in their practice, and second, we sought to help the students in their self-development and personal struggles. To ignore the students' problems would have been insensitive and unkind, even unprofessional, and would have created an artificial learning environment. For example, to teach about empathy while not showing it is bad teaching; however, the potential to teach about empathy in a meaningful way while demonstrating it is enormous. Similarly, when we as teachers respond to a student's disclosure of sexual abuse or the details of her past struggles with alcohol addiction by listening, facilitating input from other students, and providing information on the topic, we are teaching in a very immediate and concrete way. As well, we are modelling good practice while enhancing the students' professional learning and personal development.

The challenge for us as teachers has been to deal sensitively and effectively with the students' issues, while at the same time maintaining a focus on the teaching. Given the painful material often expressed, this has not always been easy and there have been many occasions where the difficult and emotional issues threatened to overwhelm the class, with no resolution and little or no teaching of the course content. As others have found (Wright, 1993) we find the issue to be one of *balance*—to listen and facilitate discussion on the personal issues and then to link it to the topic of the class. We try to move beyond the pain to understanding and learning. Thus, no matter how emotional or painful the topic that students raise, we always try to bring some kind of closure by the end of the class by refocusing on the course topic.

In addition, while we used our therapeutic skills in our responses, it was clear to us that we could not fully act as therapists in the classroom. For example, whereas in a counselling situation it would be appropriate to probe certain situations for more information, such questioning would be inappropriate in the classroom and would cross an important and necessary boundary. At the same time, however, we remained very conscious of the individual student's situation and, if necessary, would see the student individually for further discussion and perhaps refer him or her to a counsellor.

Impact on the Students

Course evaluations, student feedback given verbally or in logs, and our own observations have provided us with a sense of how this form of teaching has affected the students. While we can certainly make improvements, the response has been almost uniformly positive both in terms of acquiring social work knowledge and skills, and in personal self-development. The students have been most emotive about their own healing, making such statements as: "All the information and material has helped me deal with and understand in depth these patterns [of family violence], and has helped me further my healing journey, a journey I will live until I have changed a horrible legacy left to me from generation to generation. I have learned that I have things I need to work on and things that make me the unique person that I am." Others have written that the program "has been inspiring and enlightening in terms of self-discovery and personal growth. It helped greatly in creating in me a positive world view, in a time when for far too many Native peoples life is simply tragic" (P. Bailey, personal communication, 2000).

Discussion and Conclusions: The Teaching-Healing Model

In writing about the experience at Grant McEwan College, Pelech (1993) points out that social work educators have two choices when they are training Native social workers. The first is to continue the colonial process and train Aboriginal students only in the Western way of helping, maintaining the more typical teacher/student relationship, which is based on the authority of the teachers. This only continues "the missionization and alienation of Native students from themselves" (Pelech, 1993, p. 161). The alternative is to include Aboriginal material and approaches to helping and to pay attention to and respect the personal experiences of the students, thereby equalizing and transforming the student-teacher relationship. The students' own personal issues are an invaluable source of Native content for a social work program. As a microcosm of their communities, their problems represent a cross-section of the social, political, and personal problems that exist in Native communities (Pelech, 1993). The opportunity to deal with some of their own personal problems in the classroom empowers them both personally and professionally; they begin to overcome some of their traumas while making immediate links between theory and practice, thereby fostering the development of the knowledge and practice skills that will enable them to better help their communities.

The kind of teaching in a social work program that is described in this paper, what perhaps can be called a teaching-healing model, is a real challenge and is often emotionally draining. However, its value lies in the vital opportunity it provides for learning and personal growth. This is true for both teachers and students alike. The personal stories of the students provide a richness of material and an immediacy that cannot be found in any textbook or role-play material. There are a number of elements in this teaching-healing process that seem to facilitate the students' healing, such as a catharsis of the painful emotions, the experience of giving and receiving support from other students, and the realization that he or she is not isolated in these experiences. Furthermore, the information that the course content provides on the particular problem experienced by the student lends objectivity to the issue, in turn enabling the student to begin to master the problem. Many Aboriginal students feel a great deal of shame and guilt about the problems they and their families have endured, unaware that the major causes of these lie outside of themselves. Morrissette, McKenzie, and Morrissette (1993) have stressed the importance of the development of Aboriginal awareness about the impact of colonization as a first step to empowerment: "healing begins with a reframing of conventional views of Aboriginal reality, and this can help individuals to make clearer distinctions between personal responsibilities and structural causes" (p. 95). We observed major changes in the students' awareness when they began to understand and recognize the various sources of the problems, including the oppressive and abusive political structures and policies to which Native peoples have been subjected.[4] While they initially react to this "new" information with a range of strong emotions, including sadness and anger, eventually the students express an enhanced sense of pride and empowerment as Native peoples.

Most of our students are mature women with extensive and difficult life experiences. For them, the decision to return to school is often an important step in their healing. This is particularly true, given that the majority of them had very negative experiences in educational institutions. A similar finding was reported in an interesting study of older female students that compared the college experiences of those who had been subjected to sexual abuse in childhood with those who had not (LeBlanc, Brabant & Forsyth, 1996). This study showed that those with histories of abuse did consistently better than those who had not been abused. However, this group also indicated the need for further healing in the college experience and the study recommended that support groups be set up for such students. "For these women, return to college does not reflect closure or complete healing; these have yet to occur at this stage. Rather, their involvement in higher education represents for them a movement toward that goal, a vehicle through which healing may ultimately take place" (LeBlanc et al., 1996, p. 472).[5] More recently, Bruyere (1998) has observed that "often the pursuit of a social work education is considered by Aboriginal students to be part of their healing, and the wounds may still be tender" (p. 174).

Social work education has been largely based on a Eurocentric world view, which values linear, scientific thinking. The teaching-healing model of instruction, which allows the students to narrate their stories, is a marked deviation from this and reflects a traditional, holistic way of knowing. Furthermore, it is a natural development from ancient Native healing practices. Based on the ancient concept of the

Medicine Wheel, Aboriginal peoples have been using the "circle" as a means of helping for centuries (see, for example, Absolon, 1993; Hart, 1996). "The sacred circle or medicine wheel is a traditional symbolic circle," which "can be used as a philosophical framework for developing healing pedagogy" (Weenie, 1998, p. 60). Thus, it is a natural development for the "Healing Circle" to become a "Sharing Circle," which can be applied to teaching (Hart, 1996), thereby becoming a "Learning Circle" (Nabigon, Hagey, Webster & Mackay, 1999; Zapf et al., 2003). Regnier (1994) describes the Sacred Circle or Medicine Wheel concept as "part of the critical theory of education committed to human emancipation" (Regnier, 1994, p. 129). Furthermore, the Sacred Circle concept can be used as a "process pedagogy of healing" (Regnier, 1994, as cited in Weenie, 1998, p. 61) consisting of three phases: belonging, understanding, and critical reflection. "By using the circle, the teacher can make the classroom a healing community" (Weenie, 1998, p. 61). It would seem that we did this inadvertently. When we arranged the classroom seating by ensuring that we sat in a circle, albeit around tables, we were not conscious that we were following the Sacred Circle concept, only that we wanted to facilitate discussion. And, as described, the discussions enhanced both the learning process and healing process.

Katz and St. Denis (1991) attest that "teaching must welcome back the healing dimension" (p. 25), adding that this redefinition of teacher as healer "fosters the connections between the student, the community and the culture" (Katz & St. Denis, 1991, p. 24). This approach is appearing in other programs of research (Nabigon, Hagey, Webster & Mackay, 1999) and social work education with Aboriginal peoples (see, for example, Castellano, Stalwick & Wein, 1986; Colorado, 1993b; Kelley & Nelson, 1986; Pelech, 1993; Yellow Horse Brave Heart, 1998; Young, 1999; Zapf, 1997, 1999a; Zapf et al., 2003).

In a teaching-healing model of social work education, the attitude and behaviour of the teacher need to be similar to that of a therapist. We are not acting as therapists, but perhaps as therapeutic teachers. Carl Rogers, a major figure in the healing profession, has described the three conditions necessary for successful therapy as congruence, unconditional positive regard, and empathy (Rogers, 1980). He believed that they were also key to successful teaching. This approach was strongly endorsed in the Grant McEwan social work program, which believes that "being there" (Rogers, 1980) is absolutely essential in working with indigenous populations (Wright, 1993). Rogers elaborated on the importance of this for teachers, advocating that "when the facilitator is a real person, being what he or she is, entering into relationships with the learners without presenting a front or a facade, the facilitator is much more likely to be effective" (Rogers, 1980, p. 271). This approach equalizes the relationship between teacher and student wherein both learn from each other.

We wish we could state that we were like this right from the beginning of the program. We were not. However, in response to the students and over time, we changed our way of teaching and "being" in the classroom and are convinced that if we had not altered our methods and our presence, the program would not have lasted. In describing the impact of the program on his life, one of our students wrote that "one of the highlights of the program is that you get to learn from real people, who have lived or are living what they teach. I believe them to be true humanitarians" (P. Bailey, personal communication, 2000).

This model of teaching social work "moves far beyond the conventional concept of instructor to a point where the roles of teacher and social worker become confused and blurred" (Zapf, 1993b, p. 41). Referring to the work of the distinguished social work educator Sophie Freud (1987), who has described social work education as a social work method, Zapf suggests that "such blurring could well be the future direction of the social work profession" (Zapf, 1993b, p. 41). Our experience has been that such "blurring" of the roles of social worker and teacher in the classroom is essential in a Native program and while it is certainly more demanding for both teachers and students, it is ultimately more rewarding.[6]

In summary, the reasons behind the need for a teaching-healing model in a Native social work education program are tragic, embedded in the shameful past of the colonial oppression of Canada's Aboriginal peoples. However, our experience has demonstrated to us that out of the suffering can come healing—Aboriginal peoples have great resilience and strength, both in themselves and in their communities. The challenge for social work educators in mainstream universities is to adapt their knowledge and teaching methods to create the best healing and learning environment for Aboriginal peoples and, more importantly, to give these students a respectful place where they can develop the necessary confidence to begin to trust their abilities to heal, learn, and become "healing" social work practitioners.

Notes

1. It is important to be very clear that the Native students are victims and are not responsible for the high level of problems they and others in their community may experience. In fact, as Chrisjohn and Young (1997) suggest in their analysis of the residential school experience, the pathology lies with the oppressors.
2. In particular, see Colorado (1993a, 1993b); Feehan (1993a, 1993b); Hannis (1993a, 1993b); Lalonde (1993); Peacock (1993); Restivo (1993); Zapf (1993a, 1993b). Helpful material from non-Aboriginals includes Dean (1998) and Shulman (1987).
3. Both are present as co-coordinators and/or teachers. However, Gail, a Mohawk woman, is the cultural mediator in all of the classes.
4. This awareness was considerably enhanced when they took the course on the history of the relationship of Euro-Canadians and Aboriginal peoples. Because of the complexity of the course material, it was not offered until the last year of their three-year program. However, the material allows many of them to build on and consolidate the healing and learning they have already experienced in the classroom.
5. See also Higgins (1994).
6. While it is beyond the scope of this chapter to fully explore the possibility of applying the teaching-healing model to the teaching of non-Aboriginal social work students, it is an interesting concept to consider. In their paper on the importance of developing an Aboriginal model of social work practice, Morrissette and his colleagues recommended that "all social workers need to view developments in Aboriginal practice as potential, new forms of practice in the non-Aboriginal community" (Morrissette, McKenzie & Morrissette, 1993). This observation is equally applicable to the teaching of social work. Commenting on the leadership role that Aboriginals need to take in developing Aboriginal-centred, relevant social work education programs in Canada, Bruyere (2007) writes that this leadership role "also invites us [Aboriginal peoples] to share those traditional values, beliefs, and practices in a way that enriches students from all racial and ethnic groups that comprise Canadian society" (p. 429). This suggests that the teaching-healing model of course delivery could be applied to teaching non-Aboriginal students in a mainstream program with beneficial effects on the personal and educational development of the students. While it is unlikely that the majority of the students in a mainstream social work program would have the extent or severity of problems that Aboriginal students are burdened with, certainly a number have experienced trauma of some kind and many have issues related to loss, personal relationships, family dysfunction, and health problems, among others. There are also students from oppressed minorities who have experiences similar to those of the Aboriginal students. A teaching approach that encourages students to speak about their experiences in a safe environment would be of benefit to all students and contribute to their personal wellness, an essential element in their professional development. As in Aboriginal programs, it also has the potential of modelling good practice for the students.

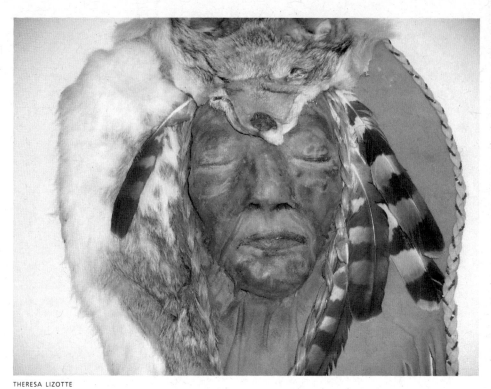

THERESA LIZOTTE

Out Where We're Supposed to Be, a mask by Theresa Lizotte

Aboriginal Healing Practices in Mainstream Social Work Education Programs ... Sagacity or Sacrilege?

Nicki Garwood and Jean Stevenson

Introduction

> ... trivialization of our oppression is compounded by the fact that nowadays anyone can be Indian if she or he wants to. All that is required is that one be Indian in a former life, or take part in a Sweat Lodge, or be mentored by a "medicine woman" or read a how-to book. (Smith, 1991, p. 45)

Within this paper, we attempt to look at the appropriateness or inappropriateness of including Aboriginal healing practices as an element of mainstream social work education. We choose to open the debate with Smith's quote, in order to emphasize the controversy of such an idea. The concept that Aboriginal healing practices could be "taught" as part of mainstream social work education, and included in mainstream curriculum—not simply as a way of having non-Aboriginal students develop a better understanding of their Aboriginal clients, but for possible use *by* non-Aboriginal social workers *with* non-Aboriginal clients—would certainly create strong debate among, and possibly protest from, many Aboriginal groups. We recognize that Aboriginal students might appropriately include class discussion of their healing practices in a culturally oriented curriculum to better respond to an Aboriginal clientele, but what would it mean if non-Aboriginal students dealt with such material? The idea seems to resonate with the same colonialism as Native[1] land appropriation.

Transferring aspects of one particular culture to another comes easily to the global village in which we live, particularly within a global economy and with the facility of the Internet. However, Hopi and Anishnabek prophecies foretold the coming of the Seventh Fire at a time when a web covers the Earth, a time of purification when Evil will be destroyed to make way for the New Age. These prophecies might imply that increased global interaction, as with all interactions, would have positive and negative aspects that would require balancing.[2] Increased global communication may lead to homogenization of cultures and societies. Whether, in the long run, homogeneity will be considered as an "Orwellian Evil" or as a "New Age Good" we cannot yet know. Therefore, when we consider the implications of lending or adapting Aboriginal healing practices to mainstream social work through education programs, we know, as

Inuit winter hunters know, that we need to recognize the colour of the ice before we step on it.

Aboriginal world views cannot be considered homogeneous since not only do Aboriginal peoples disagree on the subject of sharing Aboriginal healing practices with non-Native people, but also dissension occurs between proponents of various beliefs held by Aboriginal peoples as to what kinds of practices may be considered "healing." Traditional teachings encourage Aboriginal peoples to understand that all cultures reflect one another, as do human individuals, in a way that precludes judgment of one another. This non-judgmental attitude encompasses the acceptance of difference (Commanda, 2001; Storm, 1972). However, a complex variety of beliefs exists between and within Aboriginal groups, among which intolerance of difference flourishes. For example, in First Nations, Métis, and Inuit communities where proselytization has worked very strongly in favour of Christian religions, not only do conflicts exist between those who are of the Christian faith and those who choose to remember "traditional" (i.e., pre-colonial) healing activities, but also, conflicts exist between Aboriginal Christians of various denominations to the point where one group will not socialize with another (personal interviews with the Cree and Inuit of northern Quebec). Some First Nations members of the Christian churches regard the use of traditional Aboriginal healing practices as pagan or "of the Devil" (personal interviews). Similarly, among those who practise pre-colonial healing activities, disagreements occur over methods of, and meanings behind, symbolic healing.[3] Some Aboriginal individuals who promulgate the idea that traditional, pre-colonial rituals and ceremonies *define* the concept of traditional healing practices frown upon sharing the innermost secrets of these practices with other cultures. However, many Aboriginal peoples have a broader sense of spiritual healing that is not confined to ritual and ceremony, and which they happily share with their non-Native brothers and sisters.

At a pragmatic level, since the Indian Act of 1876 deprived Aboriginal peoples of their rights to freely practise their traditional (and, in comparison with colonial understanding of the human psyche at that time, avant-garde) healing methods, it comes as no surprise that protectionism around those means to healing would result after 75 years of their suppression by non-Native criminal law.[4] Thus, when we begin a discussion on the implications of introducing Aboriginal healing practices to non-Native social workers as part of their education—not only to have them acquire a deeper understanding of First Nations, Métis, and Inuit clients, but also as a means to self-healing for themselves and their non-Native clients—we need to understand and consider both the macrocosm and microcosms of Aboriginal cultures.

What Constitutes a Healing Practice?

In examining North American Aboriginal healing practices, we must first elucidate the various meanings of "healing" and "healing practices" as understood by Aboriginal peoples. As noted above, spiritual rituals and ceremonies as a means of symbolic healing—particularly those practices that belonged to pre-colonial Aboriginal cultures—would be too narrow a definition of "Aboriginal healing practices."

Colonization caused a schism in the Aboriginal collective memory by outlawing many traditional healing practices such as the Sweat Lodge and Sun Dance ceremonies. This interruption of traditional practices disrupted the passing on of oral history and customs. Now, every Aboriginal person needs to define his or her own sense of what constitutes "traditional" healing.

While the term "healing practices" includes ceremonies and rituals, other means also invoke healing for Aboriginal peoples, including some that originated in non-Aboriginal cultures but which have been adopted as traditional[5] to some Native groups. Drawing from our own and others' experience, we can identify the following practices as recognized healing methods among Aboriginal peoples: the use of traditional medicines[6] for spiritual, mental, emotional, and physical recovery, interception between physical and spiritual realities, hunting and trapping, storytelling and traditional teachings, dream interpretation, soul retrieval, massage and chiropractics, art and artifacts, dance, music, singing, and drumming, Christian religious practices, language and identity retrieval, education, protest and activism, psychotherapy and psychiatry, and community restoration[7]—all of which carry healing power for those who choose them. Moreover, within and between these practices, practitioners disagree on the "right" path to healing. The rivalries in the general non-Native population between the major world religions also exist in the equivalent microcosmic competitiveness among Aboriginal peoples in defining healing and the means to achieving it. Differences of opinion abound on the means to healing, depending on geographical location and the socio-political and psychosocial history of its proponents. Standard, subdued, Euro-Canadian religious activities rub shoulders with dramatic spiritual interception by medicine people or evangelical healers, for example. An Inuk might describe his spiritual tradition as "Anglican" and consider First Nations' ceremonies as "works of the Devil," but he would happily regale any listener with teaching stories that tell of shamans and shape-shifters[8] as if he were narrating history. So, too, those Aboriginal individuals whom the federal residential schools acculturated may recount the *facts* of Adam and Eve, and Heaven and Hell, while participating in, for example, smudging ceremonies.

With regard to traditional (i.e., pre-colonial) practices like ceremonies and rituals, disagreements about protocols and competitiveness arise between full-bloods and half or less bloods, between those brought up on reserve and those raised in urban centres, between young and old, between those adopted out and those never adopted, between those who only accept teachings that are passed down and those who accept experiential or life teachings, and between those who speak Aboriginal languages and those who speak only French and/or English. Additionally, between the 11 major Canadian Aboriginal language groups, differences of world views emanate from language construction. For example, among the Cree of James Bay, the word for "health" (*miyupimaatisiuu*) translates as "being alive well" (Cree Board of Health and Social Services of James Bay, 2006). For the Inuit of northern Quebec, when speaking of "holistic healing," *mamisarniq*, the Inuktitut word implies a renewal of emotional, physical, mental, and spiritual life in much the same way as some Inuit people speak about born-again Christianity.

However, Inuit individuals have many views as to the meaning of, and means to, healing, as do other groups. At a Healing Camp for Inuit survivors of the federal school system, held in Nunavik in 2003, participants cited the following as *meanings* of healing: grieving; changing negative behaviours; acting as a role model for others; understanding God's love; finding compassion for oneself and others; sharing pain with each other as well as one's life; listening to healthy elders; recognizing unhealthy behaviours; recognizing the needs of youth; forgiveness of oneself and others; living more in the moment than in the past; recognizing the consequences of one's actions; communicating better with one another; learning to be better parents; and *angiarigijarniq*, "getting rid of secret things."9 When asked to identify their values, the group produced a list that had similarities to their concepts of the healing process, i.e., mutual understanding, family, and love of each other; faith in God and the health of the soul; leadership and the knowledge of healthy elders; communal prayer; children and their future; Inuit culture and language; the community; relationships with other communities; comradeship between Christians; companionship in marriage; hunting and the country food that God provides; freedom of expression; the ability to love; sobriety; life itself; community support; physical abilities; peace and harmony; music and song; education, justice, and knowledge of the land; skills of both men and women; and opportunities to renew physical, mental, emotional, and spiritual aspects (Garwood, 2003).

Krawll (1994) defines "healing process" in terms of individual and community wellness. She identifies that healing occurs through community involvement; the development of trust, sharing, and caring; the use of intergenerational wisdom; improved communications with the elimination of blaming and shaming; the acceptance of personal responsibility; and a sense of connectedness. She describes healing as beginning with a movement from a personal, internalized process to one that touches the family and the community in a holistic manner. Ross (1996) refers to a traditional definition of personal imbalance as a disconnection from healthy relationships, or connections with unhealthy relationships, or, more severely, the avoidance of all connections. In his assessment, healing comes with repairing broken relationships. Waldram (1997) describes individual change as occurring through symbolic healing and, by way of suggestion, catharsis, placebo effect, social restructuring, and psychochemical reaction. Zapf (2004) brings to our attention the important, essential connection between environment, spirituality, and the Aboriginal individual, extending the question, "What does it mean to live well in this place?" posited by Haas and Nachtigal (1998), to "What does it mean to live well *as* this place? ... thereby rejecting the fundamental distinction between person and place in favour of a unifying spiritual connection" (p. 12). In this way, healing would imply the process by which we may reveal the truth of our being within the "Whole." Kirmayer, Simpson, and Cargo (2003) emphasize the need for social solutions, and for a re-evaluation/validation of an Aboriginal collective identity. The latter process would be achieved through positive interaction with the larger cultural environment in which the Native identity finds itself. Consensus from among the proponents of various healing methods among Aboriginal peoples indicates that any activity that strengthens the functioning of individuals, families, and communities contributes to a healing process. Thus, present-day change through Aboriginal healing practices, in an era of major paradigm shifts, involves mental, spiritual, physical, and emotional (i.e., holistic) transformation (Duran & Duran, 1995).

We can see that within the rich panoply of Aboriginal beliefs is an enormous range of traditional healing ceremonies, rituals, and activities, as well as a wide range of beliefs about their power to heal. Therefore, we raise the question as to how social work course planners might reach consensus about which particular Aboriginal healing activities could be included in a non-Native social work education program, designed to service non-Native students and their future non-Native clientele. Although we do not purport to know the answer to this question, we do believe that Aboriginal involvement in curriculum development would be essential.

The Challenges of Healing in Aboriginal Communities

Understanding the conflict that the ubiquitous medical terminology of "wounds" and "healing" depict in modern Aboriginal cultures gives deeper insight into the meaning of healing processes for Aboriginal peoples. Non-Aboriginal social work students need to know what Aboriginal peoples are healing from, in order to assess the appropriateness of Aboriginal means of healing for non-Native social work clients. Evidently, the wounds borne by most contemporary Aboriginal peoples generally do not come from the cut and slash of open war with non-Native people, as in the past;[10] rather, they are more insidious, denoting disease of spirit. Evidence of the present epidemic of multigenerational trauma appears as waves of psychic pain, which surface as mental, physical, emotional, and spiritual violence committed by one Aboriginal person against another (Aboriginal Healing Foundation, 2003; Benson, 1991; Corrado, 2003; Cummins, 2003; Cunneen, 2001; Nielsen & Silverman, 1996; Solicitor General Canada, 1998). The suppression and oppression endured by Aboriginal peoples, and the attempts by successive Canadian governments at their assimilation have resulted in waves of lateral violence. The residential school system created community environments where sexual and physical abuse still flourish (Aboriginal Healing Foundation, 2003; Milloy, 1999), while yet other Eurocentric systems have had equal importance in wounding the collective identity of Aboriginal peoples. The Sixties Scoop[11] still exists for Aboriginal families four decades later as lack of resources for Aboriginal family preservation results in children being separated from their families (Fontaine, 2005). The devastating outcomes in terms of multigenerational losses for Aboriginal peoples, e.g., of language, culture, land, self-identity, and a sense of belonging, continue to deeply affect Aboriginal families whose children social workers may remove unnecessarily for lack of appropriate cultural understanding (Aboriginal Healing Foundation, 2004; Collier, 1984). We can also look at systemic prejudices encountered on a daily basis by Aboriginal peoples involved in education and justice to understand why many question whether we really do live in a post-colonial era (Duran & Duran, 1995; Woo, 2005).

We need to remind ourselves too that enforced change within some Aboriginal societies over the last 90 years has been rapid and devastating. In Inuit populations, the fine balance of relationships between men and women has been disturbed by contact with non-Inuit values (McElroy, 1975). Paradigm shifts have occurred in the traditional Inuit value system, one that The People[12] based on survival of the group in a challenging environment, and wherein traditional concepts of equality recognized the value of each contributor to group survival. Now, individual needs begin to have some predominance over the utilitarian needs of the group as they often do in non-Inuit cultures, e.g., once-sacred carvings, which in pre-colonial times acted as symbolic healing devices for the group, now act as mere means of generating income for individuals gifted in carving. "Well-meaning" colonists encouraged the trade in Inuit artifacts as a means of economic development, which they believed to be in the interests of The People (Houston, 1995). First Nations communities have had to contend with reserve living and displacement, the latter being identified as one of the greatest influences on suicide rates for Aboriginal peoples (Brant, 1985; Canadian Psychiatric Association Section on Native Mental Health, 1986)

Not to place all the blame on the larger society in which the Aboriginal collectivity finds itself, we mention here that the process of enlightened transformation in Aboriginal communities has been subverted, in many instances, by repetitious psychic defence strategies. These negative strategies block transitional healing for Aboriginal individuals and communities. The enormous psychic energy involved in maintaining these defence strategies depletes creative resources that could otherwise be used to build a new and positive reality. The attempt to maintain an unhealthy homeostasis results in individual and community implosion. For example, gatherings of Aboriginal peoples at conferences and workshops sometimes act as a platform for individuals who seek a "healing path," but who have not yet found their personal direction. Gatherings can become places to express grievances or misdirected anger, with little regard to the integration of real grief or ways of focusing it on therapeutic solutions. Additionally, some Aboriginal helping organizations claw their way through daily life, seemingly energized only by the despair of the people who work in them, and by a capricious law of nature that allows helpers to assist others while being seemingly incapable of helping themselves. This happens even though many healing organizations simultaneously and sincerely promote self-healing among their workers (Hodgson, 1991; Solicitor General Canada, 1997). Some individuals remain powerless to instigate personal change, while they either distance themselves entirely from the intimacy of their own pain, or wallow in it to the exclusion of all other realities.

Certainly, such dynamics exist en masse in non-Aboriginal populations, but from an Aboriginal perspective, the traditional values of caring, sharing, honesty, and respect can seem like a twisted shadow of their former meaning. For example, revenge becomes mistaken for honour and justice ("I'll get him"; "I have to …"); relationship becomes ownership ("She's mine"; "I can do what I want with her …"); tradition becomes manipulation and control ("You can't speak yet—you're interrupting what I was going to say …"); self-assertion becomes aggression ("Violence is part of our culture …"); non-interference becomes neglect ("It's none of my business …"); silent observation becomes egocentricity ("It's definitely none of my business …");

survival becomes blood quantum ("He doesn't belong here"; "there's not enough to go around ..."). Spiritual ceremonies once used as rites of passage and socialization can become means of manipulation and social control (Charlie, 2005). Individuals purporting to be Medicine Men and Medicine Women can operate for self-aggrandizement, monetary gain,[13] or sexual gain. Grieving becomes a ritual that lasts for years, long after its true purpose (integrating the trauma and moving on) is past.[14]

Individual and communal understanding of the systemic injustices, that form the basis of these aforementioned survival strategies, and educating Aboriginal and non-Aboriginal students of social work in these narratives, can contribute significantly to the latter's effectiveness when putting their training into practice. Otherwise, the enormity of personal challenge faced by many Aboriginal individuals, particularly women and children, can seem overwhelming from the perspective of both worker and client.

Healing Practices with Universal Application?

Pre-colonial spiritual ceremonies, such as the Sun Dance and the Sweat Lodge, have a large element of prayer for the people through self-sacrifice. Spirituality reveals itself through placing oneself in a situation of potential, if not real, physical discomfort and pain (Weekes, 1994), an activity with which some Christian religions identify in mortification. We choose not to describe here the details of these kinds of multifaceted ceremonies because of their many interpretations and misinterpretations. Also, such spiritual ceremonies require enormous commitment on the part of the participant, including learning from elders and devotion to prayer. Preparation takes many years, and would be unlikely to fit in the time span of an academic program, even if it were deemed appropriate.

Since experience of spiritual ceremonies is utterly subjective, we have chosen to describe only a few ceremonies from among those of which we have had personal experience, and then from among those that we recognize as having potential for a wide application in general social work practice, i.e., the Healing Circle, the Letting-Go Ceremony, and Family Group Conferencing. We also attempt to describe the healing qualities of these activities. We do not pretend to prescribe these activities for use by either Native or non-Native social work exponents, but merely offer them as possibilities for consideration.

The Healing Circle[15]

The Healing Circle is perhaps the most well-known and commonly used healing tool among Aboriginal "traditionalists." In Aboriginal cultures, the Circle becomes significant in symbolic healing: dancers weave a circle; round Sacred Drums become the heartbeat of ceremony; Sweat Lodge participants build the round Lodge as preparation for the Sweat; a circle denotes the placement of a Tipi, and also the shape of the Medicine Wheel. Within its sacred symbolism, many Aboriginal cultures, particularly First Nations, use Healing Circles as a tool for addressing a multitude of issues such as addictions, abuse, grief, and trauma of all kinds. Within Aboriginal communities, addressing the legacy of multigenerational abuse becomes a daily challenge. In a Healing Circle, individuals might deal with personal losses incurred as a result of systemic injustice, prejudice, and toxic shame. Participants might also deal with issues of self-identity, deaths within the family, victimization, or being a victimizer. The Circle becomes a forum for healing through mutual, non-judgmental support and sharing. "There is no one way or right way of running a circle. Circles have different names; they are sometimes called Healing Circles or Talking Circles but they all have the same goal, providing loving support for someone …" (Sandy, 1996). In traditional Aboriginal societies, sharing life's journey is a great teacher, acknowledging that the shared experience of pain, laughter, and love can bring people closer together.

A Healing Circle invokes traditional Aboriginal values of respect, honesty, wisdom, love, bravery, and humility. It teaches compassion, responsibility, co-operation, and commitment. As with any ceremony, protocols guide the holding of a Circle, with expectations regarding attitudes and ways of behaving. Although protocols do vary from one group to another, the basic premise of a Circle remains the same: that participants show mutual and self-respect, have an attitude of non-interference with others, and recognize the presence of the Creator and the Spirits of the Ancestors within the Circle.

A Circle begins with a Smudging Ceremony[16] for purification, during which time one of the group will burn Sacred Medicines—sweetgrass, tobacco, cedar, or sage. Cleansing through Smudging rids participants of negative thoughts, bad spirits, or negative energy, in order to be ready for self-healing or to help heal another.[17] The participants pass an Eagle Feather or a Talking Stick[18] from one to another, either clockwise or counter-clockwise,[19] giving each participant the opportunity to speak about himself or herself, uninterrupted, for as long as the participant feels the need to do so (Society of Aboriginal Addictions Recovery, 1994). A participant may also hold the Eagle Feather in silence, or pass it directly on to the next person without speaking. Once the Circle has begun, no one disrupts the proceedings by arriving late or getting up and leaving, as participants consider these actions disruptive to the healing energy created within the Circle. Healing Circles may take many hours to complete, depending on the number of participants and their ability to stay focused without straying into prolonged "streams of consciousness." Once the Eagle Feather has made a complete circle, a participant will say a closing prayer.

In a study of Healing Circles conducted by Stevenson (1998) at the Native Friendship Centre of Montreal, long-time participants offered opinions on their healing experiences. Stevenson makes useful comparisons in her study between the benefits of Healing Circles and those of non-Native therapeutic group work. She notes that in non-Native therapeutic groups, the "professional" generally takes a stance outside of the experience of the participants, and exceptionally shares personal experience. In the Circle, recognition of the equality of all participants as human beings facing the challenges of past, present, and future is a given. As with the Alcoholics Anonymous movement, merely being willing to follow the protocols of the Circle, and having a belief in spiritual connection, qualifies an individual to participate in this ceremony. Inside the spiritual environment of the Circle, no direct interventions take place by either the Circle Keeper or the other participants. "The [social] worker's role as therapist is much stronger than that of a Circle Keeper—the worker in a therapeutic group might interpret what is happening in a group setting, while a Circle Keeper would not" (Stevenson, 1998, p. 40). Any reference to the sharing of others is done by indirect reference to one's own relevant experience, when appropriate. Thus, the process of the Circle drastically reduces group dynamic role-playing. Many Aboriginal peoples take the stance of observer (Brant, 1990), sometimes interpreted as "shyness," before entering into open self-expression in group work. In contrast, the format of the Circle allows participants to predict and anticipate the arrival of the Feather into their hands, and prepare themselves accordingly. The sacred object facilitates the ability of each person to speak from the heart after listening intently to the sharing of others.

Stevenson's summary indicates the following perceptions of the healing process reported by the participants of the Healing Circles: non-judgment, equality, confidentiality, trust, letting go, giving and receiving support, belonging, reality, learning about self and others, spirituality, and culture. Their combined experiences indicate a means of taking on the transformation implied in healing through the spirituality of the Circle process. Additionally, the process emphasizes the *timing and voluntary nature* of healing, i.e., participants choose whether to attend sporadically or regularly. Healing Circles may also be used as a part of a conflict-resolution process, allowing all parties to have input without fear of judgment or recrimination, and for debriefing. For conflict resolution and debriefing, the cultural background of the participants would be immaterial, and might usefully be used by non-Native social workers and their clients.

Healing with the Family Group Conference

New Zealand Maori culture has examples of traditional means of healing and conflict resolution through community circles (McConchie, 2003; Walker, 1996). Equally, in Inuit, First Nations, and Métis traditions, individuals and families in conflict used their own skills to resolve problems between themselves. Necessarily, before the advent of "social work" and colonial values in indigenous communities, the process essentially required the wisdom of elders and communal co-operation, with the utilitarian goal of devising the best outcome for the good of the group. Family group conferencing (FGC), also known as family group decision making (FGDM), reflects traditional methods of conflict resolution and closely resembles its cousin, the Healing Circle (Burford, Pennell & MacLeod, 1995). In modern times, FGC/FGDM provides a basis for resolving practical and emotional conflict, and uses a structure that adapts well to a variety of cultural contexts, while bridging the gap between non-Aboriginal policy and traditional world views (Hall, 2000; Hart, 1996, 2002).

Several versions of FGC currently promote conflict resolution across Canada, in New Zealand, and in Britain (Aboriginal Justice Learning Network, 1997; LaPrairie, 1995). In Canada, such entities as the Department of Justice strongly support the FGC process. The protocols of these Circles differ from region to region, and are eminently adaptable to local situations. Memorial University of Newfoundland conducted a study of the use of FGC among the Inuit of Nain, Labrador, as well as among non-Inuit, non-Native families in the Labrador region. They identified long-term benefits for both Inuit and non-Inuit groups (Burford et al., 1995).

FGC hands back responsibility to families for resolving potentially negative situations, rather than leaving the decision making totally in the hands of service providers, who may be Aboriginal and/or non-Aboriginal. The process works through referral, implementation, monitoring, and evaluation, with carefully structured preparation and support, and with priority given to participant safety. Where appropriate, the relevant authorities provide the participants with necessary information, and then the family deliberates in private and produces a plan of action. During the latter part of this process, participants have the opportunity to express their emotional, mental, spiritual, and physical needs. The sessions also become a forum for the expression of unaddressed fears in a safe environment, and thus act as a preventative measure against participants' possible reactive behaviours (Burford et al., 1995).

During follow-up, service providers oversee the implementation of any conflict-resolution plan devised by the participants and ensure that they meet the safety needs of everyone concerned. If necessary, service providers also plan subsequent sessions to deal with new issues as they arise. Whether used for resocialization, prevention, or diversion purposes, FGC requires community co-operation—i.e., involvement of public authorities, government representatives, and community groups, such as police, parole officers, child welfare, women's groups, elders, educators, health workers, addiction workers, and counsellors. Political will makes an important contribution to this type of healing process, as does the existence of genuine community spirit. Where this kind of co-operation exists, it matters little whether the participants are Aboriginal or non-Aboriginal for the results to be beneficial for all involved (American Humane Association, 1996).

In Nunavik, Quebec, FGC has become an important part of recent program development at the Makitautik Community Residential Centre. In citing the benefits of FGC for the 14 communities of Nunavik, the centre hopes to promote a better quality of life among the families of the victimizers; support for victims; communication improvements between family members; a reduction in incidents of violent behaviour; a better understanding of individual roles and responsibilities; an increase in community responsibility for prevention and intervention in conflicts; a greater confidence among community workers that they are making some headway in the battle against multigenerational trauma; a greater knowledge among community members of the dynamics involved in violent behaviour (and, consequently, a greater knowledge of the peripheral issues, such as drug and alcohol abuse); a greater definition of the boundaries between the generations through greater understanding of roles and responsibilities; a better understanding of the meaning of "reintegration" of offenders, and a reduction in the number of individuals experiencing the "revolving door syndrome" in the correctional system (Garwood, 2000).

FGC has proven to be successful for First Nations groups in other parts of Canada, as in Hollow Water, where, for 15 years, the whole community has involved itself in addressing rampant multigenerational sexual abuse (Hollow Water Community Services, 1993; Native Counselling Services of Alberta, 2001). A major aspect of the project has been the resolution of criminal acts at their source, within the community, through the auspices of a crisis response committee that, in turn, responds to a community advisory group. The solicitor general credits the Hollow Water First Nation's project with significantly reducing alcohol abuse, improving educational standards, and increasing the number of programs for infants, children, and youth in the community. Cost saving has been significant for the federal government and the province of Manitoba, at over $3 million in justice costs for the first 10 years (Solicitor General Canada, 2001).

In considering FGC's application to non-Native social work, we can certainly be guided by the successful projects already accomplished by McMaster University, which included a non-Native population (Burford et al., 1995). FGC would be eminently transferable to social work in a non-Aboriginal environment, wherever there might be a strong sense of *community*.

Grieving and Forgiveness: The Letting-Go Ceremony

One of the most important challenges that we all share as human beings, regardless of colour or creed, is the process of grieving and forgiving. Certainly, the last 500 years for Aboriginal peoples have given lifetimes of practise in the art of grieving. Losses have been mental, physical, spiritual, and emotional: loss of culture, identity, language, political responsibility, meaningful employment, meaningful education, land, health, sexual integrity, self-esteem, sense of belonging, pride of heritage, quality of life, living environment, and, of course, the loss of close family members through suicide, illness, and accident in greater numbers than in the general Canadian population (Canada, 2004; Kirmayer, 1994). In pre-colonial times, prolonged grieving by an Aboriginal person, e.g., a hunter incapacitated by grief, might cause grave problems for the survival of a group. Elders and shamans devised ways of facilitating the grieving process, and often did so in recognizing the connection between mind, body, spirit, and environment. At the death of a close relative, for example, a grieving Northern Cree might be set to meticulously clean a moose hide; another might use "Tree Wounding";[20] an Athabascan family might spend many months preparing for a "Stickdance,"[21] along with other community members (Jefferson, 1994). Although we recognize the benefits of using a Healing Circle as part of the process of grieving, we also recognize the necessity of employing such mental, spiritual, physical, and emotional means of release as targeted by other traditional ceremonies and rituals for the healing of Aboriginal peoples. Those of us in clinical practice may recognize the convoluted path of the grieving process as expressed through Aboriginal clients. We see the avoidance of confronting deep feelings of loss in many behaviours: addictions, anxiety disorders, violence, emotional withdrawal, suicide, and para-suicidal behaviour. We see dramatic behaviours targeting those most vulnerable (often women and children) in the place of righteous anger directed at the real source of pain (e.g., the sexual abuse, the abandonment). We see clients misled into bargaining through promiscuity for the love and security that they so justly deserve. Holistic intervention through ritual can address this painfully contorted healing path.

Ross (1996) refers to the Letting-Go Ceremony, a grieving ritual prescribed by a Cree elder in Alberta to assist in the healing process following a death. Some groups of Cree participated in the Letting-Go ritual if, after one year following a death, family members of the deceased still held on to their grief. A marker stone for the grave would be placed on a sledge with ropes tied at both ends. Anyone who still felt the pain of loss would do his or her best to pull the sledge away from the burial ground, while others tried to drag the gravestone to its appropriate resting place. The sheer expenditure of physical, mental, emotional, and spiritual energy facilitated the grieving process for those who had not been able to let go of their pain.

This type of ritual can be usefully adapted for the grieving of all kinds of losses that continue to affect the spirit, e.g., loss of relationships, childhood losses, and to confront perceived negative aspects of the self in self-forgiveness.[22] The ceremony's power comes from the interaction of mental, spiritual, physical, and emotional aspects, regardless of the cultural background of the participants. Although the ceremony's title implies a sloughing off of grief—like shedding a snakeskin—in practice, it integrates trauma through a cathartic experience that accesses "Spirit" via physical means. Each person participating in such an experience, whichever end of the rope he or she chooses to pull, becomes deeply involved in confronting his or her own truth.

Questions of Evaluation

We may now consider how Aboriginal and non-Aboriginal social work students might usefully include Healing Circles, the Letting-Go Ceremony, and FGC in their practice. However, we would need to recognize that non-Aboriginal students might attempt to impose an Aboriginal world view onto a Eurocentric world view. The struggle persists in persuading non-Native systems such as justice, health, education, and child welfare to give Aboriginal world views a prominent place in programming supposedly designed *for Aboriginal peoples.* For example, in cases of violence between a couple, court-mandated restraining orders for Aboriginal peoples work against healthy reconciliation where FGC is available. In some federal prisons, non-Native guards intrude on sacred ceremonies to "supervise." In urban child welfare,[23] Inuit children are considered a minority and often placed in foster care with non-Aboriginal minority families, rather than being fostered in the North. Introducing a Native world view to non-Aboriginal clients would need to be accomplished with close supervision from Native practitioners, but could facilitate cross-cultural understanding.

The challenges of competing world views are not insurmountable, given the benefits of multiculturalism. However, most non-Aboriginal programs contain an element of evaluation as to the efficacy of the program concerned. How, then, might we evaluate the efficacy of Aboriginal elements within a Eurocentric program? Pipe-Carrier Joseph Couture (1993, 1996) responded to the question of evaluating the efficacy of Aboriginal programming for Aboriginal inmates within the federal penitentiary system. He suggested that there may be mutually acceptable lists of behaviours that can be used by the institution and by the "healer" as indicators of healthy transformation.[24] Couture made useful observations as to how the world view of a non-Native system could be satisfied, while respecting the Aboriginal world view. Hodge (2001) contributes to the discussion of evaluating the spiritual aspect of an individual's involvement with an interpretive anthropological framework, with the proviso that the worker cannot take on the role of spiritual adviser, must avoid imposing spiritual beliefs on the client, and must not lose focus on the practical tasks at hand. Hodge describes the framework as an intervention in itself, allowing the client to have a better self-awareness of his or her strengths and resilience.

Spiritual genograms (Bullis, 1996; Hodge, 2000, 2001) give insight into the client's spiritual world, but merely answer the question as to whether spirituality has importance to personal change in the client's life. Hodge also notes that quantitative assessment not only needs an expert clinician to interpret the measures but also carries the implication that the client might be comparatively deficient in some way. An evaluation that takes the form of an interpretive framework would benefit the client's process of transformation; however, the challenge remains as to how holistic elements (mental, physical, emotional, and spiritual) could be evaluated for non-Native clients of non-Native workers trained in Aboriginal concepts. Certainly, some aspects would be easier to evaluate than others, since outcomes would be clear through observable short-term and long-term changes in participants' behaviour.

Discussion

We have described several meanings attributed by Aboriginal peoples to the terms "healing" and "healing practices." We have identified several schools of thought among Aboriginal peoples with regard to sharing Aboriginal healing practices of a ceremonial nature, i.e., those who believe that no Aboriginal ceremonies and rituals should ever be shared in any way with non-Aboriginal people; those who believe that only pre-colonial ceremonies and rituals should not be shared; those who believe that non-Native people may participate in Aboriginal ceremonies without offence, but may not appropriate them for their own or that of other non-Native individuals' use; and those who not only freely invite non-Aboriginal people to participate, but also accept the transposition and adaptation of ceremonies to other cultures without offence. We have also described three Aboriginal ceremonies—the Healing Circle, the Letting-Go Ceremony, and Family Group Conferencing—as examples for discussing the relevance and appropriateness of lending/transposing them to non-Aboriginal social work education programs.

Social work training encourages the idea of social workers as agents of change. In our rapidly changing North American society, "change" does not necessarily equate with "improvement" as we try to find ways to curtail misuse of new technologies (e.g., child pornography on the Internet). Similarly, social workers need prudence in making changes to social work approaches merely to include something "different." In speaking of using Aboriginal healing practices in a non-Aboriginal context, we need to avoid the romanticized view that somehow Aboriginal practices could not only effectively facilitate healing for non-Native people, but that such practices somehow would do so *more* effectively than non-Native practices. Mohawk teacher Gail Stacey Moore reminds us that each culture has its own healing practices, some of which have been lost or forgotten (personal communication). Perhaps a retrieval process on the part of non-Native communities and social work program developers would be in order before looking to "borrow" from elsewhere (personal interview).

For reasons mentioned in the introduction, many Aboriginal peoples frown upon non-Native individuals who conduct Native ceremonies, or even to participate in such. The opening quotation from Smith (1991), referring to the trivialization of the oppression of Aboriginal peoples, speaks of the last 500 years of suffering, which Smith and many others believe entitles Aboriginal peoples to keep traditional methods of healing for themselves—somewhat like a badge of honour, and one that no non-Native can claim to have earned. Additionally, (mis)appropriation of Native ceremonies by non-Aboriginal people may simply exemplify an attempt to satisfy the non-Native individual's need for the mystical. "New-Agers" may be tolerated, but not taken seriously. On the other hand, with regard to Healing Circles, non-Native individuals who demonstrate a genuine understanding and empathy for co-participants may be welcomed as a participant, or be invited to act as a Circle Keeper. Participation by non-Native individuals in Healing Circles may be acceptable to some Aboriginal peoples, only if the non-Native participants in question draw the line at (mis)appropriation. However, other Native peoples willingly invite non-Native people to conduct Circles. Indubitably, the answer to how a healing practice like the Healing Circle could be appropriately useful to non-Native social work would necessarily invoke the spirituality of the non-Native group involved. Such a transfer could include the use of traditional Aboriginal Medicines since some Aboriginal peoples do not believe in the *ownership* of such gifts from the Creator.

We question the cultural relevance of transposing most pre-colonial spiritual ceremonies, such as the Sun Dance and Sweat Lodge, from Aboriginal cultures to non-Aboriginal social work students and their clients. Some of these ceremonies take many years of self-preparation, and contribute to a lifelong healing journey. Teaching such healing methods as part of a social work education program for use by non-Aboriginal workers and their non-Aboriginal clients would seem ironic as a means for further developing a Eurocentric, colonial construction such as social work, unless its adoption would symbolize a major paradigm shift from systemic patriarchy. Certainly, workers, teachers, and students need to respect many spiritual Aboriginal peoples' strong belief that cross-contamination is a real possibility, i.e., that negativity can result if participants disrespect spiritual ceremonies. Aboriginal and non-Aboriginal social workers would benefit from understanding the purposes of healing practices, in order not to denigrate or avoid them in discussions of treatment with the Aboriginal client whose particular cultural background indicates their acceptable use. Aboriginal clients would also benefit if social workers had knowledge of pertinent resources within the community, such as the whereabouts of elders, Pipe Carriers, Native pastors, and Healing Circles.

In Quebec, fundamentalist Christianity drives the healing practices of large groups of Inuit and First Nations peoples, some of whom completely reject the idea of psychotherapeutic intervention in favour of a world view that places healing directly and firmly in the hands of God alone. Native and non-Native proponents of this view would have little use for social workers. However, effective psychotherapeutic intervention with Aboriginal peoples is holistic and client-oriented, with emphasis on the quality and closeness of the therapeutic relationship. Mainstream psychotherapy already shares this approach; therefore, expounding it within a social work education program would not be such a stretch. Teaching it, however, would necessarily involve the teacher's removal from the usual hierarchy of teacher-student relationships.

Healing for many Aboriginal individuals first begins with the acceptance of one's essential self as spiritually immutable. Open-mindedness around, if not belief in, concepts of spirituality would be necessary in teaching and practicing such healing activities. In a social work program, voluntary Healing Circles for students, whether Aboriginal or not, could address the necessary need for debriefing over personal issues that are touched upon in training, and could provide a model of worker wellness for the student to take into the workplace. If Aboriginal approaches and healing practices can offer hope in the face of seemingly overwhelming challenges, perhaps they may also offer hope to non-Aboriginal workers and their clients who are similarly overwhelmed.

Notes

1. Within the context of this paper, we use the terms "Aboriginal" and "Native" to refer to First Nations, Inuit, and Métis peoples.
2. The vision of North American indigenous elder, William Commanda, Algonquin, Keeper of the Seven Fires Prophecy Wampum Belt, reads: "This difficult age we live in was foreseen by spiritual visionaries across the world. My ancestors warned us about the years of struggle that would lead us to a crossroad and to the choices we would be called to make at the turn of the century. This vision was inscribed in the Seven Fires Prophecy Wampum Shell Belt in the late 1400s. The Seven Fires Prophecy holds a vision for a future where we: honour our relationship and responsibility to Mother Earth and all creation; celebrate our individual gifts and diversity; and still recognize and respect our place within the Circle of All Nations. The steps to this future are few: First, we look within, so we know ourselves best. We recognize, acknowledge, and forgive ourselves our shortcomings and any failure to achieve our best potential; we forgive others any hardship and pain they may have caused us and our communities—we trust that this energy will transform them spiritually; we recognize that our thoughts, words, and actions affect ourselves, Mother Earth, and all creation, and we embrace peace mindfully; we listen to our minds, but we trust our hearts above all. This path will lead us to love, sharing, respect, responsibility, compassion, healing, justice, and reconciliation. It is of crucial importance that the world respond immediately to the plight of the many oppressed by exploitation, social injustice, racism, and war; animate the human capacity for forgiveness, compassion, love, and reconciliation; and create a global synergy to ensure the improvement of the lives of all. We shall then light the Eighth Fire together and we will become 'A Circle of All Nations,'" August 2001. Info@circleofallnations.com.
3. The term "symbolic healing" used throughout this text indicates healing through symbolism.
4. Ceremonies like the Sweat Lodge were only decriminalized in 1951 by alteration to the Indian Act (S.C. 1951, c.29, Arts. 2–84, abrogated by s.123(2)).

5. "Traditional" in this context includes the idea of culture as adaptive and ever-changing, rather than immutable.

6. For example, tobacco, sweetgrass.

7. We recognize that this list of healing practices is not definitive.

8. Shape-shifters are believed to have the power to change at will from human to animal form. Belief in active present-day shape-shifters currently exists among some of the Kahnawake Mohawk, as well as in other groups (personal interviews).

9. It is worth noting that the Inuit participants interpreted the English word "meanings" as having a practical, active sense, i.e., it is in *doing* that we heal.

10. Some notable recent exceptions that resulted in actual violence include the events in Saskatoon of deliberate exposure of three Native individuals by police, causing the deaths of two of them (1990, 2000); during the Oka crisis (1990), when Mohawk elders, women, and children were stoned by non-Native people; at Ipperwash, where police shot Dudley George (1995); and at the Burnt Church standoff, where Native and non-Native fishermen clashed (2000).

11. The Sixties Scoop refers to that period when "well-meaning" social workers removed thousands of Aboriginal children from their families and placed them in non-Native homes.

12. "Inuit" is Inuktitut for "the people."

13. For a bona fide Medicine person to receive monetary compensation for his or her spiritual work is considered absolutely appropriate in this day and age when such a person cannot rely on community support to take care of his or her needs, as was the custom in the past.

14. These statements have been drawn from Ms. Garwood's clinical practice, and from various interactions with co-workers.

15. Otherwise referred to as the Talking Circle or Sharing Circle.

16. The Smudge bowl and its burning contents are offered to participants to move the smoke over their bodies in a ritual of cleansing and prayer. During the Smudging there may be drumming, singing, or other kinds of prayer.

17. Often the Circle Keeper will remind the women in the group that any of them who are "on their moon," i.e., menstruating, should stand back from the Circle during the cleansing. Tradition for some Nations dictates that menstruating women are not in need of extra cleansing, and that menstruation brings with it a powerful force that could be disruptive to others. Similarly, some believe that menstruating women could be more vulnerable to negative energy from others. For this reason too, in accordance with the beliefs of some, women do not touch sacred objects or may not even take part in ceremonies at this time.

18. A Talking Stick may be carved specially for Healing Circles, and takes diverse forms.

19. Direction depends on the Nation of that particular group, or Circle Keeper, if the group is of mixed Nations.

20. A man might walk into the bush and choose a particular tree from which to pull a section of bark. He would then revisit the tree on subsequent occasions to look at the healing wound as a visual confirmation of his own psychic healing (Jefferson, 1994).

21. A grieving family might take many months to prepare the gifts for a Potlatch (Give-Away Ceremony) in honour of the departed as part of the Stickdance. When they had worked on the artifacts necessary for the Give Away, they would erect a decorated pole around which they would dance for many hours. Other community members would join in, and a feast of traditional food would be shared (Jefferson, 1994).

22. The following is an eyewitness account of a Letting-Go Ceremony, conducted for a victimizer in the Quebec bush. The man had served a penitentiary sentence for manslaughter, but had not been able to process his grief over the losses he had caused and incurred after his release. An intelligent man, his inability to contribute to his community because of his prolonged grief represented a great loss for his family and for community wellness. He understood the ceremony and voluntarily agreed to participate.

   The men were experiencing intense heat, despite being shaded on one side by ancient pine trees and, on the other, by emerald fronds of tall ferns. They were already sweating profusely. One man, a healer, unravelled a long coil of thick rope and tied a large marker stone to its central point. The stone lay heavy in the centre, while the rope stretched to the North and South. After some discussion, four men took the southern end of the rope, while one lone man (the subject of the ceremony) took a stance on the northern side, wrapping his end of the rope around his waist and taking the strain over his shoulder. For a few minutes none moved. There was the sound of the low murmuring voice of the healer, guiding the man who faced his grief, and then the struggle began. As the physical effort increased, the lone man's breath began to quicken. Although he was one against four, his strength seemed magnified by the power of his long-suppressed sadness, frustration, self-hatred, and anger. Dark patches of sweat appeared down the back of his white vest, his arms gleaming. Tears and sweat poured down his face. Sounds began to emerge from his throat like the cracking of a tree when it falls. The men on the other end took the strain; felt the strain run through their own bodies. In feeling his grief, they too appeared to begin to feel their own. They pulled even harder in the opposite direction, eyes fixed on an animal skull, the symbol of endings and new beginnings, which had been placed in front of them on the ground. The lone man had resolutely dug his heels into the earth, but began to struggle against the force pulling from behind him. He dropped to one knee, and the healer immediately motioned to the other men to counterbalance, but not pull. They waited patiently while he sucked in his breath and tried to control the heaving in his chest and stomach. Then with the rope over his shoulder, he was up on his feet again, running desperately into the space before him, and yelling the name of the victim of his crime of passion. The rope caught him and stopped him as he lunged, and he sank to the ground again. Through his choking grief, he begged forgiveness from the spirit of his victim. After nearly an hour, he seemed to allow himself to re-experience his drunken jealous rage, the death, his culpability, the awful awareness of his dreadful act. When the struggle had finished with the stone lying beside the skull, the man's negative energy seemed to have emptied out. He walked out of the bush to a nearby lake, where he immersed himself in the water. He rose and fell through the dark green surface of reflected pine trees like a salmon swimming upstream. (A version of this account first appeared in Garwood, 1997.)

23. Montreal region.

24. We repeat the lists here as a practical guide, since these items become useful as target indicators for healer, institution agent, and participant as to the existence of an active healing process.

Institutional List
- elimination of drugs—abstinence
- observed/reported changes in anti-social attitudes and behaviours
- social shift in peer associations
- increase in familial affection
- increase in self-control through interiorization of locus of control, self-reliance, and self-management
- release of lying, stealing, aggression tendencies
- granting of parole
- completion of programs
- reduction in swearing and cursing
- attitudinal and behavioural shifts observable on the ranges, e.g., diminishment and/or cessation of bullying, muscling, fighting, verbal abuse
- post-release recidivism (although this is not a direct indicator of change along the way)

Healer List
- degree of participation in sweats and other ceremonies and circles
- Native Brotherhood involvement
- regular talks with Elders
- confiding completely in healers/Elders

- feeling not judged for one's feelings and desires
- development of a sense of sacredness/holiness of body as requiring respect of one's own body and the body of others
- emergent signs of forgiveness of self, of Creator, of others
- praying for those harmed
- first touching, shaking hands with each other, giving hugs, sharing innermost feelings
- becoming motivated to take the non-Aboriginal programs, and/or further Native-related programs (Couture, 1996, pp. 17–19)

MIKE PATTEN

Untitled frame from Mike Patten's *Lost Thoughts* series (2006). We have chosen Patten's images to represent the experience of many Aboriginal students struggling with a sense of lost personal identity. In non-Native educational establishments, Aboriginal people are confronted with conflicts of world view. Personal toxic shame contributes to the denigration of Aboriginal perceptions. Fragments of Aboriginal thought appear as disjointed reflections of traditional patterns. There is a stark contrast between Patten's self-expression and that of the Elder Agnes McKenzie Carriere, whose focused and methodical beadwork appears at the end of this chapter.

"Mike Patten's art relates to the notion of self-censorship…. Patten is in the habit of writing personal notes into his hand-held computer using his stylus pen. He then revises his electronic journal and erases personal or embarrassing thoughts, again with the wave of the tiny stylus wand. Several hundred of these pages are projected briefly on a gallery wall. The words become quite abstract, intriguing clusters of black fragments that look like something viewed through a microscope" (Lehmann, 2006).

CHAPTER 12

Walk a Mile in Social Work Shoes:
The One on the Right Is a Moccasin and the Left Is a Sensible Flat: Aboriginal Cross-cultural Social Work Education

Anne Acco and Nicki Garwood

The programs of Aboriginal social work education described in this book exemplify cross-cultural social work at its most challenging. We are faced with the conundrum of how best to share information in a balanced way, benefiting students and teachers alike, regardless of cultural background. Ideally, all involved come together to better themselves and the people with whom they interact. This process steps out of the Euro-Canadian academic hierarchical model in which teachers educate/lead, and students learn/follow, and in which the latter are then evaluated by the former for their ability to reproduce what they have learned. For example, in the McGill Aboriginal Certificate Program, we observe the need for an exchange of roles between leaders and followers, and the need to acknowledge that for many Aboriginal peoples, "education" means self-awareness and healing. In effect, the moccasin could represent the original sensible flat.

Actively acknowledging the needs of both teachers and students requires delicate balancing, in order to achieve effective exchange at a holistic level. We are not in competition for what is "right," but are exploring healing and consensus, regardless of cultural background. Whenever cultural mix exists, human beings naturally struggle to find the best and the seemingly non-relinquishable aspects of their own particular culture to validate their own values and particular existence, but eventually we must adapt or be set aside since culture cannot stagnate. Through this process of attrition emerge cultural change and the formation of "new traditions," which encourage psychic growth and the reduction of cultural ego. Since social work education, by definition, responds to human growth, it has the challenge of justifying itself through its ability to be responsive to multiculturalism in the classroom. The real challenge comes in identifying differences of perception and world views, and distinguishing them from difference in individual personalities, innate racism, and prejudice.

Personal and systemic prejudice both play a part in the struggle to reach consensus of direction in Aboriginal education. In his survey of the needs for social workers in Aboriginal communities in Canada, Fiddler (2000) identifies the present challenges in Aboriginal social work issues and observes that "systemic racism is perceived to be increasingly contributing to the inequalities, disparities and gaps in the level of funding and scope of social programs and services available to Aboriginal communities in comparison to the mainstream institutions ..." (p. 173).

Prejudices of both Aboriginal and non-Aboriginal individuals, organizations, and government systems combine with systemic racism in defining the *raison d'être* of Aboriginal social workers. Inevitably, the education of those social workers becomes key in helping to elaborate the function of social work within an Aboriginal environment. In order for learning to be reciprocal, courses particularly designed for Aboriginal students require both students and teachers, whether Aboriginal or non-Aboriginal, to address their own prejudices about themselves and about the "otherness" of those of a different culture. This view assumes that students and teachers have something to share with each other, i.e., information that may not be mutual to both collectivities, but could contribute to learning on both sides. As Freire (2003) noted, vigilance is necessary in identifying the barriers to such a reciprocal process, where, ideally, the roles of student and teacher merge.

In the face of systemic prejudice, no matter how professionally skilled one might be, inequalities stand in the way of knowledge transference, acquisition, development, implementation, and client satisfaction. Much of this inequality lies within the ongoing effects of a colonialism that relegated Aboriginal peoples to a tertiary position within society. Aboriginal peoples speak of "Native Pride" in the same way that homosexuals speak of "Gay Pride," i.e., as a way of self-affirmation in the face of prejudice. Prejudice is multifaceted: A Mohawk youth once said, "I don't have to wear moccasins to be Indian." Although his statement appeared to promote the notion of a modern Native individual, proud of his culture and sure of his self-identity, nothing could have been further from his truth. He was reacting at a time when the psychic bruises of the Oka crisis of 1990 were still fresh in his mind and in that of all the Mohawk people.[1] He was dealing with a two-pronged dilemma in identifying himself at all as being Native in any outward way,[2] first, because of the hatred that had reigned unchecked as rocks were thrown at children and elders of Kahnawake by the non-Native local population during the crisis and, second, because of the toxic shame that he had inherited from years of multigenerational abuse, both from within the Aboriginal collectivity and from without.

In order to respect one's own culture and that of others, we must first accept ourselves as human beings, so that we can then become part of the creative expression of any particular group of people or culture. The youth's comment was an expression of his own prejudice against himself as an Aboriginal individual; against his problem-ridden family; and against the collective toxic shame shared by the people of Kahnawake. In order to bridge the gap between mainstream social work education programs and the Aboriginal reality, courses need to prepare graduates from both the mainstream and Aboriginal programs to act as supporters and advocates for the Aboriginal clientele they may serve. They also need to be prepared to counteract racism and prejudice wherever they find it.

An Official Overview of the Miles to Come

For many individuals and groups, years of struggle against assimilation have obfuscated what it means to be valued as an Aboriginal person. The Mohawk individual mentioned above had to deal with the fact of being a visible minority, attempting from time to time[3] to deal with the non-Native majority. The lack of self-identity as an Aboriginal individual has been exacerbated by systemic prejudice in health, education, and justice, which the mainstream majority controls.[4]

In order to re-establish self-respect, and a realistic view of "Self" within Canadian society, Aboriginal peoples have begun to engage actively in community-supported healing, with the proactive support of non-Aboriginal mainstream systems. However, without a strong sense of "Self," approaching these systems can be hugely daunting for an individual uncertain of himself and his place in society (Bruyere, 1998). As Fiddler (2000) stated, social work has a responsibility to advocate for equity of treatment for our First Peoples, and to identify when world views clash to the detriment of the health of Aboriginal individuals, families, and communities. His survey indicates that there has been an increase in the employment of Aboriginal social workers, and that "positive trends towards increased Aboriginal control and delivery of programs and services ..." are improving "the quality and standards of life in Aboriginal communities ..." (Fiddler, 2000, p. 173). However, the question remains as to how much personal prejudices on both sides are interfering with, and holding back, these trends. Those who work within the penitentiaries, for example, know that regardless of policy makers, within the prison system it is the guards who run the show. Similarly, in the welfare system, it is the worker at the front desk who tells a homeless urban Aboriginal person that he is not eligible for welfare because he is Indian and therefore already well enough taken care of, according to several personal accounts. Of course, Aboriginal peoples are entitled to complain about this kind of ignorant prejudice, but it takes a kind of courage and self-confidence that many Native individuals lack.

In order to achieve personal wellness, first we need to have the intention of heading for a goal, and then, despite the ensuing chaos of the holistic work required, have the power to keep our eye on the target, i.e., the creativity of personal growth. This is also true for families and communities. Social work has relevance in clarifying the natural chaos through eliciting priorities and acting as a guide, particularly in cross-cultural work at the individual and social levels, and reducing the incidence of prejudicial actions. This may seem to be self-evident, and we may believe that the social work profession has taken great strides in reducing the gap between the mainstream systems and those of the founding Nations. However, the challenge is ongoing on a daily basis for many urban and rural Aboriginal peoples, and for the Native and non-Native social workers who advocate for them.

We Are All Prejudiced Because the Shoe Is Always on the Other Foot

The richness of human society necessarily assures that there will be many different world views. An exasperated probation officer, having interviewed a bemused Inuk client about his residency condition of staying in a halfway house in Montreal for at least six months, sighed deeply and pronounced, "They just don't understand, do they?" He did not seem to appreciate the explanation given by the social worker in residence that he (i.e., the Inuk in question) certainly did understand, but that they (i.e., other Inuit in the same predicament) just did not *agree* with being kept in a foreign environment in an urban setting for an indeterminate amount of time. It was not long after that exchange when another probation officer, taking a more "Freudian" approach with the same client, sat silently waiting for the Inuk to share his thoughts with him. Not receiving anything from the ensuing void in communication, the probation officer left, muttering about the client's lack of co-operation. As the government official retreated, the client asked with genuine concern, "Why wasn't he talking? Is he sick?"

Fortuitously, since that time, the Quebec provincial government has supported the opening of an Inuit halfway house in Nunavik, where Inuit men who are serious about their recovery choose to reside. Makitautik Community Residential Centre seems like the answer to compromise, especially when one walks in and is invited to share the most recent catch of char or ptarmigan spread out on the floor. The game has come from the on-land program that teaches traditional values to young men who have spent time in the provincial prisons. But, in the middle of winter or summer, all the windows are open in this centrally heated, air-conditioned environment. The reason for the fresh air is that, with the windows closed, the place swelters in winter and freezes in summer because the controls are in Montreal 1,000 miles away! It would appear as if the Inuit management cannot be trusted to be judicious—an example of how subtle prejudice can be. However, we have come some way from the 1980s, when bureaucrats sent new housing to the Innu of Davis Inlet that was fully equipped with baths and kitchen sinks; this was in spite of the fact that the only house boasting running water was that of the minister. Some residents adapted, and erected their tents inside as a cultural compromise. Meanwhile, the general poverty of the Innu and their parlous social problems continue with minimal human resources and no means of solving the conundrum of how a community wracked with social problems could produce Native (i.e., Aboriginal and native to the community) social workers without the input of non-Aboriginal/non-Innu educators.

Ironically, the mainstream justice system, with its mandate to legislate the regulation of prejudice, continues with its own struggles to deal with the Aboriginal reality. Finding equity for Aboriginal offenders is an ongoing battle that demands a response from the social work profession in advocacy for both victims of crime and offenders. In a Quebec courthouse in 1997, a young Mohawk before the court on a minor charge asked to be sent to a treatment program for his alcohol abuse. Although he had been instructed to arrive at the court at 9:00 a.m., he waited all day for the case to be called, along with several community workers and his parents; this is not such an unusual wait in our overloaded system. However, shortly before the end of the day, the case was called and immediately postponed, with a verbal message from the Crown prosecutor that he had seen enough Indians [*sic*] already; that in any case, treatment programs didn't work for them; and if he were pressured into being present in the case, he would ask for the strongest possible sentence. The Aboriginal workers simply shrugged their shoulders and explained to the non-Native social worker present that they were not angry because "This is how it is." The non-Native social worker became the advocate in this case, sending a letter of complaint to the minister of justice, and receiving a reasonable reply, as observed by one of the authors of this chapter, Nicki Garwood.

However, in 1999, the Supreme Court decided that there were strong mitigating circumstances for offences committed by Aboriginal individuals who had attended residential school (Gladue Decision, 1999), the inference being that the circumstances for an Aboriginal offender are "unique." The subsequent law reform, section 718.2(e), stipulates that judges use restraint in imprisoning Aboriginal offenders, and that alternative sentences be given priority. A lenient sentence, such as house arrest, for an Aboriginal person living in a large urban environment seems to comply with the spirit of the law. House arrest for an urban Aboriginal sex offender might bring out the "Not in My Backyard" groups, but does not present a significant danger to the neighbourhood, since statistics show that most Aboriginal sex offenders offend against other Aboriginal peoples and not against non-Natives (Bonspiel, 2006). However, when it comes to Aboriginal sex offenders living in small Aboriginal communities, a sentence of house arrest makes very little sense for the offender, the victim, or the community, where often no infrastructure exists to back it up. Offenders use regular day passes, attend social events, and shop at the local store where they may encounter their victims. The result is dissatisfied family members of victims, who want to take matters into their own hands; other victims who do not disclose because they believe "nothing will be done," leaving victimizers free to reoffend; and victims who feel ignored or, worse, alienated as "trouble makers" (Bonspiel, 2006). Yet, at the time of writing, these are the kinds of sentences being handed down for Aboriginal pedophiles and other sex offenders in such places as Mistissini, Quebec, even though treatment resources for the victims and offenders are sparse, and community workers remain relatively untrained to deal with the situation. Hollow Water, Manitoba, set the stage for providing an infrastructure that addresses the needs of all those involved in lateral abuse (Hollow Water, 1993), and did so with the full co-operation of their provincial justice system. Information about their successes has been disseminated widely through gatherings and media, and other communities have taken up the challenge for self-healing. However, legislation has no teeth unless those in the mainstream system have the political will to contribute to Aboriginal community healing, first, by recognizing that the Aboriginal collectivity is not comprised of a homogeneous *lumpen* proletariat that all legislation will fit and, second, by recognizing that Aboriginal social work education and the social workers who emerge from those programs form an integral part of actual implemented change through their role as advocates whether they are Native or non-Native.

When the urban family court in Montreal considers the situation of Aboriginal clients with child protection and custody issues, it benefits from the presence of a cultural broker. Brokerage facilitates mutual understanding. Unfortunately, where cultural anomalies exist, lawyers can take advantage of cultural difference merely to win a case, rather than to work solely in the interest of the child. They can do this by quoting cultural differences as if those differences are *reasons* for not considering different world views; e.g., "Living in the [named] community is more dangerous than living in Montreal ...," a reason cited for giving custody to a Montreal-based parent over his community-living partner, and also sometimes given as a reason by parole boards for not returning Aboriginal offenders to their home communities upon release. In whose view might it be more dangerous? Such statements vilify Aboriginal community living and encourage an integrationist approach. Many Aboriginal clients are unaware that child-protection cases can be transferred to protection agencies in the home community when that agency expresses an interest in taking on the case management. Instead, Aboriginal parents in particular spend many months trying to figure out a system that appears to deprive them of all parental responsibility by placing the children in foster care with limited access, while at the same time placing conditions on them to behave as if the children were still in their custody.

Confusion also arises concerning Inuit adoptions. In the North, sometimes in situations where the birth mother is not able to take care of the child, or where another family member has few or no children of her own, it is still common for children to be given over for adoption at birth to an extended family member, who is then recognized as the child's mother. Baptismal certificates are often the only proof of such adoptions. Although these arrangements are well understood in the North, lawyers in the South can use such situations to prolong court proceedings to their advantage. In these kinds of circumstances, the presence of a professional social worker as a cultural broker facilitates the reduction of prejudicial action. The social work profession needs recognition as an educational tool for the mainstream systems whether the worker is Native or non-Native, and education programs need to emphasize the importance of the social worker's role in advocating for Aboriginal peoples who feel powerless in mainstream society.

Waiting for the Other Shoe to Drop

Residential schooling contributes to the difficulties that many Aboriginal adult survivors have in integrating into post-secondary mainstream education. Those challenges have four distinct roots. First, "schooling" in most residential institutions related more to the use of the word as applied to fish than to children. Children were gathered into institutions far from their homes, and frequently (although not always) offered a low standard of education in a second language. Second, since academic standards were mostly kept low, entering post-secondary education required enormous effort for many to catch up with their non-Native peers. Third, post-traumatic stress interferes with many survivors' ability to simply *be* in the classroom due to the abuses that they suffered. Fourth, Native world views differ greatly from those of the hierarchical, patriarchal mainstream majority, requiring copious amounts of self-assertion and self-confidence on the part of Native students wishing to have their views respected, heard, and understood in a post-secondary classroom (Canada, 1996a; Chansonneuve, 2005).

But prejudice runs deep on both sides. The worst kind of insult from one First Nations individual about another can be, "Red Apple!" i.e., having red skin, but essentially being full of White ideas and White education, rather than adhering to an Aboriginal cultural heritage. Aboriginal peoples educated within the mainstream system risk being labelled as "Red Apples," and thus find themselves alienated from the very people they have educated themselves to help. The Sixties Scoop[5] and residential schooling (Bennett, Blackstock & De La Ronde, 2005) contributed in a major way to the formation of such prejudice, and to the creation of divisions within communities between those who were educated in residential or mainstream schools and those who were not. For example, in the early 1960s, the Canadian federal government experimented with Inuit children who had been carefully selected for their high intellect, removing them to schools in Churchill and Ottawa. Well-known Inuk chronicler, Zebedee Nungak, of Kangirsuk, Nunavik, was one of those children. He reports that these self-described "experiments" produced a large group of youth, well-educated academically, who returned to their home communities from the big city having lost the survival skills of hunting and fishing, and were alienated from those who did not have a *Qallunaat* (White) education. They were greatly ridiculed for their lack of useful survival skills by members of the community who had stayed home (Nungak, 2000).

Abuse from residential schools reverberates throughout the communities to this day as ex-students achieve powerful positions in the non-Native-imposed, governmental community structures, e.g., Band Council positions, which require more than a modicum of literacy; a broad comprehension of the English language, as well as non-Native world views and value systems; and a working knowledge of law. Although many First Nation Band Council members hold office for the betterment of their communities, they do wield, and sometimes misuse, power in the communities to the detriment of community health and healing (Fiddler, 2000; Teichroeb, 1997). This need for negative power emanates from being victims of the destructive power of physical, mental, sexual, and emotional abuse experienced by countless Aboriginal individuals who survived residential schooling. For many survivors, turning tragedy into triumph has meant repeating the cycle through lateral violence within their home communities (Mussell, 2005). Prejudicial power acts by way of nepotism, sexual and physical abuse, power brokerage, and drug trafficking, with the larger families having the edge in voting. Multigenerational abuse allows the pattern to continue.

Leave Your Boots Outside

As described in the preceding chapters on the McGill Certificate Program in Aboriginal Social Work Practice, in particular chapters 4, 5, and 10, within the classroom of this program can be found the principles of reducing the barriers of prejudice constructed by both teachers and students. Reduction in these prejudicial barriers contributes to a reduction in systemic racism and prejudice. These principles may be summarized as follows:

1. Respect the students' ability to learn new skills, techniques, and strategies, and provide them with the tools to adapt methods to resonate with their own particular culture.

2. Acknowledge the expertise of both the designated teachers and their students.
3. Ensure an atmosphere that gives the students a sense of support, belonging, and significance in the process of learning.
4. Encourage the understanding of the importance of verbal and written communication skills to promote one's point of view.
5. Educate administrators about Aboriginal ways and means of life.
6. Give legitimacy to mutual benefit, reciprocal learning acquisition, i.e., for both designated teachers and students, and acknowledge that this process leads to healing and growth for the students.
7. Acknowledge that Aboriginal teachers act as valuable conduits between their non-Aboriginal colleagues and the students, facilitating a fast free-flow of information while respecting their colleagues' knowledge base.
8. Acknowledge that once students acquire social work skills, they will take up any of a variety of roles, and could expect advancement in their chosen field.
9. Acknowledge the multiculturalism among Aboriginal students, and encourage the formulation of individual solid cultural identity.
10. Encourage the students to consider further education.
11. Acknowledge the reality of difference of capacity and pace for learning among individuals, but underline all positive progress in individual development.
12. Acknowledge the progress achieved in overcoming mainstream system barriers.

Achievement of these 12 points will lead to taking down the barriers to an authentic "education" for Aboriginal peoples.

Unfortunately, due to their necessarily colonial approach to acquiring land and natural resources through assimilation of Aboriginal populations into the mainstream, it has never been in the interest of colonial governments to strengthen the health of Aboriginal communities. Historically, suppression of a people through suppression of education has proved to be effective for long periods of time (e.g., outlawing teaching slaves to read in the southern states). Echoes of that suppression currently exist in the lack of public libraries in Aboriginal communities in Quebec.[6] As well as books, well-funded public libraries provide journals, magazines, Internet access, music, videos, and meeting places to gather. They are portals to the larger world and to international connections. They are also a way of promoting cultural continuity and a sharing of tradition. Similarly, providing culturally appropriate environments for education, both in terms of curriculum and classroom, has been a low priority for governments.[7]

The challenge has been well described by Archibald (2006) in her report on the colonization, decolonization, and healing among indigenous peoples in Canada, Australia, New Zealand, and Greenland. She writes that "the central lesson learned about promising healing practices is the immense value and efficacy of incorporating history and culture into holistic programs based on Indigenous values and worldliness" (Archibald, 2006, p. viii). We can identify a genuine post-colonial movement of culturally appropriate programming for Aboriginal education in the First Nations Adult and Higher Education Consortium Social Work Task Force

(FNAHEC) in Alberta. This organization pools cross-cultural Aboriginal talent to provide a culturally appropriate academic learning environment. As an indigenous body, FNAHEC places emphasis on affirming the capacity for healing and sharing between Aboriginal workers and their community members, and encouraging the use of Aboriginal ways and language to promote well-being (Zapf et al., 2003). The experience of FNAHEC seems to justify the structure of the learning environment of the McGill Certificate Program, in as much as the course work and space to learn responded to the Aboriginal collectivity of the students. Education as healing takes place in a collaborative synthesis of beliefs and value systems.

Traditionally, the efforts of Medicine people (whose role was often that of teacher) recognized the organism and dynamism of the individual, using a set of methods exploring the aptitude of the mind, the whole body systems, the state of spirit, and the attitude of heart. Certain conditions needed and still need to exist for effective rebalancing to take place, i.e., compassion for the one who suffers; knowledge of the body systems; insight into the relationship between the body systems and the environment; recognition of the need to harmonize internal and external relationships; understanding of cause and effect; purification; an atmosphere of trust; and informality of relationships and sharing, while maintaining the protocols of symbolic healing. All of these conditions speak of the needs of Aboriginal education.

Reviving the Sole/Soul of Aboriginal Education as Healing

Even our favourite shoes get worn down by overuse, moccasins or not. We recognize the need for repair when we feel it. So too, each Aboriginal community knows exactly how it may be failing to thrive. The factors of breakdown may include the transition from one way of life to another by the forces of nature, economy, or attempts to control. Old ways and familiar scenery are gone and replaced by new languages of communication and alien world views. Social growth requires facilitation according to the present situation *in relation to* the past. Social workers need to see the whol(istic) picture, and therefore need to learn the holistic landscape. Their attitude needs to be that of "the informed not knower" (Dean, 2003; Laird, 1998). Remembering becomes a necessity for each community in addressing present social ills. Aboriginal social work education needs flexibility to address the "how" of approach in all its aspects, as well as the "what" of community realities, as students find the self-confidence to adapt their synthesized learning to the particularities of their eventual practice.

Native leaders are working very hard to give hope to their youth, a population that is growing very rapidly. As revealed in several chapters of this book (chapters 5, 6, and 10), what happened in the learning is very sobering. People were willing to reveal their brokenness and sorrow, yet decided to forge ahead and learn how to heal. There is an art to all of that—one of acceptance of the causes and effects of the past wrongs and reaching out to accept Aboriginal peoples as they are at the moment. "The lives of Aboriginal individuals are like frosted breath in an early spring morning" (Acco, 2006); we know that as human beings we must tread softly regardless of which shoes we are wearing.

Notes

1. For a description of the Oka crisis, please see note 1 in Chapter 5
2. Although the youth had the classic look of a dark-haired, dark-eyed, dark-skinned "Indian" as portrayed in the movies, he could easily have been mistaken for a Spanish or Chilean immigrant. For him, wearing any artifact that might identify him as North American Aboriginal, let alone Mohawk, was an anathema.
3. More than 15 years after the Oka crisis, there are still many community members in Kahnawake who become anxious at the idea of crossing onto the Island of Montreal, just a few kilometres away.
4. The Cree of James Bay and the Mohawk of Kahnawake are exceptions in Quebec, where negotiations have taken place over some aspects of health, justice, and education.
5. The Sixties Scoop describes a period of time during the 1960s when well-meaning, but misguided, non-Native social services removed thousands of Aboriginal children from their homes and communities and placed them with non-Native adoptive parents. These actions were taken as social services judged thousands of Aboriginal parents to be neglectful and abusive. Residential school syndrome had not yet been recognized. However, in many cases, poverty was the only issue (Bennett, Blackstock & De La Ronde, 2005; Fournier & Crey, 1997).
6. Kahnawake is an exception to this rule in Quebec, but only because of the sterling efforts of a young Mohawk volunteer.
7. However, at the time of writing, the Quebec Liberal government has announced the investment of $3.8 million in the Université du Québec en Abitibi-Témiscamingue for the construction of a First Nations education building in Val d'Or in northern Quebec.

Beadwork moccasin by Agnes McKenzie Carriere (1995–2003), Cree

References

Aboriginal Healing Foundation. (2003). *Aboriginal domestic violence in Canada.* Ottawa: Aboriginal Healing Foundation.

Aboriginal Healing Foundation. (2004). *Historical trauma and Aboriginal healing.* Ottawa: Aboriginal Healing Foundation.

Aboriginal Justice Learning Network. (1997). *Building community justice partnerships: Community peacemaking circles,* ed. Barry Stuart. Ottawa: Minister of Justice and Attorney General of Canada.

Absolon, K. (1993). *Healing as practice: Teaching from the medicine wheel.* Commissioned paper for the WUNSKA network, The Canadian Schools of Social Work. Unpublished manuscript.

Acco, A. (2006). *Aboriginal social work education.* Unpublished manuscript.

Alcoze, T., & Mawhiney, A. (1988). *Returning home: A report on a community-based Native human services project.* Sudbury: Laurentian University Press.

American Humane Association. (1996). Family group decision-making: Its potential contributions to child welfare reform. *The Practice and Promise of Family Group Decision-Making, 12*(3), 1.

Antone, B., & Hill, D. (1990). *Traditional healing: Helping our people lift their burdens.* London: Tribal Sovereign Associates.

Anzaldua, G. (2002). (Un)natural bridges, (un)safe spaces. In G. Anzaldua & A. Keating (Eds.), *This bridge we call home: Radical visions for transformation* (pp. 1–15). New York: Routledge.

Apple, M. (1989). Social crisis and curriculum accords. *Educational Theory, 38*(2), 191–201.

Archibald, L. (2006). *Decolonization and healing: Indigenous experiences in the United States, New Zealand, Australia, and Greenland.* Ottawa: Aboriginal Healing Foundation.

Armstrong, R., Kennedy, J., & Oberle, P.R. (1990). *University of education and economic well-being: Indian achievement and prospects.* Ottawa: Indian and Northern Affairs Canada.

Assembly of First Nations. (1994). *Breaking the silence: An interpretive study of residential school impact and healing as illustrated by the stories of First Nation individuals.* Ottawa: Assembly of First Nations.

Ayala, J., & Weiden, T. (2003). *The University of Calgary BSW Access Program: The first five years—A progress report.* Calgary: University of Calgary Faculty of Social Work Centre for Social Work Research and Development.

Bannerji, H. (1991). But who speaks for us? Experience and agency in conventional feminist paradigms. In H. Bannerji et al. (Eds.), *The university as a site of feminist struggles* (pp. 67–107). Toronto: Women's Press.

Barden, J., & Boyer, P. (1993). Ways of knowing: Extending the boundaries of scholarship. *Tribal College Journal of American Indian Higher Education, 4*(3), 12–15.

Barnhardt, R. (1991). Higher education in the fourth world: Indigenous people take control. *Canadian Journal of Native Education, 18*(2), 199–231.

Bastien, B. (2004). *Blackfoot ways of knowing: The world view of the Siksikaitsitapi.* Calgary: University of Calgary Press.

Battiste, M. (1998). Enabling the autumn seed: Toward a decolonized approach to Aboriginal knowledge, language, and education. *Canadian Journal of Native Education, 22*(1), 16–27. Retrieved August 8, 2006, from http://mrc.uccb.ns.ca/battiste1.html

Battiste, M., Bell, L., & Findlay, L.M. (2002). Decolonizing education in Canadian universities: An interdisciplinary, indigenous research project. *Canadian Journal of Native Education, 26*(2), 82–95.

Beaulieu, B. (1993). A new vision. In K. Feehan & D. Hannis (Eds.), *From strength to strength: Social work education and Aboriginal people* (pp. 195–196). Edmonton: Grant MacEwan Community College.

Begg, A.C., & Begg, N.C. (1980). *The world of John Boultbee.* Auckland: Whitcoulls.

Bennett, M., Blackstock, C., & De La Ronde, R. (2005). *A literature review and annotated bibliography on aspects of Aboriginal child welfare in Canada* (2nd ed.). Winnipeg: First Nations Research Site of the Centre of Excellence for Child Welfare and the First Nations Child & Family Caring Society of Canada.

Benson, G.F. (1991). *Developing crime prevention strategies in Aboriginal communities.* Ottawa: Solicitor General, Ministry Secretariat.

Bodor, R., & Zapf, M.K. (2002). The learning circle: A new model of rural social work education in Canada. *Rural Social Work, 7*(2), 4–14.

Bonspiel, Steve. (2006). Does the punishment fit the crime? *The Nation, 13*(16), 10–23.

Borg, D., Delaney, R., & Sellick, M. (1997). Traditional healing practices: Contextual patterning strategies for northern social work practice with First Nation communities. In K. Brownlee, R. Delaney & J.R. Graham (Eds.), *Strategies for northern social work practice* (pp. 129–141). Thunder Bay: Lakehead University Centre for Northern Studies.

Brant, C. (1982). *Native ethics and principles.* Text of an address to the workshop organized by the Union of Nova Scotia Indians and the Maritime School of Social Work. Retrieved from http://mrc.uccb.ns.ca/brant.html.

Brant, C. (1985). *Suicide in the North American Indian.* Ste-Foy, QC: Canadian Psychiatric Association.

Brant, C. (1990). Native ethics and rules of behaviour. *Canadian Journal of Psychiatry, 35,* 534–539.

Briggs, J.L. (2000). Conflict management in a modern Inuit community. In P.P. Schweitzer, M. Biesele & R.K. Hitchcock (Eds.), *Hunters and gatherers in the modern world: Conflict, resistance, and self-determination* (pp. 110–124). Oxford: Berghahn Books.

Brown, L.A. (1992). Social work education for Aboriginal communities. *The Canadian Journal of Higher Education, 22*(3), 46–56.

Bruyere, G. (1998). Living in another man's house: Supporting Aboriginal learners in social work education. *Canadian Social Work Review, 15*(2), 169–176.

Bruyere, G. (1999). The decolonization wheel: An Aboriginal perspective on social work practice with Aboriginal peoples. In R. Delaney, K. Brownlee & M. Sellick (Eds.), *Social work in rural and northern communities* (pp. 170–181). Thunder Bay: Lakehead University Centre for Northern Studies.

Bruyere, G. (2007). Picking up what was left by the trail: The emerging spirit of Aboriginal education in Canada. In J. Coates, M. Gray & M. Yellowbird (Eds.), *Indigenous social work around the world: Towards culturally relevant education and practice* (pp. 408–430). London: Ashgate.

Bullis, R.K. (1996). *Spirituality in social work practice*. Washington: Taylor & Francis.

Burford, G., Pennell, J., & MacLeod, S. (1995). *Family group decision-making project*. St. John's: Memorial University of Newfoundland.

Cairns, T., Fulcher, L., Kereopa, H., Nia Nia, P., & Tait-Rolleston, W. (1998). Nga pari karangaranga o puao-te-ata-tu: Towards a culturally responsive education and training for social workers in New Zealand. *Canadian Social Work Review, 15*(2), 145–167.

Callahan, M., & Wharf, B. (1989). Distance education in social work in Canada. *Journal of Distance Education, 4*(2), 63–80.

Canada. (1867). The Constitution Act, 1867 (UK), 30 & 31 Victoria, c. 3.

Canada. (1985). Indian Act, RSC 1985, c. I-5, ss.10(a), 12, 17–20.

Canada. (1996a). Royal Commission on Aboriginal peoples. *Report of the Royal Commission on Aboriginal peoples: Looking forward, looking back* (vol. 1), (pp. 333–386). Ottawa: Canada Communications Group Publishing.

Canada. (1996b). Royal Commission on Aboriginal peoples. *Report of the Royal Commission on Aboriginal peoples: Reconstructing the relationship* (vol. 2). Ottawa: Minister of Supply and Services.

Canada. (1996c). Royal Commission on Aboriginal peoples. *Report of the Royal Commission on Aboriginal peoples: Gathering strength* (vol. 3). Ottawa: Minister of Supply and Services.

Canada. (2001a). *Comparison of socio-economic conditions, 1996 and 2001: Registered Indians, registered Indians living on reserve, and the total population of Canada*. Ottawa: Indian and Northern Affairs. Retrieved April 11, 2007, from http://www.ainc-inac.gc.ca/pr/sts/csc/csc_e.pdf.

Canada. (2001b). *Overview of DIAND program data*. Ottawa: Indian and Northern Affairs. Retrieved April 11, 2007, from http://www.ainc-inac.gc.ca/pr/sts/ove_e.pdf.

Canada. (2001c). *Policy research for Canadian youth: Social work transitions*. Retrieved November 22, 2004, from www11.sdc.ca.

Canada. (2004, January). *Premature mortality in health regions with high Aboriginal populations*. Ottawa: Statistics Canada.

Canadian Association of Schools of Social Work. (1987). *Resolution on social work education and Aboriginal peoples*. Ottawa: CASSW.

Canadian Psychiatric Association Section on Native Mental Health. (1986). *Proceedings on depression in the North American Indian, causes and treatment*. Edmonton: Nechi Institute, Poundmakers Lodge.

Cardinal vs. Attorney General of Alberta. (1974). 40 DLR (3rd) 537 (SCC).

Carriere-Laboucane, J. (1997). Kinship care: A community alternative to foster care. *Native Social Work Journal, 1*(1), 43–53.

Castellano, M.B., Stalwick, H., & Wein, F. (1986). Native social work education in Canada: Issues and adaptations. *Canadian Social Work Review, 3*(1), 167–184.

Certificates in Aboriginal and Northern Social Work Practices. (1994). Paper presented at the Steering Committee, School of Social Work, McGill University.

Challen, D., & McPherson, D. (1994). Community-based social service organizations and the development of an economically sound model for sustainable community development. In B. Galaway & J. Hudson (Eds.), *Community economic development: Perspectives on research and policy* (pp. 194–202). Toronto: Thompson.

Chansonneuve, D. (2005). *Reclaiming connections: Understanding residential school trauma among Aboriginal people*. Ottawa: Aboriginal Healing Foundation.

Charlie, S. (2005, February 1). Native spirit dances: A rite of passage gone wrong. *The National Post*, p. A5.

Cheers, B. (1998). *Welfare bushed: Social care in rural Australia*. Aldershot: Ashgate.

Chrisjohn, F., & Young, S. (1997). *The circle game*. Penticton: Theytus Books Ltd.

Christenson, C.P. (1991). *Social work education at the crossroads: The challenge of diversity*. Report of the Task Force on Multicultural and Multiracial Issues in Social Work Education. Ottawa: Canadian Association of Schools of Social Work.

Ciaccia, J. (2000). *The Oka crisis: A mirror of the soul*. Dorval, QC: Maren Publications.

Collier, K. (1984). *Social work with rural people*. Vancouver: New Star Books.

Colorado, P. (1991). A meeting between brothers—indigenous science (Interview with J. Carroll). *Beshara, 13*, 20–27.

Colorado, P. (1993a). Coherence: A process of social work education with Aboriginal students. In K. Feehan & D. Hannis (Eds.), *From strength to strength: Social work education and Aboriginal people* (pp. 79–94). Edmonton: Grant McEwan Community College.

Colorado, P. (1993b). Healing the wound and the promise of the New Sun. In K. Feehan & D. Hannis (Eds.), *From strength to strength: Social work education and Aboriginal people* (pp. 139–145). Edmonton: Grant McEwan Community College.

Colorado, P. (1995). Who are you?: How the Aboriginal classroom sparks fundamental issues in human development. In K. Feehan & D. Hannis (Eds.), *From strength to strength: Social work education and Aboriginal people* (pp. 65–78). Edmonton: Grant McEwan Community College.

Commanda, W. (2001, August). *A circle of all nations*. A treatise explored at a Gathering in Maniwake.

Cook, Captain J. (1900). *The journals of Captain James Cook on his voyages of discovery*. London: Hakluyt.

Corrado, R. (2003). *Mental health profiles for a sample of British Columbia's Aboriginal survivors of the Canadian residential school system: Prepared for the Aboriginal Healing Foundation*. Ottawa: Aboriginal Healing Foundation.

Couture, J. (1993). *Culture and Native inmates, an overview: Assessment issues and possibilities*. Saskatoon: Corrections Canada.

Couture, J. (1996). *Coming together: Proposal for high-intensity pilot project for Aboriginal sex offenders*. Saskatoon: Aboriginal Programs Directorate, Correctional Services.

Cram, J.M. (1978). Training Inuit teachers in northern Quebec. *British Journal of Teacher Education, 4*(3), 203–209.

Cree Board of Health and Social Services of James Bay. (2006). *The gift of healing: Health problems and their treatments*. Chisasibi: Author.

Cummins, B.D. (2003). *Aboriginal policing: A Canadian perspective*. Toronto: Prentice Hall.

Cunneen, C. (2001). *Conflict, politics, and crime: Aboriginal communities and the police*. Crows Nest: Allen & Unwin.

Dean, R.G. (1998). A narrative approach to groups. *Clinical Social Work Journal, 26*(1), 23–38.

Dean, R.G. (2003). *The myth of cross-cultural competence*. Unpublished paper.

Delaney, R., & Brownlee, K. (1996). Ethical dilemmas in northern social work practice. In R. Delaney, K. Brownlee & M.K. Zapf (Eds.), *Issues in northern social work practice* (pp. 47–69). Thunder Bay: Laurentian University Press.

De Montigny, G. (1992). Compassionate colonialism: Sowing the branch plant. In M. Tobin & C. Walmsley (Eds.), *Northern perspectives: Practice and education in social work* (pp. 73-82). Winnipeg: University of Manitoba.

De Montigny, G. (1995). The power of being professional. In M. Campbell & A. Manicom (Eds.), *Knowledge, experience, and ruling relations* (pp. 209–220). Toronto: University of Toronto Press.

Dickason, O. (2002). *Canada's First Nations: A history of founding peoples from earliest times* (3rd ed.). Don Mills: Oxford University Press.

Dodson, M. (2003, June). *Violence and dysfunctional Aboriginality*. Presentation to the National Press Club, Canberra.

Dominelli, L. (1997). *Anti-racist social work*. London: MacMillan Press Ltd.

DuBray, W. (1985). American Indian values: Critical factor in casework. *The Journal of Contemporary Social Work, 66*(1), 30–37.

Dulac, G. (1996). *Certificate in northern social work practice: Evaluation of the program*. Unpublished report. Montreal: The Centre for Applied Family Studies, School of Social Work, McGill University.

Duran, E., & Duran, B. (1995). *Native American post-colonial psychology*. New York: New York State University Press.

Durie, M. (1998). *Te Mana Te Kawanatanga the politics of Maori determination*. Auckland: Oxford University Press.

Durie, M. (2003). *Launching Maori futures*. Wellington: Huia.

Fairclough, N. (1995). *Discourse and social change*. Cambridge: Polity Press.

Feehan, K. (1993a). Cherishing the sacred. In K. Feehan & D. Hannis (Eds.), *From strength to strength: Social work education and Aboriginal people* (pp. 19–30). Edmonton: Grant McEwan Community College.

Feehan, K. (1993b). Vision and values. In K. Feehan & D. Hannis (Eds.), *From strength to strength: Social work education and Aboriginal people* (pp. 7–18). Edmonton: Grant McEwan Community College.

Feehan, K., & Hannis, D. (Eds.). (1993). *From strength to strength: Social work education and Aboriginal people*. Edmonton: Grant McEwan Community College.

Fiddler, S. (2000). Part 3: Aboriginal overview. In M. Stephenson, G. Rondeau, J. Michaud & S. Fiddler (Eds.), *In critical demand: Social work in Canada* (pp. 171–193). Ottawa: The Social Work Sector Study.

Fiddler, S. (2001). *In critical demand: Report on strategic human resources: Analysis of Aboriginal social work sector*. Ottawa: CASSW.

Foley, D. (2003). Indigenous epistemology and indigenous standpoint theory. *Social Alternatives, 22*(1), 44–52.

Fontaine, P. (2005, January 11). Indian affairs funding is flawed. *The Gazette* [Montreal], p. A21.

Four B Manufacturing Ltd. vs. United Garment Workers of America, 102 DLR (3rd) 385 (Ontario Divisional Ct. 1979).

Fournier, S., & Crey, E. (1997). *Stolen from our embrace: The abduction of First Nations children and the restoration of Aboriginal communities*. Vancouver: Douglas & McIntyre Ltd.

Freire, P. (1970). *Pedagogy of the oppressed*. (M.B. Ramos, Trans.) New York: Herder & Herder.

Freire, P. (1985). *The politics of education: Culture, power, and liberation*. (D. Macedo, Trans.) South Hadley: Bergin & Garvey.

Freire, P. (2000). *Pedagogy of the oppressed* (30th anniversary ed.). (M.B. Ramos, Trans.) Edgware: Continuum International.

Freire, P. (2003). *Pedagogy of hope: Reliving pedagogy of the oppressed*. New York: Continuum International Publishing Group Inc.

Freire, P., & Shor, I. (1987). *A pedagogy for liberation*. London: Macmillan.

Freud, S. (1987). Social workers as community educators: A new identity for the profession. *Journal of Teaching Social Work, 1*(1), 111–126.

Freud, S. (1993). A grand lady's voyage into nowhere land. In K. Feehan & D. Hannis (Eds.), *From strength to strength: Social work education and Aboriginal people* (pp. 111–138). Edmonton: Grant McEwan Community College.

Friesen, D.W., & Orr, J. (1998). New paths, old ways: Exploring the places of influence in Aboriginal teacher identity. *Canadian Journal of Native Education, 22*(2), 188–200.

Garwood, N. (1997). Tug-of-war. *The Waseskun Circle* 1(1), 3.

Garwood, N. (2000). *Submission to the Aboriginal Healing Foundation.* Unpublished document.

Garwood, N. (2003). *Report to the Aboriginal Healing Foundation.* Ottawa: Kangirsuk Healing Camp.

German, N.R. (1997). Northern student education initiative. *Native Social Work Journal,* 1(1), 33–41.

Gilchrist, L. (1997). Aboriginal communities and social science research: Voyeurism in transition. *Native Social Work Journal,* 1(1), 69–85.

Gladue, R.V. (1999). 2. C.N.L.R. 252.

Green, R. (2000). Rural social welfare: Preparing students to work effectively in rural communities: An Australian experience. In J.C. Montgomery & A.D. Kitchenham (Eds.), *Issues affecting rural communities* (Vol. 2, pp. 280–283). Nanaimo: Rural Communities Research and Development Centre, Malaspina University College.

Grenier, A. (2001). *Student assessment of McGill University's certificate program in Aboriginal social work practice: Building on five years of partnership.* Unpublished report.

Grieves, F. (1992). My first year. In M. Tobin & C. Walmsley (Eds.), *Northern perspectives: Practice and education in social work* (pp. 67–68). Winnipeg: University of Manitoba.

Griffin-Pierce, T. (1997). When I am lonely the mountains call me: The impact of sacred geography on Navajo psychological well-being. *American Indian and Alaska Native Mental Health Research,* 7(3), 1–10.

Haas, T., & Nachtigal, P. (1998). Place value: An educator's guide to good literature on rural lifeways, environments, and purposes of education. In M.K. Zapf (Ed.), *Profound connections between person and place: Exploring location, spirituality, and social work.* Paper presented at the 3rd Annual Canadian Conference on Spirituality and Social Work, University of Manitoba, Winnipeg, June 2004.

Haig-Brown, C. (1989). *Resistance and renewal: Surviving the Indian residential school.* Vancouver: Tillacum Library.

Haig-Brown, C. (1995). *Power and contradiction in First Nations adult education.* Vancouver: University of British Columbia Press.

Hall, B.L. (2000). *Indigenous knowledges in global contexts: Multiple reading of our world.* Toronto: OISE/ University of Toronto Press.

Hannis, D. (1993a). Evaluating excellence: What the research had told us. In K. Feehan & D. Hannis (Eds.), *From strength to strength: Social work education and Aboriginal people* (pp. 175–184). Edmonton: Grant McEwan Community College.

Hannis, D. (1993b). Liberation or assimilation: What are adult educators trying to do? In K. Feehan & D. Hannis (Eds.), *From strength to strength: Social work education and Aboriginal people* (pp. 45–56). Edmonton: Grant McEwan Community College.

Harris, B. (2005). What can we learn from traditional Aboriginal education? Transforming social work education delivered in First Nation communities. *Canadian Journal of Native Education,* 29(1), 117–134.

Hart, M. (1996). Sharing circles: Utilizing traditional practice methods for teaching, helping and supporting. In S. O'Meara & D. West (Eds.), *From our eyes: Learning from indigenous peoples* (pp. 59–72). Toronto: Garamond Press.

Hart, M. (2001). An Aboriginal approach to social work practice. In T. Heinemen & L. Spearman (Eds.), *Social work practice: Problem solving and beyond* (pp. 239–256). Toronto: Irwin.

Hart, M.A. (2002). *Seeking Mino-Pimatisiwin: An Aboriginal approach to helping.* Halifax: Fernwood.

Hesch, R. (1996). Antiracist educators *sui generis?* The dialectics of Aboriginal teacher education. *Canadian Review of Sociology and Anthropology, 33*(3), 269–289.

Higgins, G.O. (1994). *Resilient adults overcoming a cruel past.* San Francisco: Jossey Bass Inc.

Hodge, D. (2000). Spiritual ecomaps: A new diagrammatic tool for assessing marital and family spirituality. *Journal of Marital and Family Therapy, 26,* 229–240.

Hodge, D. (2001). Spiritual assessment: A review of major qualitative methods and a new framework for assessing spirituality in social work. *Social Work, 46*(3), 203.

Hodgson, M. (1991). *Shattering the silence: Working with violence in Native communities.* Edmonton: Nechi Institute.

Hodgson, M. (1992). *From anomie to rebirth: The eagle has landed.* Edmonton: Nechi Institute.

Hollow Water Community Services. (1993). *Community holistic Healing Circles.* Hollow Water, MB: Author.

hooks, b. (1990). *Yearning: Race, gender, and cultural politics.* Toronto: Between the Lines.

Houston, J. (1995). *Confessions of an igloo dweller.* Toronto: McClelland & Stewart.

Inuit Tapiriit Kanatami. (2000). *Evaluation of models of health care delivery in Inuit regions.* Retrieved October 26, 2006, from http://www.itk.ca/publications/200403-healthcare-evaluation.pdf.

Jack and Charlie vs. The Queen. (1985). 21 DLR (4th) 641.

Jefferson, C. (1994). Conquest by law. *Aboriginal peoples collection.* Ottawa: Supply and Services Canada.

Jewison, C. (1995). Our students, our future: Innovations in First Nations education in the NWT. *Education in Canada, 33*(1), 4–11.

Katz, R., & St. Denis, V. (1991). Teacher as healer. *Journal of Indigenous Studies, 2*(2) 23–36.

Kelley, M.L., & Nelson, C.H. (1986). A nontraditional educational model with Indian Indigenous social service workers. *Canadian Journal of Native Education 13*(3), 20–31.

Kirkness, V.J., & Barnhardt, R. (1991). First Nations and higher education: The four R's—respect, relevance, reciprocity, responsibility. *Journal of American Indian Education, 30*(3), 1–15.

Kirmayer, L.J. (1994). Suicide among Canadian Aboriginal peoples. *Transcultural Psychiatric Research Review, 31,* 3–58.

Kirmayer, L., Simpson, C., & Cargo, M. (2003). Indigenous populations healing traditions: Culture, community, and mental health promotion with Canadian Aboriginal peoples. *Australasian Psychiatry, 11,* S15–S23.

Krawll, M.B. (1994). *Understanding the role of healing in Aboriginal communities.* Ottawa: Solicitor General of Canada.

Laird, J. (1998). Theorizing culture: Narrative ideas and practice principles. In M. McGoldrick (Ed.), *Re-visioning family therapy* (pp. 20–36). New York: Guilford.

Lalonde, P. (1993). In retrospect. In K. Feehan & D. Hannis (Eds.), *From strength to strength: Social work education and Aboriginal people* (pp. 197–200). Edmonton: Grant MacEwan Community College.

LaPrairie, C. (1995). Altering course: New directions in criminal justice sentencing circles and family group conferences. *The Australian and New Zealand Journal of Criminology* (Special Supplementary Issue), 78–99.

Lather, P. (1991). *Getting smart: Feminist research and pedagogy within the postmodern.* New York: Routledge.

LeBlanc, J.B., Brabant, S., & Forsyth, C.J. (1996). The meaning of college for survivors of sexual abuse: Higher education and the older female college student. *American Journal of Orthopsychiatry 66*(3), 468–473.

Lehmann (2006, April 15). Read between words at must-see show. *The Montreal Gazette*, p. E4.

Leonard, P. (1994). Knowledge/power and postmodernism: Implications for the practice of a critical social work education. *Canadian Social Work Review, 11*(1), 11–26.

Lippitt, R., & Romero, M. (1992). More than 400 years in creation: The path of American Indian education. In D. Ray & D.H. Poonwassie (Eds.), *Education and cultural difference: New perspectives* (pp. 127–151). New York: Garland Publishing Inc.

Lippman, L. (1975). Aboriginal education: Center for research into Aboriginal affairs. *Australian & New Zealand Journal of Sociology, 11*(2), 13–19.

Long, D. (1992). Culture, ideology, and militancy: The movement of Native Indians in Canada, 1969–91. In W.K. Carroll (Ed.), *Organizing dissent* (pp. 118–134). Aurora: Garamond Press.

Lonne, B., & Cheers, B. (2000). Personal and professional adjustment of social workers to rural and remote practice: Implications for improved retention. In J.C. Montgomery & A.D. Kitchenham (Eds.), *Issues affecting rural communities* (Vol. 2, pp. 48–53). Nanaimo: Rural Communities Research and Development Centre, Malaspina University-College.

Lorde, A. (1983). The master's tools will never dismantle the master's house. In C. Moraga & G. Anzaldua (Eds.), *This bridge called my back: Writings by radical women of color* (pp. 98–101). New York: Kitchen Table, Women of Color Press.

MacPherson, J.C. (1991). MacPherson report on tradition and education: Towards a vision of our future. Ottawa: Indian and Northern Affairs.

Marker, M. (2002). Theories and disciplines as sites of struggle: The reproduction of colonial dominance through the controlling of knowledge in the academy. *Canadian Journal of Native Education, 28*(2), 102–120.

Martinez-Brawley, E.E. (1986). Issues in alternative social work education: Observations from a Canadian program with a rural mandate. *Arete, 11*(1), 54–64.

Mastronardi, L. (1990). The Inuit community workers' experience of youth protection. In L. Davies & E. Shragge (Eds.), *Bureaucracy and community: Essays on the politics of social work* (pp. 103–145). Montreal: Black Rose Books.

May, L. (1996). *Perspective of an Inuk teacher.* Paper presented at the Inuit Studies Conference Social Work Caucus, St. John's.

McAlpine, L., Cross, E., Whiteduck, G., & Wolforth, J. (1990). Using two pairs of eyes to define an Aboriginal teacher education program. *Canadian Journal of Native Education, 17*(2), 82–88.

McClure, M. (1998). *A civilized community.* Auckland: Auckland University Press.

McConchie, P. (2003). *Elders: Wisdom from Australia's indigenous leaders.* Cambridge: Cambridge University Press.

McElroy, A. (1975). Canadian Arctic modernization and change in female Inuit role identification. *American Ethnologist, 24,* 662–686.

McKenzie, B., & Mitchinson, K. (1989). Social work education empowerment: The Manitoba experience. *Canadian Social Work Review, 6*(1), 112–125.

McLaren, P., & Leonard, P. (1993). *Paulo Freire: A critical encounter.* London: Routledge.

McLaughlin, A. (1982). *Native content in the social work curriculum.* Victoria: University of Victoria School of Social Work.

McLean, S. (1997). Objectifying and naturalizing identity: A study of adult education in the Canadian Arctic. *Canadian Journal of Sociology, 22*(1), 1–29.

McMahon, A., & Allen-Mearers, P. (1992). Is social work racist? A content analysis of recent literature. *National Association of Social Workers, 37,* 533–539.

Meawasige, I. (1995). The healing circle. In R. Delaney & K. Brownlee (Eds.), *Northern social work practice* (pp. 136–146). Thunder Bay: Lakehead University Centre for Northern Studies.

Mesher, D., with Woolam, R. (1995). *Kuujjuaq: Memories and musings.* Duncan: Unica.

Miller, J.R. (1996). *Shingwauk's vision: A history of Native residential schools.* Toronto: University of Toronto Press Inc.

Miller, N.B. (1982). Social work services to urban Indians. In J.W. Green (Ed.), *Cultural awareness in the human services.* Englewood Cliffs, NJ: Prentice-Hall.

Milloy, J. (1999). *A national crime: Canadian government and the residential school system.* Winnipeg: University of Manitoba Press.

Mohanty, C. (2003). *Feminism without borders: Decolonizing theory, practising solidarity.* Chicago: Duke University Press.

Monette, D.R., Sullivan, T.J., & DeJong, C.R. (1998). *Applied social research: Tools for the human services* (4th ed.). Fort Worth: Harcourt Brace & Co.

Morrissette, V., McKenzie, B., & Morrissette, L. (1993). Towards an Aboriginal model of social work practice: Cultural knowledge and traditional practices. *Canadian Social Work Review, 10*(1), 91–108.

Mussell, B. (2005). *Warrior-caregivers: Understanding the challenges and healing of First Nations men.* Ottawa: Aboriginal Healing Foundation.

Nabigon, H., Hagey, R., Webster, S., & MacKay, R. (1999). The learning circle as a research method: The trickster and windigo in research. *Native Social Work Journal, 2*(1), 113–137.

National Native Association of Treatment Directors. (1992). *The right to be special: Native alcohol and drug counselor's handbook. Working with sexual abuse disclosure.* Calgary: National Native Association of Treatment Directors.

Native Counselling Services of Alberta. (2001). *A cost-benefit analysis of Hollow Water's community holistic circle healing process.* Ottawa: Solicitor General Canada.

Native Women's Shelter of Montreal. (1993–1994). *Director's report.* Montreal: Native Women's Shelter of Montreal.

Nelson, C.H., Kelley, M., & McPherson, D.H. (1985). Rediscovering support in social work practice: Lessons from Indian indigenous human service workers. *Canadian Social Work Review, 2*, 231–248.

New Zealand. (2000). *Ministerial review of the Department of Child Youth and Family Services.* Wellington: Government of New Zealand.

Nielsen, M., & Silverman, R. (Eds.). (1996). *Native Americans, crime, and justice.* Boulder: Westview Press.

Nungak, Z. (2000). Experimental Eskimos. *Inuktitut, 87*, 4–17.

Obomsawin, A. (1993). *Kanaehsatake: 270 Years of resistance.* National Film Board of Canada.

Obomsawin, A. (2000). *Rocks at Whiskey Trench.* National Film Board of Canada.

Pace, J.M., & Smith, A.F.V. (1990). Native social work education: Struggling to meet the need. *Canadian Social Work Review, 7*(1), 109–119.

Paine, R. (1977). The nursery game: Colonizer and colonized in the eastern Arctic. In R. Paine (Ed.), *The white Arctic: Anthropological essays on tutelage and ethnicity* (pp. 105–131). St. Johns: Memorial University Press.

Pauktuutit Inuit Women of Canada. (1989). *The Inuit way: a guide to Inuit culture.* Ottawa: Author.

Paziuk, L. (1992). The northern BSW program: Maintaining community connections. In M. Tobin & C. Walmsley (Eds.), *Northern perspectives: Practice and education in social work* (pp. 69–72). Winnipeg: University of Manitoba.

Peacock, C. (1993). Growing together and finding the balance. In K. Feehan & D. Hannis (Eds.), *From strength to strength: Social work education and Aboriginal people* (pp. 188–194). Edmonton: Grant MacEwan Community College.

Pelech, W. (1993). A return to the circle. In K. Feehan & D. Hannis (Eds.), *From strength to strength: Social work education and Aboriginal people* (pp. 147–162). Edmonton: Grant McEwan Community College.

Perley, D.G. (1993). Aboriginal education in Canada as internal colonialism. *Canadian Journal of Native Education, 20*(1), 118–128.

Pinderhughes, E. (1994). Empowerment as intervention goals: Early ideas. In L. Gutiarrez & O. Nurius (Eds.), *Education and research for empowerment practice* (pp. 46–60). Seattle: University of Washington School of Social Work.

Rangihau, J. (1986). *Puao-te-Ata-tu (Daybreak): Report of the ministerial advisory committee on a Maori perspective for the department of social welfare.* Wellington: Department of Social Welfare, Government of New Zealand Printing Office.

Ray, D., & Poonwassie, D.H. (1992). An assessment: Implications for schooling and teacher education, the social context—a summary and evaluation. In D. Ray & D.H. Poonwassie (Eds.), *Education and cultural difference: New perspectives.* New York: Garland Publishing.

Régie Régionale du Nunavik. (1995). *Annual report 1994–1995.* Unpublished report.

Regnier, R. (1994). The sacred circle: A process pedagogy of healing. *Interchange, 25*(12), 129–144.

Restivo, G. (1993). The power of healing. In K. Feehan & D. Hannis (Eds.), *From strength to strength: Social work education and Aboriginal people* (pp. 185–187). Edmonton: Grant McEwan Community College.

Rogers, C. (1980). *A way of being.* Boston: Houghton Mifflin.

Rogers, G. (1998). *Alberta social work degree accessibility plan—Virtual learning circles: A BSW for rural, remote, and Aboriginal communities.* Unpublished report. University of Calgary Faculty of Social Work, Calgary.

Rosenman, L.S. (1980). Social work education in Australia: The impact of the American model. *Journal of Education for Social Work, 16*(1), 112–118.

Ross, R. (1996). *Returning to the teachings: Exploring Aboriginal justice.* Toronto: Penguin Books.

Ruttan, L. (2000). *Issues in shared schools in mixed Aboriginal and non-Aboriginal school systems.* Nanaimo: Rural Communities and Identities in the Global Millennium.

Sandy, E. (1996, February). Talking circles have guidelines based on respect for people. *Anishinabek News,* p. 1.

Santé Québec. (1994). *A health profile of the Inuit: Report of the Santé Québec health survey among the Inuit of Nunavik 1992.* Montreal: Ministère de la Santé et des Services Sociaux, Gouvernement du Québec.

Savage, J. (1807). *Some account of New Zealand.* London: Union Printing Office St. Johns Square.

Senkpiel, A. (1997). Side by side in the Yukon: The development of the northern human service worker/BSW program. In K. Brownlee, R. Delaney & J.R. Graham (Eds.), *Strategies for northern social work practice* (pp. 29–44). Thunder Bay: Lakehead University Centre for Northern Studies.

Services, N.H. (1995). Information package, Nishnaabe Kinoomaadwin Naadmaadwin. Honours, Bachelor of Social Work, Laurentian University School of Social Work.

Shulman, L. (1987). The hidden group in the classroom: The use of group process in teaching group work practice. *Journal of Teaching in Social Work, 1*(2), 3–31.

Slack, D. (2005). *Bullshit, backlash, and bleeding hearts.* Auckland: Penguin Books.

Smith, A. (1991, November–December). For all those who were Indian in a former life. *Ms Magazine,* 44–45.

Smith, L.H. (1999). *Decolonizing methodologies, research, and indigenous people.* Dunedin: University of Otaga Press.

Society of Aboriginal Addictions Recovery. (1994). *The Substance Abuse Treatment Readiness Program: Men.* Calgary: Author.

Solicitor General Canada. (1997). *Responding to sexual abuse: Developing a community-based sexual abuse response team in Aboriginal communities.* Ottawa: Author.

Solicitor General Canada. (1998). *Understanding and evaluating the role of elders and traditional healing in sex offender treatment for Aboriginal offenders.* Ottawa: Author.

Solicitor General Canada. (2001). *Mapping the healing journey: The final report of a First Nation research project on healing in Canadian Aboriginal communities.* Ottawa: Author.

Stairs, A. (1993). Learning processes and teaching roles in Native education: Cultural base and cultural brokerage. In M. Danesi, K.A. McLeod & S. Morris (Eds.), *Aboriginal languages and education: The Canadian experience* (pp. 85–101). Oakville: Mosaic Press.

Statistics Canada. (2003). *Aboriginal peoples survey 2001—Initial findings: Well-being of the non-reserve population.* Statistics Canada catalogue no. 89-589-XIE. Retrieved March 10, 2007, from http://www.statcan.ca/english/freepub/89-589-XIE/89-589-XIE2003001.pdf.

Stevenson, J. (1998). *Healing circles: How are they effective for the healing process?* Unpublished thesis, McGill University School of Social Work.

Stevenson, J. (1999). The circle of healing. *Native Social Work Journal, 2*(1), 8–21.

Storm, H. (1972). *Seven arrows.* New York: Ballentine Books.

Sturmey, R. (1992). *Educating social welfare and community workers for rural/remote areas.* Portland & Armadale: The Rural Development Centre.

Tastsoglou, E. (2000). Mapping the unknowable: The challenges and rewards of cultural, political, and pedagogical border crossing. In G. Sefa Dei & A. Calliste (Eds.), *Power, knowledge, and anti-racist education: A critical reader* (pp. 98–121). Halifax: Fernwood.

Teichroeb, R. (1997). *Flowers on my grave.* Toronto: HarperCollins.

Thompson Cooper, I. (1995). *Proposed certificate program in Aboriginal social work practice.* Unpublished paper.

Thompson Cooper, I. (2004). The development of the McGill Certificate Program in Aboriginal social work practice: Overcoming resistance and building bridges. *Women in Welfare Education, 7,* 88–105.

Thompson Cooper, I., Stacey Moore, G., & Priestley, K. (2002). *Follow-up of graduates of McGill Certificate Program in Aboriginal social work.* Unpublished report.

Tobin, M., & Walmsley, C. (1992). *Northern perspectives: Practice and education in social work.* Winnipeg: University of Manitoba Press.

Trigger, B.G. (1987). *Natives and newcomers: Canada's "heroic age" reconsidered.* Kingston & Montreal: McGill University Press.

University of Regina School of Social Work. (1982). *Indian and Native Social Work Education Project.* Unpublished conference report. University of Regina School of Social Work, Saskatchewan.

Urtnowski, L. (1996). *Education for social work in Nunavik: The McGill Certificate Program in Northern Social Work Practice.* Unpublished manuscript.

Usher, R., & Edwards, R. (1994). *Education and postmodernism.* New York: Routledge.

Waldram, J.B. (1997). *The way of the pipe: Aboriginal spirituality and symbolic healing in Canadian prisons.* Peterborough: Broadview Press.

Walker, H. (1996). Wanua Hui, family decision-making, and the family group conference: An indigenous Maori view. *Protecting children: The practice and promise of family-group decision-making, 12*(3), 8–10.

Walmsley, C. (2005). *Protecting Aboriginal children.* Vancouver: University of British Columbia Press.

Waterfall, B. (2003). Native peoples and the social work profession: A critical analysis of colonizing problematics and the development of decolonised thought. In A. Westhues (Ed.), *Canadian social policy: Issues and perspectives* (3rd ed.), (pp. 50–66). Waterloo: Wilfrid Laurier University Press.

Webster, S., & Reyno, R. (1999). Conducting community-based research in First Nations communities. In R. Delaney, K. Brownlee & M. Sellick (Eds.), *Social work in rural and northern communities* (pp. 182–191). Thunder Bay: Lakehead University Centre for Northern Studies.

Weekes, M. (1994). *The last buffalo hunter.* Saskatoon: Fifth House Publishers.

Weenie, A. (1998). Aboriginal pedagogy: The sacred circle concept. In Lenore Stiffarm (Ed.), *As we see: Aboriginal pedagogy* (pp. 56–66). Saskatoon: University of Extension Press, University of Saskatchewan.

Welsh, E., & Ayala, J. (2005). *The University of Calgary BSW access program learning circles: A participatory evaluation.* Calgary: University of Calgary Faculty of Social Work Centre for Social Work Research and Development.

Wesley-Esquimaux, C., & Smolewski, M. (2004). *Historic trauma and Aboriginal healing.* Ottawa: Aboriginal Healing Foundation.

Wilcannia Community Working Party Workshop. (2001). Wilcannia workshop: Booklet two. Retrieved May 23, 2007, from http://users.tpg.com.au/hope2/CWP/Booklet_2.htm.

Woo, G.L.X. (2005). *The decolonization of democracy: Indigenous rights and constitutional integrity in Canada.* Unpublished doctoral thesis, Montreal.

Wright, M. (1993). Being there: Applying Rogerian concepts in the classroom. In K. Feehan & D. Hannis (Eds.), *From strength to strength: Social work education and Aboriginal people* (pp. 57–64). Edmonton: Grant McEwan Community College.

Yellow Horse Brave Heart, M. (1998). The return to the sacred path: Healing the historical trauma and historical unresolved grief response among the Lakota thru a psychoeducational group intervention. *Smith College Studies in Social Work, 68*(3), 287–305.

York, G., & Pindera, L. (1991). *People of the pines: The warriors and legacy of Oka.* Toronto: Little Brown & Co.

Young, M.I. (2003). *Pimatisiwin: Walking in a good way: A narrative inquiry into language and identity.* PhD thesis, University of Alberta.

Young, W.D. (1999). Aboriginal students speak about acceptance, sharing, awareness, and support: A participatory approach to change and community college. *Native Social Work Journal, 2*(1), 21–58.

Zapf, M.K. (1993a). Methods instruction as a two-way process. In K. Feehan & D. Hannis (Eds.), *From strength to strength: Social work education and Aboriginal people* (pp. 95–110). Edmonton: Grant McEwan Community College.

Zapf, M.K. (1993b). Who is the client?: Contracts and social work outreach program in Native communities. In K. Feehan & D. Hannis (Eds.), *From strength to strength: Social work education and Aboriginal people* (pp. 31–43). Edmonton: Grant McEwan Community College.

Zapf, M.K. (1997). Voice and social work education: Learning to teach from my own story. *Canadian Social Work Review, 14*(1), 83–98.

Zapf, M.K. (1998). Crossing cultural and social boundaries: Teaching social work courses in Aboriginal outreach programs. In L. Ginsberg (Ed.), *Social work in rural communities* (3rd ed.), (pp. 233–246). Alexandria: CSWE.

Zapf, M.K. (1999a). Bi-cultural teaching of helping approaches: Integrating Native Indian and Western perspectives in a social work classroom. *International Journal of Inclusive Education, 3*(4), 327–337.

Zapf, M.K. (1999b). Location and knowledge building: Exploring the fit of Western social work with traditional knowledge. *Native Social Work Journal, 21*(1), 138–152.

Zapf, M.K. (2004). *Profound connections between person and place: Exploring location, spirituality, and social work.* Paper presented at the 3rd Annual Canadian Conference on Spirituality and Social Work, University of Manitoba, Winnipeg.

Zapf, M.K., Bastien, B., Bodor, R., Carriere, J., & Pelech, W. (2000). *The learning circle: A new model of BSW education for Alberta's rural, remote, and Aboriginal communities.* Nanaimo: Rural Communities and Identities in the Global Millennium.

Zapf, M.K., Pelech, W., Bastien, B., Bohor, R., Carriere, J., & Zak, G. (2003). The learning circle. *Tribal College Journal, 15*(2), 52–58.

Zintz, M. (1963). *Education across cultures.* Dubuque: Kendall/Hunt Publishing.

Index

A

Aboriginal and Torres Strait Islander
Commission, 130
Aboriginal Peoples
ambivalence towards education, 6, 26,
28, 56, 89, 101
Academia's historical relationship to, 69,
78, 79
Australian social work education
programs for. *See* Australian social
work education
Canadian social work education for,
5–27, 33–40, 42, 47–49, 60–63, 70, 71
healing practices of, 3, 22, 41, 85–88, 90,
118–119, 144, 148–151, 153–157, 159–170
mainstream education intersecting with
healing practices of, 153, 154, 165–167
New Zealand social work education
programs. *See* New Zealand, social
work in
and negative experiences within
university systems, 48, 49, 100
and their relationship to non-Aboriginal
instructors in social work education.
See Certificate Program in Aboriginal
Social Work Practice
Aboriginal Peoples Survey (2001), 55
academia and Aboriginal experience. *See*
Aboriginal Peoples.
Acco, Anne, 3
affiliated autonomous, as educational model,
93
Akwesasne, 56
alcohol abuse, 8–9, 16, 59, 80–81, 104, 143–146,
162
Alcoholics Anonymous, 160
birth defects from, 55
treatment programs for, 163, 176

Allen-Mearers, P., 65
Anglem, Jim, 3
Annahatak, Lolly, 3, 10, 28
Anzaldua, G., 34
Aotearoa, social work in. *See* New Zealand,
social work in
Apple, M., 39
Archibald, L., 180
Armstrong, R., 56
Aronoff, Leiba, 76
assimilation, 3, 35–36, 40, 75, 102, 106, 157, 174,
180
Australian social work education, 3, 64, 93, 111,
118, 121–132
and the Diploma of Human Services, 131
and social inequalities, 121–122
and Technical and Further Education
(TAFE), 128–129
autonomous, as educational model, 93

B

Banks, Joseph, 134
Barnhardt, R., 38, 48, 93
Battiste, M., 98
Boultbee, John, 134
Borderland, 34
Brant, Dr. Clare, 58
Brewarrina, 121
Briggs, Jean, 25
British North American Act (1867), 66
Brownlee, K., 40
Bruyere, G., 105, 148, 151

C

Canada's Constitution Act (1867), 61
Canadian Association of Schools of Social
Work (CASSW), 40, 101, 111, 117
Canadian Charter of Rights and Freedoms, 63